SIMON SHERIDAN

The Universal State of America

An Archetypal Calculus of Western Civilisation

First edition

This book was professionally typeset on Reedsy.
Find out more at reedsy.com

Contents

Introduction

This book began with, and is a sequel to, my 2021 book titled *The Devouring Mother: The Collective Unconscious in the Time of Corona*. That book, in turn, was the product of a revelation that had occurred to me during the corona event of 2020. I had noticed that the collective psychology during that time was neither random nor a one-off state change but rather a heightened and exaggerated form of the general pattern of modern western society. What's more, I saw that this pattern also had a distinctive political aspect to it which raised a number of other interesting avenues for exploration. With a seeming abundance of possibilities requiring further research and thought, I decided to write *The Devouring Mother* from a more or less straightforwardly psychological perspective. I believe that the analysis in that book still stands as an accurate account of the collective psychology of our time and has only become more pronounced in the aftermath of the corona event.

Once the first book was published, I set out to explore the wider themes raised by the two primary archetypes of the Devouring Mother and the Orphan. I was surprised by how well these accounted for the geopolitics of the era during which the two archetypes became dominant in the West; namely, the post-Cold War years where the United States has become the global hegemon. The manner in which the USA exerts its geopolitical dominance bears a surprising resemblance to the manner in which the Devouring Mother fosters the dependence of her child, causing it to become stuck in the Orphan phase of life.

All that was curious and seemed important in ways I hadn't yet grasped. But the question which proved the most fruitful and which has led to the creation of this book was a very simple one. If I was correct in stating that the Devouring Mother and the Orphan are the dominant archetypes of our time, when did they become dominant and what archetypes, if any, preceded that change? That question led me back to the study of history, but with a new perspective, one grounded in the concept of archetypes. I was asking a question which most historians would not dream to ask since it lies beyond the usual scholarly boundaries of the subject. The question might be phrased as: *what archetypes have dominated the Collective Unconscious throughout history?* That led to another question: *if dominant archetypes can change, how and why do they change?*

The idea of collective archetypal changes, although not something that historians would think about in those terms, is nevertheless broadly compatible with historical scholarship. Almost all historians mark out history into different phases, and most would also agree that the transition between those phases is difficult, often marked by societal upheaval, war, and other major cataclysms. But there is a sub-group of historians who make this claim explicit. In the work of comparative history, I found a direct correspondence between the archetypal phases of the human lifecycle and the phases of the collective cycle of civilisation. That principle was the basis for the work of the 20th century's two greatest comparative historians, Arnold Toynbee and Oswald Spengler. We will be making extensive use of their ideas in this book.

Thus, I had found firm ground for supposing that the individual and collective archetypal progressions mirrored each other. What I subsequently realised was that there was a common pattern that sat beneath not just the human lifecycle and not just the civilisational cycle of the comparative historians, but also two related works of comparative scholarship: Arnold van Gennep's *rites of passage* and Joseph Campbell's *Hero's Journey*. Both of these posit a cyclical structure grouped into phases just like the human lifecycle and the cycle of civilisation of Toynbee and Spengler. I had stumbled across what seemed to be an underlying unity which linked psychology, anthropology, biology, literature, history and more. This was not a unity I had been looking for, and it wasn't until I started to think through the ramifications that I could see how well it worked as a conceptual framework.

It is that underlying unity that we will lay out in the first part of this book. We will show the correspondences between the microcosm (the human individual) and the macrocosm (civilisation). We will posit that those correspondences hold across three levels of being: the Physical (including the biological), the Exoteric and the Esoteric. The archetypes form the unifying concepts that link microcosm and macrocosm over the levels of being. That is where part of the title of this book comes from: *an archetypal calculus*.

The second half of the book takes the archetypal calculus and applies it to modern western civilisation with a focus on the period from the Reformation until today. It is here that we find the answers to the question: *when did the Devouring Mother and the Orphan become dominant?* The answer to that question is tied in with another: *why is the United States manifesting the Devouring Mother?* We will see that this is partly driven by the civilisational cycle and is therefore an archetypal phase of western civilisation. However, it is also a unique adaptation that follows from the individual nature of western civilisation itself.

What all this boils down to is that civilisations can be thought of as individuals with personality and character, or, as the historian Spengler phrased it, spirit and soul. But we might go one step further and say that, whatever civilisations are, they are the same kinds of things as the human individual. Just as the individual has a personal consciousness and unconscious, so too does the civilisation have these. Just as we each as individuals must go through the archetypal phases of life, and just as our individuality arises partly in our unique response to those phases, so, too, do civilisations go through archetypal phases, and so, too, do they develop a unique character. It is by understanding the unique character of modern western civilisation that we can understand both why the USA has become its Universal State and why it has manifested the Devouring Mother archetype as a result.

Putting it all together, we get the full title of this book: *The Universal State of America: An Archetypal Calculus of Western Civilisation.*

One final note.

Although this book is a sequel to *The Devouring Mother: The Collective Unconscious in the Time of Corona*, it in no way requires an understanding of the first book. In fact, although I expect readers of the first book will easily see the connections with this work, I suspect that the better order in which to read the books would be this one first, followed by the original. In any case, this book stands (or falls!) on its own merits.

With that said, let's begin.

Part 1: The Integrated Model

The Microcosmic Perspective

Although we are going to be using some fancy-sounding words in the pages ahead, the core concepts on which this book is built are some of the most basic to our daily lives. Perhaps the most important of those for our analysis is the notion of the cycle. Cycles structure our lives. What could be more fundamental than the cycle of the Earth on its axis, which gives us the alternation of day and night, or the cycle of the Earth around the sun, which gives us the progression of the seasons of the year.

It so obvious that most of us have probably never thought about it, but the cycles of the day and the year can be divided into qualitatively and quantitatively distinct sections. The words which denote these sections are some of the most basic in our languages: day, night, morning, afternoon, and evening. The qualitative differences that these words denote are uncontroversial. Everybody knows the morning is cooler than the afternoon, that night is colder than the day, and midday is brighter than midnight.

We will see in the pages ahead how quickly such simple concepts can get complicated when they are combined with each other, but, ultimately, this book is about cycles and the very simple and obvious idea that cycles can be broken up into qualitatively different sections. Later, we will apply this idea to domains that are much less obvious than the cycles of day and year, so we can use this opportunity to lay the groundwork for our analysis while we are on solid ground. We can represent the cycle of the day in the form of a diagram, which is going to become very familiar to us throughout the course of this book but which we all already know since it is nothing more than the familiar face of the clock.

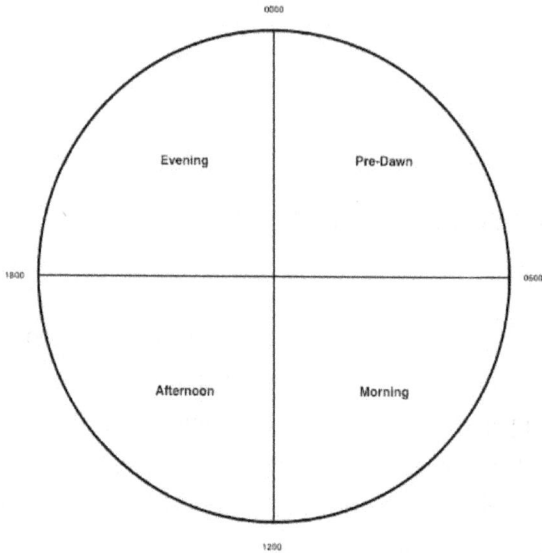

Since this representation is so familiar to us, there is no need to expand on it. Our second point will be less familiar but also follows quite straightforwardly from the relationship between the cycle of the day and the year. When we have two entities that have the same structure (a cycle with segments), we can invoke a definition that has a long theological and philosophical tradition: the microcosm-macrocosm. As the words imply, micro is the smaller and macro the larger. Given that a year is longer than a day and therefore "larger", we would call the year the macrocosm and the day the microcosm.

It is possible for the microcosm and macrocosm to be interrelated, and, given that we are talking about cycles, this refers to the confluence of two cycles. Once again, there is nothing mystical about this; it's a basic aspect of the world we live in. The cycle of the day, caused by the rotation of the Earth around its axis, interacts with and is affected by the cycle of the Earth around the sun. The segments of the cycle of the year (summer, autumn, winter, and spring) each have their own distinctive quantitative and qualitative properties, and these interact with the distinctive segments of the day. Thus, we get the hot and dry summer afternoon and the cold and damp winter morning.

More specifically, we can say that the macrocosm governs and modifies the microcosm. A day in winter is different from a day in summer, both in quantitative terms (the length of the day vs. night, temperature etc.) and in qualitative ones. The general properties of the segments of the day stay the same, but they are modulated by the properties of the segments of the year.

Many things in nature follow this same pattern of a cycle broken up into segments. One of those is the human lifecycle. Irrespective of any specific theological framework, we end life where we began it, at least in the physical realm. That is why our lives can be thought of as a cycle. Furthermore, the cycle of our lives can be broken up into quantitatively and qualitatively different segments. Nobody would deny that childhood is qualitatively different from adulthood in the same way that summer is different from winter. In this book, we will argue that there are four main segments to the human lifecycle: childhood, adolescence, adulthood, and old age. We can represent these on our cyclical diagram in the exact same way we did for the cycle of the day.

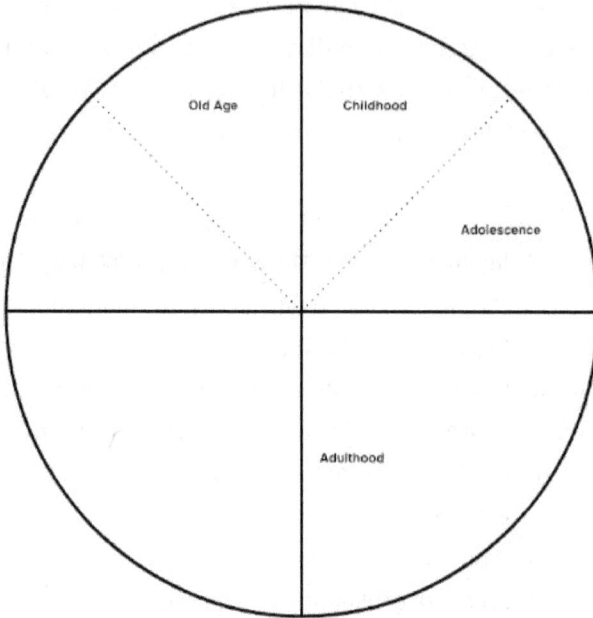

When we think of the differences between childhood and adulthood, some of the main ones that come to mind might be the physical and biological changes that occur. It goes without saying that we are bigger and stronger as adults than as children, that we are sexually mature, and that our appetites and tastes change. As adults, we have rights and responsibilities that children do not have, and these require a very different mindset from the imaginative but unfocused playfulness of childhood. Once again, we are going to give these obvious truths a fancy name and one that has a long tradition in the intellectual realm: the levels of being. We are going to use a quite specific version of the levels of being concept, so it will be worthwhile to define these clearly now. We will be working with three levels of being: the Physical, the Exoteric and the Esoteric.

By the Physical level of being, we denote all the phenomena of the world that are normally studied under the scientific disciplines of physics, chemistry, and biology. The cycle of the day and the cycle of the year can both be analysed entirely at the Physical level of being. Physics accounts for the rotation of the Earth on its axis and the rotation around the sun. Physics and related disciplines also account for the quantitative variables that change as a result of those rotations, while biology and related disciplines may also study how those effects interact with living systems.

In relation to the cycle of human life, an analysis at the Physical level of being would be mostly concerned with the biological facets of our lives. Thus, childhood brings obvious biological changes, including rapid growth, the arrival and replacement of a child's teeth, crawling, walking and more. Adolescence brings about the major changes we call puberty etc. These will all be familiar to us and uncontroversial.

The Exoteric level of being is one that most people will not have heard of. The word *exoteric* literally means *pertaining to the outside* or *external*. In relation to us as human beings, the Exoteric is about our external identity within the society and culture that we belong to. Humans are social animals, and our Exoteric existence refers to our place in society. Thus, clothing, fashion, ritual markings, jewellery, and other cultural practices that modify the human body belong to the Exoteric. The scholarly disciplines of anthropology, sociology, economics, and other *social sciences* are all concerned with the Exoteric level of being as we are defining it.

We can further identify four primary Exoteric identities that we have as humans living in society. There is our economic identity, our political identity, our sexual identity, and our religious identity. In the modern West, our economic identity is our career e.g. butcher, baker, or candlestick maker. Our political identity relates to our rights and responsibilities as citizens. Our sexual identity relates to our sexual availability and preferences. Our religious identity is marked by our affiliation with a church or spiritual tradition. Marriage is arguably the primary Exoteric institution across cultures since it entails a combination of all four primary identities.

Returning to the human lifecycle, we can see that the transition through the segments of our lives is also marked by developments at the Exoteric level of being. All cultures distinguish between at least childhood and adulthood for these purposes. Every culture has more or less formal ways to recognise when an individual is now an "adult" and the concept of adulthood comes with Exoteric changes in identity. To use the modern West as an example again, once we are recognised as adults, we are allowed to vote, to drive, to drink, to gamble etc. Thus, we can say that, at the Exoteric level of being, the segments of the human lifecycle are also demarcated. This demarcation will have some correspondence with the changes that occur at the Physical level of being, but the correspondence does not have to be temporally identical. That is part of the reason why we need to separate the Exoteric and Physical from an analytic point of view.

Finally, we have what we are going to call the Esoteric level of being. *Exoteric* means external or visible. *Esoteric* also has its etymology in Greek where it means "within" or "hidden". The word itself also has a long religious tradition. To be initiated into esoteric rites means to be given secret knowledge that is not to be shared publicly. We are going to use Esoteric to denote the variety of psychic, mental and spiritual states which are not directly visible to the senses and, therefore, are hidden from the external world. Encompassed in this definition are the disciplines of psychology, philosophy, theology, and spirituality. This might seem like an arbitrary grouping, but it's noteworthy that most spiritual mystical traditions require the adept to first master their "lower" psychological states, such as emotions, desires etc. The attainment of Esoteric mastery involves a psychological and philosophical journey through the *lower Esoteric,* across *the Abyss,* and over to the *higher Esoteric.*

If we limit ourselves to the parts of the Esoteric that are shared by all - the emotions – we can agree that the progression through the lifecycle sees a pattern of development that occurs in most people. The exuberance and enthusiasm of childhood give way to the cynicism or idealism of adolescence, the relative control and stability of adulthood, and, stereotypically, the grumpiness and curtness of old age.

The Esoteric is itself a complex domain that could be further split up into multiple extra levels of being. Since our analysis in this book aims to cover multiple different civilisations and cultural traditions, we will try to avoid making specific metaphysical commitments, and this is part of our motivation to group all of these issues together into a single category called the Esoteric. To reiterate, we include in the Esoteric level of being all of the most obvious mental and psychic faculties, including the emotions, desires, the conscious mind, the unconscious, the will, and all kinds of higher spiritual notions, including soul, spirit and Self.

When we apply this broader definition of the Esoteric to the human lifecycle, we find that it also maps to the segments we have defined earlier. Freud and Jung made a career and a legacy out of analysing and treating the psychology of childhood and adolescence. Subsequent psychologists, such as Erik Erikson, expanded the scope of psychology and found that the other segments of life also have their own unique challenges, opportunities, and qualities in the psychological domain. In relation to the other aspects of the Esoteric, such as the philosophical or spiritual, we can also say that the phases of life come with specific qualities. The later phases of adolescence, for example, often come with a desire to find meaning and purpose in life, which can be analysed as both a psychological development and a philosophical and theological one.

We can see, therefore, that the cycle of human life resonates at two levels of being that do not exist for the other cycles we looked at earlier, which exist entirely on the Physical level of being. The Exoteric and Esoteric definitely relate to the Physical but are not necessarily correlated with it. In fact, as we will see in our analysis later in the book, a great deal of human problems are caused by the asynchronous nature of the Exoteric and Esoteric realms. This is also what modern psychology found: childhood behavioural patterns can continue well beyond the time when they are appropriate at the Physical and Exoteric levels of being. Modern society designates such cases as "mental illness", but we will propose a different analysis as this book proceeds.

Another primary difference between the levels of being is their universality. At the Physical level of being, our experience throughout life is very much the same as anybody else's, at least in abstract terms. We are all thrown into this world at birth, go through puberty into maturity, and then descend into old age and, eventually, death. That much is universal. Our Exoteric experience of life shows much more variability, and our Esoteric experience shows the most variability. This is why most spiritual traditions focus on the Esoteric parts of the individual. This is also why some spiritual traditions argue that humans can eventually transcend the cycle at the Esoteric level of being.

Taking these differences into account, we can nevertheless see the correspondences between human life and the natural cycles we looked at earlier. When we talk about the segments of the human lifecycle, we are going to be using the concept of the archetypes inspired by Jungian psychology, but with the key difference that we will be extending their scope beyond the psychological and across the three levels of being that we have just identified. Thus, we will not be concerned only with the psychological facets of being an adolescent, for example, but also with the Exoteric and Physical facets. This will allow us to incorporate biological, sociological, anthropological, and spiritual perspectives alongside the more familiar psychological ones. The advantage of this should become clearer later in the book. For now, we will simply denote the names of the segments we will use in the analysis ahead as follows:-

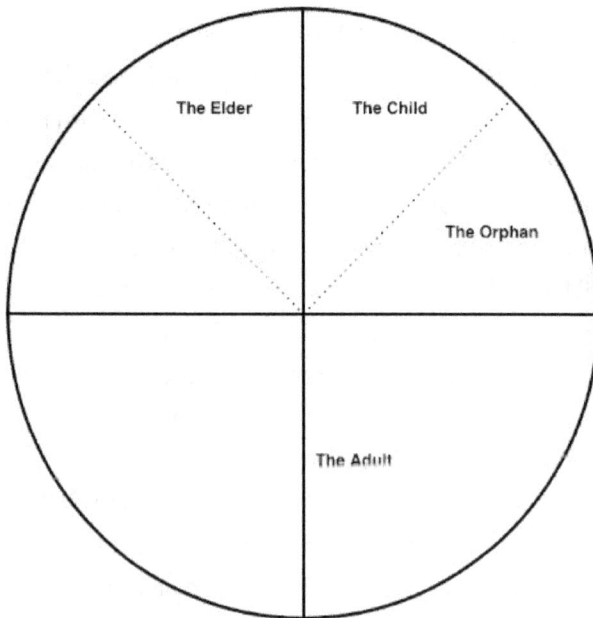

The Elder   The Child

The Orphan

The Adult

Whenever we refer to an archetype, therefore, we are not just talking about the psychological realm, which we have placed in the Esoteric level of being, but its correspondences with the Physical level of being that includes biology and the Exoteric level of being, which includes societal and anthropological factors. To give an introductory summary of what that means, we can represent the archetypes with their different resonances across the levels of being in table form as follows:-

Archetype	Level of Being			
	Physical	Exoteric	Esoteric – General	Esoteric – Dominant Faculty
The Child	Birth - Childhood	Son or daughter	Innocence, optimism, curiosity, naivete	Imagination
The Orphan	Puberty	Student, friend, protégé, initiate	Empathy, interdependence, cynicism, victimhood	Intellect
The Adult	Maturity	Husband/wife, parent, citizen, employee/boss, churchgoer	Conjugal love, ambition, achievement, domination, subjugation	Will
The Elder	Old Age - Death	Retiree, Mentor, Teacher	Wisdom, care, anger, disappointment	Soul

Reading the rows of the table across the levels of being gives us an overview of that phase of life in the general terms we have placed in the table. Reading the columns of the table from top to bottom gives us the archetypal progression through life at each level of being. For example, at the Exoteric level, it is during the Orphan phase when we begin to develop our independent identity, which will reach maturity during the Adult phase. The Elder phase then represents the time when we help the next generation through their own phases of life and we denote this with the terms mentor and teacher. Again, we will have much more to say about this later in the book, so we won't go into more detail now.

An important point about the archetypal progression through life is that it is one-directional. Once we have gone through puberty, there is no way to return to our former child's body. Similarly, an Adult who behaves like a

Child is, at best, acting inappropriately and, if the behaviour continues, may be considered to have a mental illness. Meanwhile, a loss of Exoteric identity during the archetypal phases can also be very damaging. For example, unemployment, the loss of the Adult economic identity, is linked with all kinds of negative outcomes, such as drug and alcohol abuse, depression and suicide. The archetypal wheel turns only in one direction, and this is true at the Physical (biological), Exoteric (social) and Esoteric (psychological and spiritual) levels of being.

It follows from the last point that each archetype can be thought of as a mini-life, and, since we cannot go back to earlier archetypes, the transitions between the archetypal phases can be thought of as mini-deaths. Note that this way of thinking matches some cultural traditions where the winter solstice marks a "rebirth" to a new year. We can think about the archetypal phases of our own lives in just the same way. Puberty is the "death" of the childhood body and the emergence of the new adult one. Within the cycle of our own lives, that death is final. There is no going back, although some spiritual beliefs hold that we will return in a future life to experience the same thing again.

The same is true at the other levels of being. Once we have graduated high school, for example, there is no going back and doing it again. Even if our society would allow us to go back to the beginning, we would be doing so as individuals who had already achieved the Exoteric identity of *high school graduate,* and this identity would not change a second time around. The Exoteric markers of life are at least as much about our society's demarcation of our identity as our own, and that is why repeating a rite of passage the second time has no bearing since the completion of it the first time has already changed our status from the point of view of the broader culture. There are exceptions to this, of course, such as modern marriage practices in the West.

At the Esoteric level of being, we find a classic reference to the idea that the archetypal progressions are mini-deaths when Jesus talks of being *born again* in the Bible. Jesus' interlocutor in the passage, Nicodemus, mistakenly thinks Jesus is talking about the Physical level of being. "Can he enter a second time into his mother's womb and be born?" he asks. Jesus responds that he is talking about *spirit*. In our terminology, he is talking about the Esoteric level of being. Most spiritual traditions have a concept of being born again into spirit, which is, in some sense, the beginning of the *higher Esoteric* journey through life, one that is foreign to us in the materialist modern West.

It is because the transition points between the archetypal phases of life are often painful that the characterisation of them as a mini-death also suits their psychological manifestation. This is something that Carl Jung touched on. He called it the individuation process, and Jung judged that individuation was psychically painful enough that most people will try to avoid it. This accounts for much of the difference that occurs at the Esoteric level of being. The biological progression through life cannot be avoided, but we can and do try to avoid the Exoteric and Esoteric ramifications of those changes. As both Freud and Jung found, we can try to dissociate from the archetypal changes by pushing them down into the Unconscious, from where they take on a life of their own and emerge as seemingly unrelated psychoses. Once again, this is why we need the levels of being concept, since in this way we can analytically account for a difference between the Physical and Esoteric realms.

With that, we have finished our brief introduction to what we are going to be calling the microcosmic view in this book, and, if it feels like we have covered a lot of territory in a very short amount of time, rest assured that we will be going into much more detail about these concepts in the pages ahead. Our purpose here has been just to provide the briefest overview.

We have said that the microcosm should have a corresponding macrocosm. Having defined the human lifecycle as the microcosm, that raises the question: what is the macrocosm? That is the subject to which we will now turn, and it is here that we will have to leave the relative safety of our discussion so far, which has touched upon uncontroversial matters that almost everybody would agree with. The macrocosm we are going to posit is that of civilisation and where the controversy comes in is because most people will not be used to thinking of civilisation as a cycle since our default understanding of history in the modern West is linear. That is a bias that we must now attempt to overcome.

We should remember, however, that the broader claim we are making here is that the relationship between the microcosm of the human individual and the macrocosm of civilisation is the same one we have established between the day and the year. Our own lives take place against the broader arcs of history in just the same way that each day takes place against the rotation of the Earth around the sun. Whether civilisation is cyclical or not, nobody would deny that it is qualitatively different to live in the modern world than it was to live several thousand years ago. That is what we mean when we say that the macrocosm of civilisation (or society and culture more broadly) plays a major governing role in our own lives and the lives of every person. This follows from the obvious fact that humans are social animals. Let's now turn to our introductory analysis of the macrocosm.

The Macrocosmic Perspective

At the very beginning of his TV series entitled *Civilisation*, the historian, Kenneth Clark, admitted that he could not define the concept of civilisation in abstract terms but that he knew it when he saw it. He then turned to look over his shoulder at Notre Dame Cathedral in the background. What a cathedral represents is not just order and structure but, more importantly, meaning. It is the physical expression of a set of ideas that form a coherent whole. Civilisation, therefore, also resonates across all three levels of being we have defined earlier, with the highest manifestation being at the Esoteric level: the set of ideas that unify a culture. Notre Dame was built during the emergence of modern European culture in the Gothic era of the 12th century. Since the Catholic Church was crucial not just in the construction of cathedrals but in the entire culture itself, the cathedral stands as a symbol of the unity of belief which held that civilisation together.

The concept of civilisation may be hard to define, but one thing we can say for sure is that it sits above political groupings such as tribes, nations etc. If a civilisation revolves around a core set of beliefs and ideas, it's also true that those ideas can manifest with different local flavours while still retaining an overall unity, in much the same way that a language can have many regional dialects while still being a single language. Thus, we don't talk of British, French, or German civilisation but of European civilisation.

Modern European civilisation was literally born in the ruins of the Roman Empire, and this has given it a peculiar obsession with both the Classical civilisation that preceded it and history more generally. With the expansion of European civilisation around the world, particularly in the 18th and 19th centuries, Europeans applied that historical perspective to other civilisations and came to the realisation that it was not just Rome that had "died". Numerous civilisations have existed and then perished. What Europeans in the 18th and 19th centuries came to realise was that the death of any given civilisation was not just possible but likely, perhaps even inevitable. This included, of course, their own civilisation. The poet, Shelley, captured some of the sentiment that this realisation evoked in his famous poem, Ozymandias:

"My name is Ozymandias, King of Kings;
   Look on my Works, ye Mighty, and despair!
   Nothing beside remains. Round the decay
   Of that colossal Wreck, boundless and bare
   The lone and level sands stretch far away"

It was around this time that some historians began to use the accumulated knowledge that Europeans had gathered from around the world to look for common patterns across the different civilisations that had been identified. Given that civilisations must begin sometime and must also end sometime, the comparison with the human lifecycle was obvious, and a cyclical pattern of the rise and fall of civilisation was discovered. Comparative historians such as Charles Rollin, Giambattista Vico, Arnold Toynbee and Oswald Spengler all had slightly different ways of analysing the phases of the cycle of civilisation, but all agreed that it was a cycle and one that had been repeated numerous times throughout history.

Crucially for our purposes, the comparative historians identified qualitatively distinct segments within the overall cycle, thus giving us the same pattern we have identified for the microcosm of the human individual as well as the day and yearly cycles of the Earth. We can, therefore, represent the cycle of civilisation in just the same way as we have done earlier in the book. To do so, we will use the terminology and analysis of Arnold Toynbee who was arguably the most methodical and rigorous of the comparative historians. We can diagram the basics of Toynbee's cycle of civilisation as follows:-

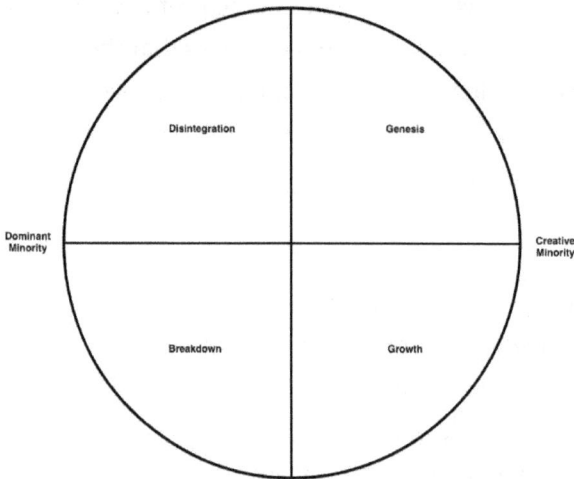

If the cycle of the day takes, well, a day, and the cycle of the human lifespan in the modern world takes about 80 years, the cycle of civilisation plays out over centuries and even millennia. Toynbee identified over 20 civilisations that are attested in the historical record. There is significant variability in how long they last. Perhaps the longest is the ancient Egyptian, while others seem to start but "die" before going through the full cycle.

Toynbee saw the cycle of civilisation as a series of challenges-and-responses that a unified group of people faces. What differentiates the growth phase of a civilisation from the breakdown phase is whether the response to a challenge leads to growth or decay. The labels that Toynbee gives to his cycle suggest a path to destruction. However, it's more complicated than that. Most of the things we associate with civilisation – law, order, power, wealth – belong to the second half of the cycle. A civilisation reaches its peak of worldly power in what Toynbee calls the Disintegration phase.

We can resolve this seeming paradox by invoking our levels of being concept. In relation to civilisation, the Physical level of being includes the non-biological world, since this makes up the natural resources that every society needs to survive and prosper. The way in which a civilisation makes use of the natural resources available to it gives it a metabolism which is directly analogous to biological entities. All of this belongs to the Physical level of being and it is, in fact, at this level of being, where Toynbee identifies the origins of civilisation which seem to stem from a crisis that forms the first great challenge that a nascent civilisation must overcome. Changing environmental conditions leading to famine or disease are a common theme in this respect.

Although these challenges take place at the Physical level of being, their effect is felt at the Exoteric and Esoteric too. Since the distribution of food is among the core functions of any society, a bad enough famine can break down the Exoteric structures that hold things together. A serious and prolonged famine can destroy those structures entirely, leading to political and economic revolution. It may well be that the Exoteric institutions that a society creates out of such crises are the very thing which propels it forward if they manifest some unique properties that lead to "success" in the broadest sense of the term. That's how Toynbee explained the beginnings of civilisation.

At the Esoteric level of being, it is clear that a famine or similar catastrophe would cause much emotional and psychological distress, but a significant enough event may go so far as to shake the theological foundations of a society. In the modern West with our secular materialist outlook, we forget that the Exoteric institutions of society, including the highest offices of politics, are justified at the Esoteric level. A bad enough crisis that calls into question the Esoteric basis of society will almost always cause the overthrow of the Exoteric institutions too, since they lose their justification. The Bible is full of exactly these kinds of crises and their ramifications at the different levels of being.

Using the work of the comparative historians, we see that civilisation is cyclical. We also see that it is made up of discrete segments and that both the whole arc of civilisation and the different segments resonate across the three levels of being. This is all prima facie evidence for a correspondence between the microcosm and macrocosm, and we are justified in thinking of the segments as archetypes in exactly the same way that we defined the archetypes of the microcosm as Child, Orphan, Adult and Elder. Following Toynbee, we name the archetypes of civilisation Genesis, Growth, Breakdown and Disintegration.

Just as the archetypal phases of the human lifecycle are qualitatively different, although unified, so too the phases of a civilisation are discrete and meaningful in themselves while also belonging to the overall cycle. We can use the levels of being concept to elaborate on these qualitative differences.

The Genesis period is one where the nascent civilisation is weak at the Physical level of being. Life during this time is nasty, brutish, and short due to the impoverished state of society. Similarly, the Exoteric institutions of society will be, by later standards, undeveloped and rudimentary during this time. Whatever hierarchies exist, there will be little power found at the top. Rather, there is decentralisation and significant heterogeneity throughout the peoples and lands where the civilisation is taking shape. What unifies the civilisation during this time can almost literally be called a "spirit" and this clearly refers to the Esoteric level of being. This spirit is almost always embodied in the religious institutions and beliefs of the new civilisation.

Civilisations start out poor and weak. On the Physical level of being, they are not much to talk about. It is at the Esoteric and Exoteric that they really take off during what Toynbee called the Growth phase. We see theological, philosophical and scientific advancements, as well as great works of art, architecture, music etc. All this happens while the general population lives in what we would call poverty and while the civilisation itself is under constant threat of being conquered militarily by powerful external enemies.

What Toynbee calls the Breakdown and Disintegration phases are actually the times when the civilisation reaches its peak at the Physical level of being.

It is now the most powerful actor, and it projects its power outward in military and economic dominance of foreign peoples. It is partly for this reason that Toynbee labels the ruling class of the late phases of civilisation the *Dominant Minority*. Whereas in the early stages the leadership class is likely to include the religious caste at the forefront, and this is what Toynbee called the *Creative Minority*, in the latter phases the leaders are usually military strongmen.

Toynbee's "breakdown" occurs at the Exoteric and especially the Esoteric levels of being. We see various crises of faith manifested in religious and political strife. More importantly, we see the seat of power shift from the land to the cities, which reflects the increasing centralisation and homogenisation of the culture. This process requires the dismantling of the old forms of society, which is why the phase *breakdown* is a good descriptor of the overall development. The general feeling at this time is of a loss of a moral authority and faith in the organic bonds which used to hold things together. Unlike a famine, a war, or some other obvious event on the Physical plane, an Esoteric crisis is much harder to identify and probably goes unnoticed for a long time until much later, when a prophet or philosopher announces that "God is dead".

A way to sum up the two halves of the civilisational cycle is that the first half is a challenge-and-response in the spiritual domain, while the second half is a challenge-and-response in the political and military domain. Oswald Spengler made this distinction by calling the first half of the cycle "culture" and the second half "civilisation". Putting all this together, we can construct an archetypal table very similar to the one we earlier showed for the microcosm. Since the phases of the civilisational cycle are less well-defined than those of the human lifecycle, we'll collapse the four archetypes into two rows as follows:-

Archetype	Level of Being		
	Physical	Exoteric	Esoteric
Growth - Genesis	Subsistence Agriculture	Decentralised political power, heterogeneity, localisation	Authority in tradition which links back to the spiritual, importance of belief and honour, ancestor worship, faith
Breakdown - Disintegration	Large scale agriculture, trade, tribute economy	Military and political institutions dominate, homogeneity and centralisation, rise of the mega-cities	Breakdown of authority in tradition, materialism, humanism, rationalism, utopianism, loss of faith

Necessarily, any analysis of civilisation is going to be more abstract and less intuitive than the simple truths we can all recognise about our own lives and those of other people. It is important to bear in mind that comparative history at the level of detail that Toynbee, Spengler, Vico and Rollin achieved was only possible with the truly global scope of European civilisation and the particular interest in history that that civilisation has always had. For this reason, we won't attempt to go into any more detail at the moment about the specifics of the civilisational cycle. This will be our focus in Part 2 of the book.

What is crucial to understand at this point is the relationship between the two cycles that we have now outlined: the microcosm and macrocosm. Once again, we can refer back to the relation between the year and the day to make this clear. Just as we can know with some certainty the properties of any day of the year if we know what season that day occurs in, what the comparative historians found was that the same is true of the civilisational cycle. To be born and to live through the Genesis period is very different than to live through the Disintegration phase. To take just one example from the table above, any individual born into the Genesis phase is almost certainly going to live in a decentralised and small scale community, while the same person born into the late phase of the cycle is far more likely to live in a giant city.

Since we have defined the Genesis and Disintegration phases as archetypes, we might already call comparative history a kind of archetypal history in that it looks for patterns that are shared across all examples of civilisation.

What we will be concerned with in this book and which differentiates this book from a standard comparative history is the way in which the interaction between the archetypes of the macrocosm and microcosm plays out. That is what the phrase from the title of the book, *archetypal calculus,* refers to. We are not just concerned, as psychologists are, with the archetypes of the microcosm and we are not just concerned, as comparative historians are, with the archetypes of the macrocosm. We want to know the relationship between the two.

All of this sounds very complicated due to the fancy word we are using when, in fact, it is just the same pattern that we observed earlier. If we call the segment of the day known as *afternoon* an archetype of the microcosm and we call *winter* an archetype of the macrocosm, it's clear that the latter archetype modulates the former. For example, we know that afternoons in winter are shorter than they are in summer. Therefore, we have shown that the archetype of the macrocosm governs a change in the archetype of the microcosm. It's this exact same pattern that we will be looking for between the microcosm of the human individual and the macrocosm of human civilisation.

When applied to the microcosm of a human individual and the macrocosm of civilisation, what we expect to see, therefore, is that the archetypal phases of Child, Orphan, Adult and Elder are modulated during the phases of the macrocosm. It was this exact phenomenon that I had accidentally discovered with my Devouring Mother analysis, where I found that the archetypes of the Devouring Mother and the Orphan seemed to dominate the collective psychology of the modern West. It was my attempt to find the beginnings of that macrocosmic development that has led to this book.

Demonstrating the truth of the above statement will take us the rest of this book and will also lead us down some fascinating back alleys away from the standard narratives that our society constructs for itself. For now, it is enough to note that we have shown that the cycle of the human lifecycle and the cycle of comparative history are identical and that this is prime facie evidence for our microcosm-macrocosm assumption. We can capture this fact in the following diagram of our integrated model, which we will be honing more in the pages ahead.

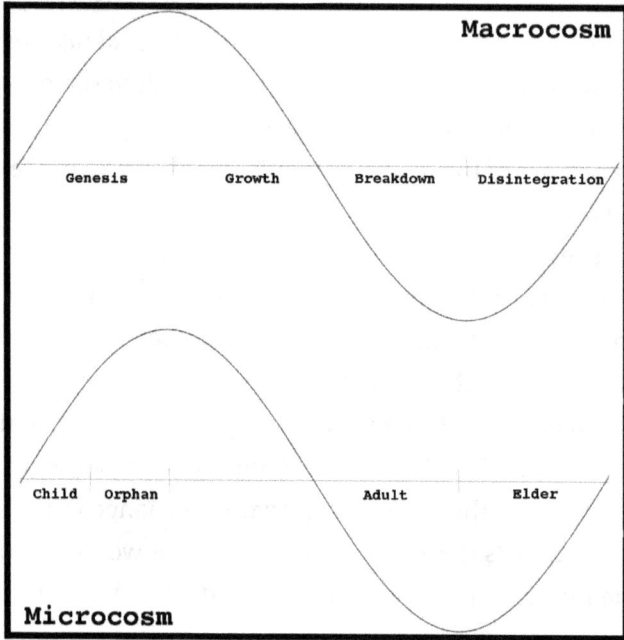

Note that we have chosen to represent the cycles as sine waves. This is both for ease of presentation, but there is an ulterior motive, which will become evident shortly.

Our diagram shows clearly that the microcosm and the macrocosm have identical underlying structures, but we have claimed that there are interrelations between the two cycles. That means we need to explain what the nature of those interrelations is, and here we will find our first surprising discovery because it turns out that two of the most important practices which link the microcosm and macrocosm also have exactly the same underlying cyclical structure. It's time to talk about Hero's Journeys and rites of passage.

The Hero's Journey

It should be a fairly uncontroversial statement to say that stories are one of the main ways in which societies and cultures hold together and, therefore, one of the ways in which the link between microcosm and macrocosm is established and then maintained. There is a reason, after all, why billions of dollars are spent every year on public relations and advertisements, and why politicians and other famous people take every opportunity to appear in all forms of media. As Plato once wrote – who tells the stories, rules society.

Another way in which stories are an obvious device of enculturation is that they are always told in a specific language and therefore belong to the culture in which that language is spoken. Fictional stories will also feature characters and settings which make sense within the culture. Stories reflect ourselves back to us. They are also especially popular with children as a way for them to become part of the culture, and, thus, children's storybooks as well as TV and film are a major way in which young people are initiated into society.

All of this is quite obvious and uncontroversial. What is less obvious, but more relevant for our analysis, is the way in which stories reflect the deeper archetypal structures that we have introduced in this book. In fact, stories have the exact same structure that we have already found in the microcosm and macrocosm i.e. a cycle that is separated into qualitatively discrete segments. The modern thinker who is known for analysing this structure in great detail is another comparative scholar, although one who was not working in history but in mythology. Joseph Campbell discovered the Hero's Journey pattern from his readings of myths from across a multitude of different cultures. He found a common structure beneath the surface differences.

Campbell was heavily influenced by Jung's idea that symbols are the key to the exploration of the Unconscious. Within our framework, we can say that symbols resonate across the levels of being we have identified. A snake is just a snake on the Physical level of being, but the danger which the snake represents in the material world may be symbolically extended to refer to a threat to our psychic equilibrium (an Esoteric danger) or even a threat to our social status and identity (an Exoteric danger). In a well-told story, we expect to see resonance across all the levels of being simultaneously in just the same way that a sophisticated piece of music resonates harmonically across different registers of the musical spectrum.

Hero's Journeys are cycles that resonate across the levels of being. That makes them comparable to the other cyclical structures we have identified. Also like those structures, the cycle of the Hero's Journey is made up of qualitatively discrete segments. How many segments there are in a story has been debated for a long time. Aristotle identified five in ancient Greek drama. This became known as Five-Act structure and was the dominant analytical paradigm during the neoclassical period (16th-18th centuries) in Europe, which is why most Shakespeare plays have five acts. In his book *The Hero with a Thousand Faces*, Joseph Campbell identified a 3-Act structure which he calls *Departure – Initiation – Return*. These can be mapped onto our now familiar cyclical diagram as follows:-

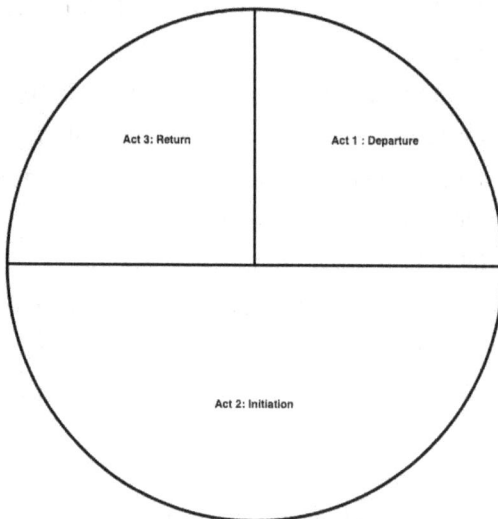

The archetypal analysis that Campbell used to define the Hero's Journey is identical to both the life cycle analysis and the analysis of comparative history we went through earlier in that it looks for the common patterns which underlie surface phenomena. Every story is different, just as every civilisation and every human are different. But it's also true that there are common patterns which underlie these differences. Everybody must go through puberty. How one navigates that phase of life is unique since, ultimately, the core of the challenge must be faced alone. The same is true of the Hero's Journey concept. Although ever story is unique and the best-written stories are the most unique and, therefore, the most interesting, it's also true that every story follows the same pattern. Every hero receives a Call to Adventure in Act 1 of the story, and every hero faces a make-or-break moment at the end of Act 2. Those are the common patterns which Joseph Campbell identified.

Very briefly, we can summarise the three archetypal phases of the Hero's Journey as follows.

At the beginning of Act 1, we find the hero in stasis. They are in their normal, everyday world, doing normal, everyday things. They might be a king in a castle, a knight at a jousting contest, a kind-hearted bandit planning the next robbery, or a princess wandering aimlessly by a stream. The hero's world is in equilibrium, and the hero is acting with the certainty that follows from being secure in the knowledge of their surroundings and their life situation.

But there is something that the hero is lacking, and that something will be embodied in the Call to Adventure which comes at the midpoint of Act 1. As the name suggests, the Call to Adventure will require the hero to depart from their normal, everyday world and step into the new world that is offered to them by a third party. The stakes are high, since the hero has something to lose, but the *Call to Adventure* also offers them something to gain.

In psychoanalytic terms, the Call to Adventure comes from the Unconscious. Something has been bubbling away in the background and has finally risen to the surface and presented itself to the conscious mind. For this reason, it's common for the *Call to Adventure* to come from a symbol of the Unconscious such as a frog, a toad, or an old hag. This is true even in high literature. In Shakespeare's *Macbeth*, the Call to Adventure comes from the three witches. In *Hamlet*, it comes from the ghost of Hamlet's father.

In *Romeo and Juliet*, the titular characters are each other's call from the Unconscious representing the Jungian *anima* and *animus* respectively.

When the hero accepts the call from the Unconscious, the *Initiation* phase of the story begins. By definition, Act 2 requires the hero to step into the unknown, and that is why Campbell described the middle phase of the journey as a descent into the Unconscious. In mythology, the Unconscious is symbolically represented by supernatural events and creatures. In secular terms, we can say that the hero enters a new world that they do not fully understand and must learn to navigate through. They might be the greatest warrior or the most powerful king, but the hero is now out of their depth. They struggle to come to terms with a situation where their old knowledge, understanding, and skills no longer work.

The *Initiation* phase of the story might involve all kinds of events and challenges on the Physical level of being but these go hand-in-hand with a challenge to the ego and to the conscious mind of the hero. Thus, there is also a resonance on the Esoteric level of being and this resonance may go all the way to challenging the basic suppositions about reality that the hero held at the beginning of the story. The hero is tested. Sometimes they win and seem to be on the verge of success. But they also fail, and the failures mount until they seem insuperable. This is the make-or-break moment that comes at the end of the second act. The hero can try to back out and return to the perceived safety of the *Old World* or they can push on towards the goal, knowing that the price of failure will now be ruinous.

In Act 3, the hero lays it all on the line and pushes on to the *Return* phase of the cycle. This is where the challenge is greatest, but the hero finds within themselves the strength to transcend to a new level. The Return phase is a return to the "real world" with the new skills, truths, and perspectives the hero has gained on their journey. Act 3 maps to what Jung called Individuation. It is the integration of what was previously unconscious into consciousness. It is precisely because the Hero returns to normality, equilibrium, and consciousness at the end of the story that the Hero's Journey is a cycle. The hero is back where they started, and it's very common for the external world to be exactly the same at the end of the story as it was at the beginning. But the hero has always changed. If there is a happy ending, the hero has successfully negotiated the challenge and transcended to a new form of life. If the story is a tragedy, the hero has failed and is brought undone.

We said at the start of this section that stories work to establish and maintain a culture through the use of a specific language, specific cultural practices, and patterns. That is certainly true. But what our brief summary of the Hero's Journey shows is that stories communicate at a deeper level, and they do so because they have the same underlying structure as the human lifecycle. Consider all that we have just described about the seemingly fictional world of the Hero's Journey and then consider that it is also a perfect description of our progress through the archetypal phases of life. Our journey from childhood to adulthood, for example, is a journey to a new form of life. Like the hero of a story, we are qualitatively different on the other side of that journey. In fact, we can state that the archetypal phases of our lives are Hero's Journeys. At puberty, the Child is given a Call to Adventure to leave their old world, the world of the Child, and step into a new one. The new world of adolescence comes with new challenges and opportunities that must be confronted. At the end of the journey, the hero is qualitatively different from where he or she started. They have transcended from the Child to the Adult. The reason stories are so popular is certainly because they sub-communicate these deeper truths that resonate with our intuitive understanding of our own lives.

As with our own lifecycle, we can also analyse the cycle of the Hero's Journey as a set of resonances across the three levels of being. The Physical relates to the actual movement of the characters and their actions in the world they exist in. Cinderella begins the story scrubbing floors in her home, gets dressed up and goes to the ball, then returns to scrubbing where the prince finds her with the shoe. What Joseph Campbell showed in great detail was that we must interpret the Physical in symbolic terms as pointers to both the Exoteric and Esoteric levels of being. A frog is not just a frog. It's a symbol of the Unconscious and, therefore, it points to the Esoteric level of being. When the beautiful princess meets the frog, this is the symbol of her confrontation with her Unconscious and the beginning of her Hero's Journey.

Of course, the very role of *princess* belongs to the Exoteric context of a story, which can also function as a symbol pointing to the other levels of being. Cinderella begins her story in the Exoteric role of a lowly washerwoman. She briefly Departs (the Departure phase of the story) from that life and gets to spend a short time in the Exoteric role of princess dancing at the ball. When we interpret this change symbolically, we find that the Exoteric washerwoman role is itself a symbol of the Physical level of being, as demonstrated by Cinderella's floor scrubbing. Meanwhile, the role of princess is far more Esoteric since royalty is a mostly symbolic position and one that certainly does not require strenuous physical activity. There is a meta-symbolism in the story of Cinderella becoming a princess. Her *Call to Adventure* is a call to transcend the Physical and Exoteric levels of being and create a life of meaning at the Esoteric level. In the Jungian sense, the handsome prince is the symbol of Cinderella's *animus*, her soul. Cinderella's soul is calling her to an adventure to create meaning for her life above and beyond the Physical and Exoteric levels where she begins the story.

Just like a complex piece of harmonic music, even relatively simple Hero's Journeys like fairy-tales resonate at multiple levels of being at the same time. The frog is both a Physical challenge, an Exoteric challenge to the extent that princesses are not supposed to associate with frogs, and an Esoteric challenge given that the princess must overcome her feelings of revulsion and pride. When she wins the handsome prince as a result, he is a combination of a Physical, Exoteric and Esoteric blessing. The overall symbolism of the Hero's Journey is that facing up to the Unconscious and overcoming its challenges brings a reward.

Since all of these meanings are embedded in the symbolic context of the Hero's Journey and also in interaction with the other archetypal elements in a story, and since most people never learn to consciously decode that symbolism, we can state that all these meanings are transmitted subconsciously through stories. But, to say it again, the reason stories resonate so strongly with us is because we intuit the underlying structural identity that they have with our own lives. The structure of the Hero's Journey is the structure of our lives. That is what we perceive subconsciously in a well-told story.

All of this is transmitted through stories, alongside the more obvious cultural markers that we mentioned at the beginning of this section, such as choice of language, culturally specific characters and settings etc. For all these reasons, we can state that stories form a bridge between the microcosm and the macrocosm. This is especially true once we understand that a great deal of the communication in our society, including in seemingly unrelated domains such as politics and religion, also consists of the telling of stories. We can represent the role that Hero's Journeys play as the link between ourselves and our society on our diagram of the integrated model as follows:-

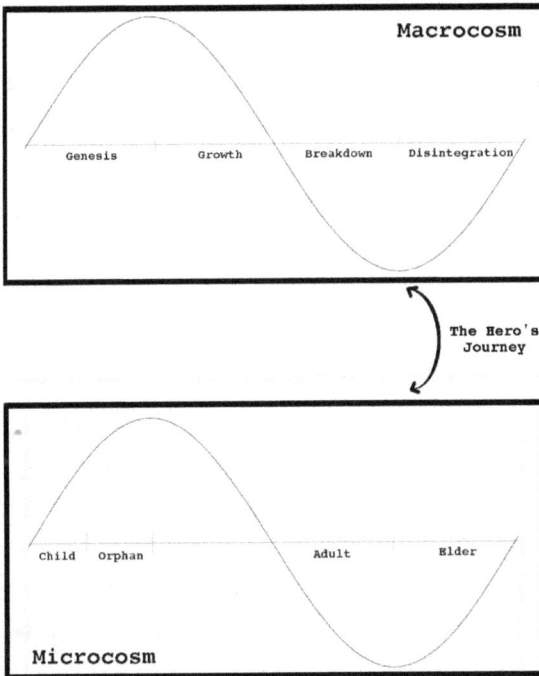

We will go into much more detail about Hero's Journeys later in the book, so this summary will suffice for now. We are now ready to move on to the second cultural practice that forms a link between microcosm and macrocosm as we review the work of anthropologist, Arnold van Gennep, and his notion of the rites of passage.

The Rites of Passage

From an anthropological point of view, one of the defining features of modern western culture is our lack of rites of passage. Marriage is perhaps the last remaining rite that is taken seriously enough to give us an understanding of what, for most cultures throughout history, was a recurring feature throughout life. Imagine the time, energy, and seriousness which go into a marriage ceremony, and then imagine that there were numerous such ceremonies throughout your life similar to that. Those ceremonies are the rites of passage. Even more obviously than for the Hero's Journeys because of their formal and overt nature, the rites of passage are the means by which the individual is inducted into the collective and are, therefore, a link between the microcosm and the macrocosm.

The anthropologist, Arnold van Gennep, coined the concept of the rites of passage in his best-known work of the same name, written in 1909. That was a full 40 years earlier than Campbell's *The Hero with a Thousand Faces*. What van Gennep showed, and Campbell later confirmed, was the underlying structural identity between Hero's Journeys and rites of passage. If you told somebody that a wedding ceremony followed the same underlying pattern as a Shakespeare play, they would no doubt be surprised, and, yet, it's true. The longevity of wedding ceremonies and Shakespeare is further evidence that the structure itself resonates with us, even though we are not consciously aware of it. We said earlier that our lives are Hero's Journeys but we might equally well say that they are rites of passage. That is what many religious traditions either imply or outright state.

The religious connection here is not arbitrary. We have just seen that Campbell analysed the Hero's Journey using a Jungian framework, which entailed a transition from consciousness to the Unconscious and back again.

32

Van Gennep posits an identical transition for the rites of passage; only the concepts he uses are profane and sacred. In the secular modern West, we have little to no understanding of the meaning of the word *sacred* and we'll need to elaborate on it a little to understand what van Gennep had in mind. There is a dual meaning at play. On the one hand, the sacred is dangerous and powerful, with connotations of illness and disease alongside the more spiritualised meanings of angry deities and spirits. On the other hand, the sacred is about holiness, healthiness, and healing. This makes sense if we think of the sacred as a process, which is exactly how van Gennep uses it in relation to the rites of passage. A rite of passage is the process of navigating through the sacred and coming out the other side. At the beginning of the rite, we step into the sacred and become unholy, un-whole and unhealthy. At the end of the rite, we are made holy, whole, and healthy again.

We can see that, even in secular terms, the rites of passage are still valid since there are dangers involved, even if only in the social sphere rather than the physical and spiritual ones. Once again, a modern marriage ceremony can serve as an example, since most of us would have a story about a wedding that went wrong, leading to various social consequences. Some people will never speak to each other again. Others will suffer the less dramatic reputational damage that comes from a best man losing the ring or a drunk father making a bad speech.

All these risks exist because of the *sacredness* of a rite of passage. We all hope to get to the *other side* unscathed. Once the danger is over and the rite is over, the initiate returns from sacred to profane status. Here, again, we see obvious parallels with the Hero's Journey since initiates who have gone through the rite of passage have now incorporated the sacred into themselves in just the same way that the hero has returned from the Unconscious at the end of their journey. To take just a couple of the more obvious examples, a woman exits the rite of passage of childbirth with a new child, and a groom exits the rite of marriage with a new bride (or groom, given recent changes to marriage laws). In less dramatic and important rites, we may come out the other side with nothing more than a pat on the back from family and friends. In any case, something must be gained on the other side, since if nothing was gained, then there must have been nothing at stake, and the rite of passage was not a true rite but an empty ceremony.

Joseph Campbell discovered the Hero's Journey by analysing the myths from a variety of different cultures. Van Gennep found the rites of passage through a similarly extensive study of ceremonial practices from around the world. Both men found the structure that we are now intimately familiar with: the cycle with qualitatively discrete segments. Van Gennep names his *Separation - Transition - Incorporation*. We can see how similar these are in meaning to Campbell's *Departure – Initiation – Return*. We can represent a rite of passage with our familiar cyclical diagram as follows:-

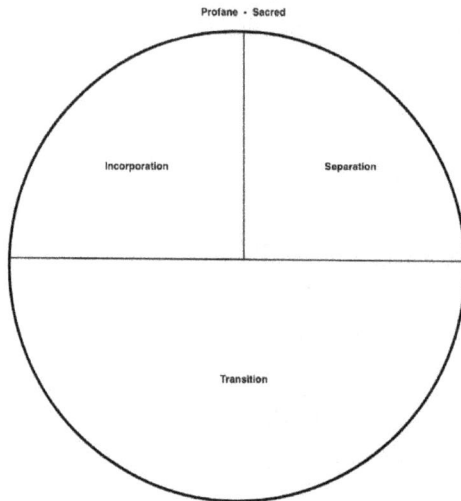

Just as we did with the Hero's Journey, let's briefly walk through each phase of the cycle, using the western marriage ceremony as an example.

The Separation phase of a rite begins at the moment when you detach from your ordinary, everyday routine and begin the preparation for the rite of passage. In relation to marriage, we can see that the Separation phase begins with the proposal of marriage, since the acceptance of that proposal brings about a new status for the future marriage partners and demarcates a new phase of life. There follows a long period of preparation for the wedding, including choosing the bridal dress, the location, the catering options, and all the other details that will go into the ceremony. Again, all of this is outside of our normal routine and therefore counts as the Separation phase of the rite.

This raises an important point which we will go into detail about shortly, but which we need to clarify now for this analysis to make sense. The individual sections of a rite of passage are also rites of passage. That is, they have the exact same structure as the overarching pattern. The same is true of the Hero's Journeys and, we will later argue, of the archetypal phases of our own lives. Thus, we can "zoom in" on the rites of passage and find that each of the segments is itself a rite of passage with its own Separation – Transition – Incorporation structure.

The marriage proposal, if done in the usual fashion where the would-be groom invites the would-be bride somewhere special, makes the proposal, and then puts the engagement ring on the finger, is itself a rite of passage. We can clearly see that the Separation phase is going to the place where the proposal will take place, the Transition phase is whatever the pair does leading up to and including the proposal, and the Incorporation phase is the placing of the ring on the finger if the woman says *yes*. But the important point to understand is that the proposal is a rite of passage, which is itself part of the larger rite of passage, which is the marriage. More specifically, the proposal constitutes the beginning of the Separation phase of the overall rite. The rest of the Separation phase includes telling friends and family that the couple is now engaged. In different cultures, the Separation phase may only conclude once the parents and other relevant parties have given their explicit and formal consent to the marriage.

If the proposal belongs to the Separation phase of the overall marriage rite, then the preparations for the marriage are the Transition phase, and the wedding ceremony itself is the Incorporation phase. But, again, the wedding day is itself a rite of passage that meets the formal structure. The Separation phase begins with the preparations to attend church, since this is an even more pronounced departure from everyday life. The Transition phase can be seen as the journey to the church, while the ceremony itself is the Incorporation phase. But we can drill down even further and see that the wedding ceremony is a full rite of passage, where entry to the church is the Separation phase, and where the father "gives away" the bride, meaning she is now symbolically *separated* from her family. We then enter the Transition phase, where there are speeches and other ceremonial happenings. Finally, the Incorporation phase includes the reading of the vows, the exchanging of rings, and the final kiss.

As if all that wasn't enough, we can "zoom out" from all of this and see that everything we have just talked about – the proposal, the preparations for the wedding, and the wedding ceremony – are all part of the Separation phase of the even larger rite of passage which marriage represents. We have to remember that marriage used to be a lifelong commitment, and the *til death do us part* promise was expected to be kept. In that case, the act of getting married forms the Separation phase of the rite; the marriage itself is the Transition phase; and the breaking of the marriage with the death of one of the couple is the Incorporation phase.

Mathematically speaking, a structure which recurs at different degrees of resolution and scale is called a fractal. We can see from these considerations that rites of passage are fractals, and so too are Hero's Journeys. Indeed, our own lives are also fractal since the archetypal phases of our lives – Child, Orphan, Adult and Elder – are *mini-lives* i.e. they have the same structure as our overall lives. We will return to the fractal nature of the cycles we have been looking at shortly.

It should be no surprise, given all the other correspondences with our previous analysis, to find that the rites of passage can also be analysed as resonances across all three levels of being. Since a rite of passage has an actual, real-world Physical component in the formal actions carried out by the participants, this constitutes the pattern of the rite at the Physical level of being. But rites of passage are primarily Exoteric in nature since they are explicitly about initiating individuals into an Exoteric institution of society. A marriage takes place in a church because, historically, in modern European civilisation, it was the church who was the keeper of marriage records and not the state. The fact that the state now supersedes the church is part of a change in the political balance of society that began in earnest in the 19th century.

In any case, at the Exoteric level of being, the outcome of the marriage rite of passage is that the two people are now considered married and that this marriage is recognised by the Exoteric institutions of society, including church and state. The marriage rings are the Exoteric markers worn by the married couple, which signal to other members of society that the individual is "taken". Other Exoteric institutions of society, such as banks, insurance companies, and the tax office, will have special categories that the newly married couple now belongs to. In the way we will be using the concept in this book, we can state that every rite of passage should have an Exoteric outcome i.e. the initiates' Exoteric status will be changed on the other side of the rite. This distinguishes the rites of passage from esoteric religious and spiritual rites, which, by definition, do not have an Exoteric component since they are carried out in secret.

The rites of passage, as we have defined them, also resonate on the Esoteric level of being. Certainly, the lower Esoteric is present in the form of heightened emotions - the anxiety, nervousness, and tension that come from the fear of "failure". Because rites of passage require public-facing actions, this nervousness is understandable since, even if you know exactly what is going to happen at the Physical level of being and have practiced your moves, that is a very different thing from actually performing those moves correctly when the heat is on.

This reveals something not just about the rites of passage but also about our lives in general. Intellectually knowing something is not the same as actually experiencing it. That is why there is an element of danger to the rites of passage captured by van Gennep's invocation of the concept of the sacred. Ultimately, there is an Esoteric leap of faith into the unknown for the initiates of a rite. A wedding ceremony has been performed millions of times before, but how you will perform it cannot be known until the rite of passage has actually been completed. Just as every story is different even though it follows the Hero's Journey pattern, so, too, is every rite of passage different even though it follows the same ceremony that has been carried out millions of times before. It is this inherently individual aspect which belongs to the highest level of the Esoteric.

Both the rites of passage and the Hero's Journeys serve to make sense of our world, to induct us into our culture, and to guide us through the archetypal phases of life. From a macrocosmic point of view, they are there to ensure the propagation of society not just at the Physical level of being through the creation of the next generation but at the Exoteric level of being through the induction of that generation into the institutions of society and the Esoteric level of being through the initiation of the next generation into the core beliefs of the culture. For these reasons, we can mark the rites of passage alongside the Hero's Journeys on the diagram of our integrated model as follows:-

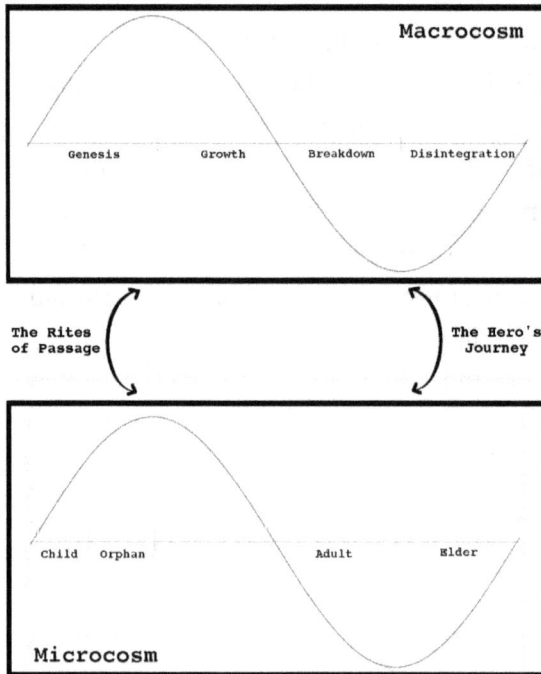

With this, we have laid out the main elements of our integrated model of civilisation. We are now ready to bring it all together.

The Integrated View: Microcosm and Macrocosm

Since we have covered a lot of ground in a very short space of time, it is worth briefly reiterating the original hypothesis that we made at the beginning of the book.

We made the claim that civilisation is the macrocosm to the microcosm of an individual human life. This means that civilisation stands in relation to human life as a year stands in relation to a day i.e. as a larger cycle which governs or influences a smaller cycle. In practice, this means that just as a day in summer is different from a day in winter, so, too, is it different to live through the different archetypal phases of the civilisational cycle. There are different challenges, different opportunities, and different emphases that mark out each phase. But this is also true of the different segments of our lives. It is different to be a Child than to be an Adult, to be an Orphan than to be an Elder. It is because of the shared underlying structure between these cycles that we can use one to describe another. Thus, we can say of a person that they are *in the summer of their life* or of a civilisation that it is *in its springtime.*

Following our original formulation of an integrated model that includes the microcosm and macrocosm, we introduced the two main cultural practices which serve as a bridge between the two, and we saw that those cultural practices shared the exact same underlying structure. The rites of passage and the Hero's Journey are both cycles demarcated into qualitatively different segments. To be consistent, we might call those segments archetypes since they map directly to the archetypes of civilisation and the human lifecycle. Crucially, we showed that the relationships between the overall cycle and the segments of the cycle were identical. That is, the archetypes or segments that we have defined within the larger cycles are also cycles with the exact same archetypal structure. In mathematics, this is called a fractal. Thus, we can say that the cyclical patterns we have identified in the microcosm, macrocosm, rites of passage, and Hero's Journeys are all fractals.

To finish Part 1 of the book and complete the basic presentation of our integrated model, we will now incorporate the idea of the fractal into the model and, in doing so, show with more clarity the relationships between the concepts we have introduced thus far.

Modification 1: The Fractal Sine Wave

We are now ready to take advantage of a modification we made earlier, whereby we represented the cycle as a sine wave, since it is much easier to represent a fractal relationship on a sine wave than on a circle. Let's begin with a fractal representation of the microcosm:-

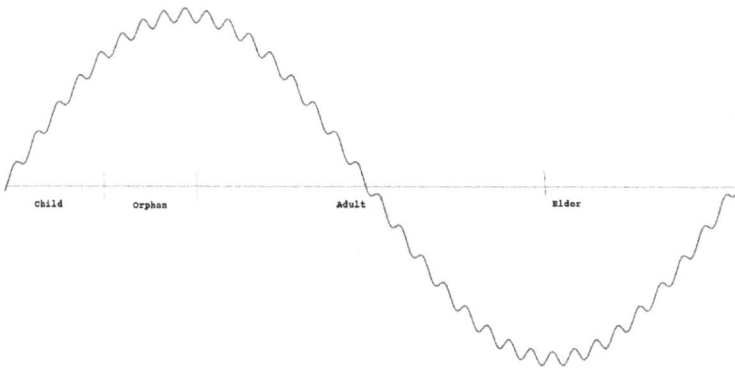

The overall arc remains the same and denotes the full cycle of a human life. The question then arises: what do the smaller sine waves represent? The answer is that they are nothing more or less than the rites of passage and the Hero's Journeys that make up our lives. The reason this works is because we know that the rites and Hero's Journeys are also cycles and can therefore also be represented as sine waves. We also know that our lives can be thought of as a series of rites and Hero's Journeys that change in nature during the different archetypal phases, beginning in childhood with the start of education, continuing through adolescence with events like a first job, a first kiss etc. and then into adulthood and elderhood.

The huge advantage of our fractal sine wave representation of the micro-cosm is that it allows us to see the full cycle at a glance while also allowing us to "zoom in" on specific rites of passage or Hero's Journeys. To demonstrate, let's choose a specific rite of passage, which we will mark in black as a single sine wave on the full lifecycle. If we were to "zoom in" on that rite of passage, we would see the familiar structure that we analysed earlier:-

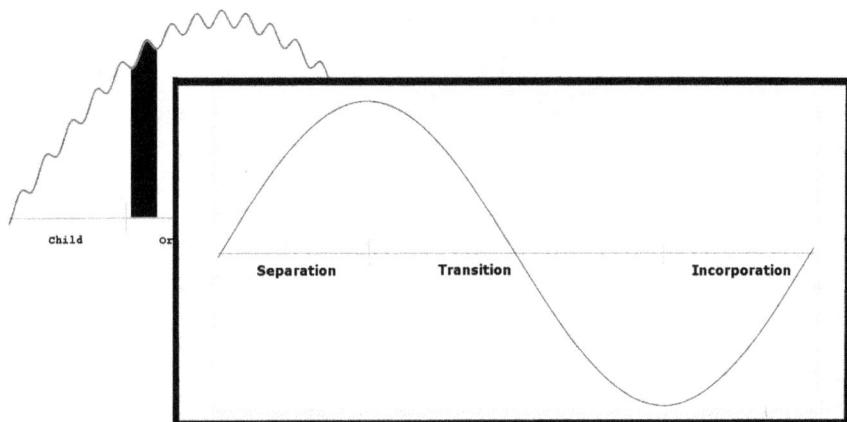

What we have represented is a rite of passage that takes place near the beginning of the Orphan phase of life. Without knowing the specifics of the rite or anything about the culture in question, we could make a very accurate guess at what type of rite of passage this will be. It will be one which inducts the initiate for the first time into an institution of society or an element of culture, since that is the overarching theme of the Orphan phase of life.

Of course, it's also true that specific rites of passage belong to specific cultures. Arguably, once we understand the universality of the underlying concept, we obtain a better understanding of how the specific content of a rite reveals something about the culture in question. Let's take an example from European civilisation that matches the diagram above. We are looking for a rite of passage that occurs at the start of the Orphan phase, and we find it in the Christian rite of Holy Communion.

Holy Communion is a rite of passage that demonstrates van Gennep's 3-part cyclical structure to a tee. The *Separation* phase of the rite is the consecration of the wine and bread. This marks the break (the Separation) between this specific rite and the rest of the Mass. The *Transition* phase is the congregation moving to the altar. The *Incorporation* phase is the receipt of the wine and bread. Holy Communion marks the Orphan transition because it is the first time the individual receives the Eucharist and, therefore, symbolises their full membership in the church. At the end of the rite, there is an Exoteric status change on the part of the individual, who is no longer one of the children but one of the adults. Hence, it belongs at the onset of the Orphan phase of life.

But the fun doesn't stop there. Holy Communion is one part of the overall rite of passage, which is the Christian Mass. It is, in fact, the Incorporation phase of the Mass. Since Mass is also a 3-part rite, containing a Separation and Transition phase too, we see a fractal relationship at play. There are, in fact, three hierarchical levels involved, with the Mass at the top level, Holy Communion at the second level, and the individual segments of Holy Communion at the third level. Technically speaking, each of these is a cycle and should therefore be represented as a sine wave.

But even that is not all, since there is another hierarchical level above the Mass. Holy Communion is itself the third and final phase of the overall rites of initiation into the Catholic Church, the first two being Baptism and Confirmation. Baptism is the Separation phase of the rite and Confirmation is the Transition phase. In the early days of Christianity, these three sacraments were all given together; only later was the process stretched out over a period of years. So, we have at least four hierarchical levels going on for just this one rite of passage. Note that this is the exact same pattern we saw earlier in relation to the completely different rite of passage of marriage i.e. a nested structure where each element in the hierarchy has the same pattern as the element above it. In fact, this is a general property of rites of passage, of Hero's Journeys, and our own lives.

What this means is that our above diagram of the fractal sine wave is missing a number of hierarchical levels, and we would need to "zoom in" at least four levels to capture the relationships that hold. Since this is all but impossible to represent on a static, two-dimensional diagram, what we can do instead is try and represent it in table form. Before we do that, let's go back to the start and work through our example again.

Level 1 is the overall human lifecycle. Level 2 is the archetypal phases of life. Our assumption is that each archetypal phase has the same structure as the overall cycle. Here we run into a small analytical problem because we have introduced two separate variations on what that structure is. We have seen that the microcosm and macrocosm have four archetypal phases, and the rites of passage and Hero's Journey have three. Since it's not important whether the numbers match up exactly, we will represent the Orphan phase of life as having a 3-part structure since that will fit within our table format. Level 3 then becomes the three phases of the Orphan period of life: initiation, adolescence, and marriage. This works because marriage has traditionally been seen as the end of the Orphan phase and the beginning of the Adult phase. Note that it's more complicated than that but, for now, this simplification works to make our point.

Since we have chosen to focus on the Orphan phase of life and the Initiation segment of the Orphan phase, Level 4 becomes an initiation rite of passage, which we have already identified as the three-part structure of Baptism-Confirmation-Communion. Level 5 is the rite of Mass, which contains the rite of Communion, which is Level 6.

Putting it all together, we get the following table:-

	Separation	**Transition**	**Incorporation**
Human Lifecycle	Child-Orphan	Adult	Elder
Orphan Phase of Life	Initiation	Adolescence	Marriage
Initiation rite of Christianity	Baptism	Confirmation	Communion
Mass	Start of Mass	Body of Mass	Eucharist (Communion)
Communion	Consecration of bread and wine	Congregation moves to altar	Receipt of bread and wine

Note that the top row in our table represents a point that we have already made, which is that the entire human lifecycle can also be thought of as a rite of passage (or Hero's Journey). This view maps directly to how a number of religious traditions think about the subject. Life is *sacred* to the extent that we are *Separated* from the spiritual realm at birth and *Incorporated* back into it at death. Our lives are the Transition phase during which we are tested and where our task is to strive for holiness (wholeness).

Another important thing to note is that once we introduce the concept of hierarchical levels, we rapidly expand the number of combinations that our model captures. With a 3-part structure at six levels, we get 3^6, which is 729 combinations. Those are just the archetypal combinations, and we haven't even thought about our three levels of being concept yet. If this sounds implausible, consider that in the above example we have chosen only one archetypal phase of life, only one segment of that phase, only one rite of passage within that segment, and only one smaller rite within the larger 3-part rite. We could do the same exercise with any other archetypal phase and any other rite of passage or Hero's Journey within it. The power of the integrated model represented as a series of fractal sine waves is that it gives us an easy shorthand to "drill down" and then "come back up" the hierarchy without losing sight of the bigger picture.

There are, however, a couple of limitations in our use of the fractal sine wave that are worth mentioning. The first is one we have already touched on, which is that our fractal sine wave diagram shows only the relation between top-level rites of passage and the overall human lifecycle. It is missing the intermediate sine wave that should represent each archetypal phase, since we have said that each of these is also a cycle (a mini-life). This is part of the broader issue that we cannot represent six hierarchical levels of fractal sine waves on a static, two-dimensional image.

The second point is less obvious than the first but no less important. For ease and clarity of presentation (and ease of generating the image in the first place!) we have chosen a homogenous fractal sine wave where each of the smaller sine waves are of the same dimension. This gives us an aesthetically pleasing image, but it misrepresents the reality, which is that not all rites of passage and Hero's Journeys are of equal importance. The birth of a child is a far more important rite than a first date. Marriage is more important than a birthday party. Holy Communion is more important than the Masses which follow it. If we were representing a generic quantity of "importance" on the implied y-axis of our sine waves, we would have to show these rites of passage and Hero's Journeys as being larger than the others. Our fractal sine wave would become lumpy, but this would reveal a crucial point, which we will explore more in Part 2 of the book, which is that the "lumps" would all congregate around the archetypal transition points since those are the most challenging times in life.

With our concept of the hierarchy, we can now see why those times are more challenging i.e. because there is a phase change at work that is higher in the hierarchy. We can make the general statement that the higher in the hierarchy a rite or Hero's Journey is, the more important it is. Let's again use the Christian rites as an example. The Eucharist is a part of the Mass and although every Mass is an invitation to go all the way "up the hierarchy" to the highest level of the Esoteric through connection with God, not every Mass demarcates a state change for the individual. Using our table, we can characterise the average Mass as follows:

	Separation	Transition	Incorporation
Human Lifecycle	Child-Orphan	Adult	Elder
Orphan Phase of Life	Initiation	Adolescence	Marriage
Initiation rite of Christianity	Baptism	Confirmation	Communion
Mass	**Start of Mass**	**Body of Mass**	**Eucharist**
Eucharist	**Consecration of bread and wine**	**Congregation moves to altar**	**Receipt of bread and wine**

The Mass which marks Communion, however, invokes three extra levels in the hierarchy since it is the completion of the 3-part rite of Christian initiation and also the transition out of the Child archetype and into the Orphan. For that reason, it resonates at the top level of the microcosmic hierarchy as follows:-

	Separation	Transition	Incorporation
Human Lifecycle	Child-Orphan	Adult	Elder
Orphan Phase of Life	Initiation	Adolescence	Marriage
Initiation rite of Christianity	Baptism	Confirmation	Communion
Mass	Start of Mass	Body of Mass	Eucharist (Communion)
Communion	Consecration of bread and wine	Congregation moves to altar	Receipt of bread and wine

It is for this reason that the rites of passage that occur at the major archetypal turning points of life are always the most important, and that also explains the significance of marriage, which represents the beginning of the Adult phase of life. Note also that this fits perfectly with our characterisation of the archetypal transitions as being Hero's Journeys. As in any good movie or book, the most dramatic moments of the Hero's Journey come at the end, when the hero must transcend to a new level. We now know what that transcendence means in relation to our lifecycle: it is the transcendence to the next archetype.

A less pragmatic and more poetic reason to prefer the sine wave representation is one that fits the idea that there are ebbs and flows within the progression of life. We have said that human life is like a rite of passage or a Hero's Journey, but it is also like a piece of music, and music can be represented as sine waves. Like music, life has a rhythm; it has an underlying structure; it has ups and downs, build-ups to dramatic moments that are the culmination and completion of what came before. This leads back to the theological question raised by our model. If our lives are pieces of music, who is the composer? Is it God? Is it some impersonal force? Or is it ourselves?

Modification 2: Unify the Rites of Passage and the Hero's Journeys

What we have done with modification 1 is to incorporate the rites of passage into the microcosmic cycle via the fractal sine wave. But we also used them interchangeably with the Hero's Journey concept. It's time now to get more precise about what exactly the difference is between these two.

We know that rites of passage and Hero's Journeys have the same under-lying structure. But there's an important difference between them that we haven't yet addressed: rites of passage are always actions. To participate in a rite of passage is to show up somewhere at a certain time and *do something*. What differentiates the actions carried out during rites of passage from the actions of everyday life is that they have explicit symbolic meaning. There are formal roles and formal expectations around behaviour, which include, for example, ceremonial costumes. The bridal gown of the marriage rite is a classic example of this, as are the outfits of the bridesmaids, the groom, and the best man. Those involved most directly in a rite of passage almost always have special outfits that separate them from the others, but, more generally, everybody in attendance is expected to wear formal clothing and to behave in accordance with their role in proceedings.

In terms of our levels of being definition, we say of rites of passage that they resonate most strongly at Exoteric level, remembering that the Exoteric refers to the exterior view of reality. That's what the special clothing represents, and that's what the formal nature of the actions carried out in a rite of passage means. Of course, what gets done in a rite of passage can have an incredible depth of meaning, which can be explored by interpreting the actions symbolically, but this doesn't detract from the point, which is that rites are primarily Exoteric in nature. Hero's Journeys, by contrast, primarily belong to what we have called the Esoteric level of being.

But perhaps this is the wrong way to think about it. Perhaps the fact that the rites are Exoteric and the Hero's Journeys Esoteric, while both have an identical structure, points to an underlying unity. If we expand the idea of a Hero's Journey beyond just fictional stories, if we consider them as representations of Esoteric experience itself, what we can now say is that the rites of passage and the Hero's Journeys are just two sides of the same coin. The rites refer to the Exoteric side of the coin, and the Hero's Journeys refer to the Esoteric side.

What does that mean in practice? Once again, marriage provides us with an ideal example to make the point clear. The marriage ceremony is the Exoteric part of the equation; it involves the formal actions that are carried

47

out, the special clothing that is worn, and all the other external and visible details of the event. But a marriage ceremony is also a Hero's Journey which is experienced by the participants involved at the Esoteric level of being. That includes all of the lower Esoteric emotions and feelings and, potentially, the higher Esoteric as well. With this idea, we capture an important fact which will become relevant in our later analysis, namely, that it is possible to have either the Exoteric or the Esoteric without the other.

What happens when you have a rite of passage that is not a Hero's Journey i.e. when you have the Exoteric without the Esoteric? You get an empty ceremony. The people involved are just *going through the motions*. They don't feel anything at the lower Esoteric and they certainly don't see any larger meaning associated with their actions that would belong to the higher Esoteric. Conversely, what happens if you have a Hero's Journey without an Exoteric component? You have a subjective experience that is not recognised by the culture or society in which you live. It is possible to fall in love without getting married or being in a relationship. It is possible to have a connection with God without belonging to a religion. It is possible to do work that you love without getting paid for it. All of these are examples where the Esoteric is present without the Exoteric. The converse is also true. You can be in a loveless marriage, conduct a spiritless religious practice, or be stuck in a stultifying job. There, you have the Exoteric without the Esoteric. You have rites of passage that are not Hero's Journeys because they are devoid of meaning.

At a mundane level, we can see that this interaction between Exoteric and Esoteric waxes and wanes throughout our own lives. We might be excited to start a new job. In that case, there is a match between Exoteric and Esoteric. Over time, the Esoteric seems to wane, and we get stuck in a rut. Maybe we manage to rediscover the Esoteric within the job, or maybe we decide to get a new job, at which point we are modifying the Exoteric to try and bring it into line with the Esoteric. The desire for an equilibrium between the Esoteric and Exoteric seems to be a basic one in human affairs. As Tolstoy put it, "If you're not enjoying your work, you should either change your attitude, or change your job." Either way, you need to bring the Esoteric and the Exoteric into harmony with each other.

This need for equilibrium also exists at the societal level, and this makes sense as we know that the Exoteric rites are the way in which the individual (microcosm) is initiated into the macrocosm. Where there is an imbalance between the Exoteric and Esoteric, this implies a mismatch between the individual and society. When the mismatch exists for a large proportion of that society, this means that the Exoteric institutions no longer reflect the Esoteric reality of the public. Such mismatches can, in special cases, change the trajectory of a civilisation, when the people decide to implement a modification of Tolstoy's advice and change the Exoteric institutions themselves.

Let's consider just one example of this dynamic using the life story of an individual we will talk about in more detail later. Martin Luther was clearly a very devout Christian who had a depth of spiritual (Esoteric) experience that was out of kilter with the institutions (Exoteric) of his time. Luther went through the initiations of the Catholic Church and would later be initiated both into university, and then a Catholic monastery. These would have required him to go through the usual rites of passage, but we know that these rites were not satisfactory to Luther. In his case, the Exoteric was not in alignment with the Esoteric.

Most of us, when confronted with such a situation, will grin and bear it. Some people will rebel against it and become outsiders in their own society. Very occasionally will there appear a rebel such as Luther who taps into a broader vein of discontent, which leads to the overthrow of the Exoteric institutions themselves. In Luther, we see the individual as Esoteric demanding the modification of the Exoteric institutions of his society. Luther might have been the very first rebellious teenager of western civilisation. He began a trend which continues to this day.

But we can now be more specific about the case of Luther because what we see in Luther's life path was a series of what we know are Hero's Journeys that did not have a corresponding rite of passage element to them. It was these Hero's Journeys, these Esoteric experiences, which primarily brought Luther into conflict with his society. One of them was an event that occurred when he was a young man. Luther was walking back to his lodgings at the university one day after an argument with his parents when a storm approached. Lightning struck nearby, which knocked Luther to the ground and apparently singed his hair. So intense was the experience that Luther believed he was going to die. He prayed for divine intervention, promising to join a monastery if he was saved. He survived the storm and went on to fulfil his promise.

Clearly, this event was not a rite of passage since it was a work of nature that occurred while Luther was alone walking in a forest. It was an Esoteric event of supreme importance to Luther, but, by definition, it had no Exoteric resonance with Luther's society. It was not a rite of passage in the technical meaning of that term, but it most certainly was a Hero's Journey. Not only was the incident itself a Hero's Journey, it became a pivotal moment in the larger Hero's Journey that was Luther's life. It was the Call to Adventure that would see Luther rebel directly against his parents and then set him on a collision course with the primary Exoteric institution of his society: the Catholic Church.

In Luther's case, the Exoteric was out of alignment with the Esoteric and he would make it his life's mission to try and bring them into alignment. In normal circumstances, such an individual would be ostracised from society or otherwise neutralised, and that's certainly what the Catholic Church attempted to do to Luther. However, Luther's Hero's Journey and the Esoteric feeling of it resonated with his contemporaries. He became a lightning rod (pardon the pun) for a societal Esoteric force that was eager to break out of an Exoteric mould that had become stifling. We said earlier that a Hero's Journey without a rite of passage is an Esoteric event that is not socially recognised. The case of Luther shows that sometimes the Esoteric demands its own recognition and restructures the Exoteric to achieve that end.

Thinking back to our new fractal diagram:-

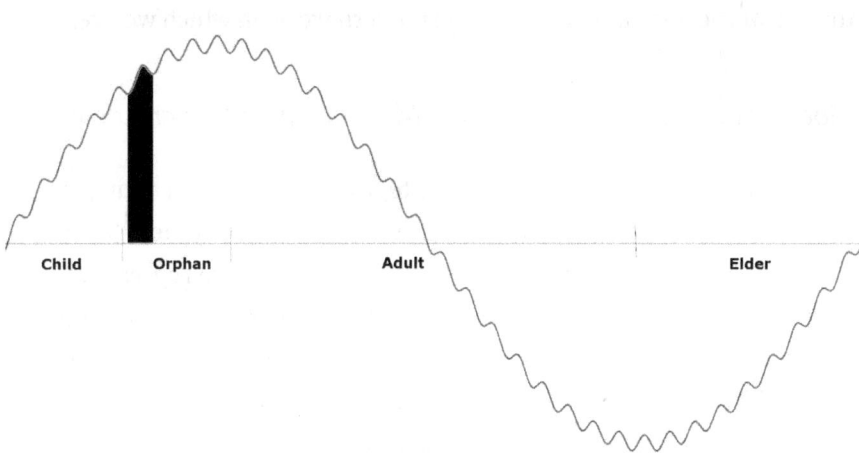

We can now see that the smaller sine waves may refer to rites of passage, to Hero's Journeys or to a combination of the two. The difference is whether or not the event resonates at the Exoteric and Esoteric levels of being. To capture this information, we could imagine a third dimension to the graph running along the z-axis, which represents the levels of being. Whether this is mathematically valid or not, it would allow us to capture the scenarios mentioned above where we can have rites that do not resonate at the Esoteric level or Hero's Journeys that fail to resonate at the Exoteric. If the above diagram represents Luther's experience of the lightning strike, we could then show that its resonance was entirely at the Esoteric but not the Exoteric, which is crucial information in order to understand both Luther's life and the way in which he changed the world around him.

This distinction is no mere analytical amusement. The case of Luther is not an isolated one. Just as the Esoteric and Exoteric waxes and wanes in our own lives and we try to bring them into equilibrium with each other, the same process happens at the macrocosmic level. This is one more piece of evidence for our hypothesis that the microcosm and macrocosm really do have the same underlying structure. The macrocosm also tries to bring about a balance between the Exoteric and the Esoteric and when this fails to happen gracefully, the result is war, rebellion, and revolution. We will go into detail about that in Part 2, and it will be the key to our analysis towards the end of the book as we analyse the modern world in which we live.

Modification 3: the Integration of Microcosm and Macrocosm

We began our presentation of the integrated model with four primary elements: the macrocosm, microcosm, rites of passage, and Hero's Journeys. We have just shown how the latter three of these can be represented in a single sine wave in fractal form (with some implied extra fractal layers that we could not fit on the diagram), and so it should be little surprise that our last modification will now incorporate the macrocosm as well, giving us, in theory, a single fractal sine wave at multiple levels of resolution. In making this integration, we will add an extra two levels to our hierarchy.

Let's begin by showing the macrocosmic wave as a fractal as follows:-

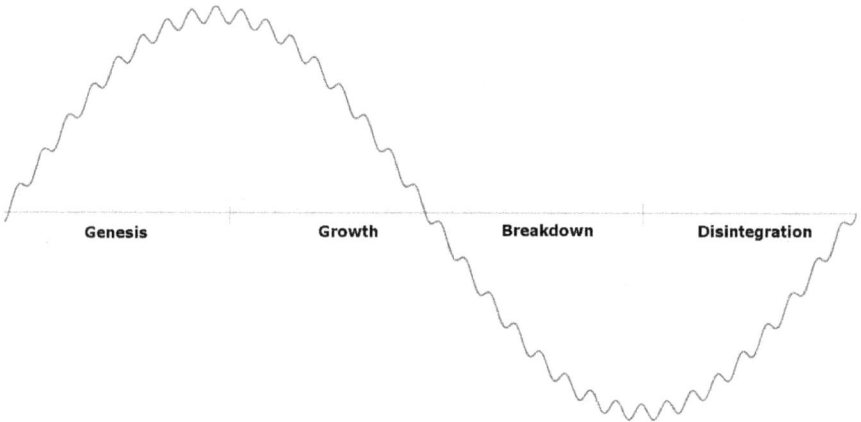

| Genesis | Growth | Breakdown | Disintegration |

Once again, we see the familiar overarching cycle of civilisation. What do the smaller sine waves represent in this view of the macrocosm? There are two perspectives we might take on this. The first is that of individual generations. A civilisation is made up of generations of people who are initiated into the civilisation before passing it on to the following one. A generation is a group of people who all go through the archetypal phases of life at more or less the same time period and are assumed, therefore, to have the same experience of the macrocosm. Since a generation is already an abstraction, our archetypal representation of the microcosm works just as well for a generation as it does for an individual.

The second perspective we might take is to see the smaller sine waves on our new diagram as the lifecycles of important individuals that lived during each phase of the civilisational cycle. Using the Martin Luther example again, we could posit that he lived during the Growth phase of modern western civilisation and we could mark that position on the macrocosmic diagram and then zoom in on the microcosmic as follows:-

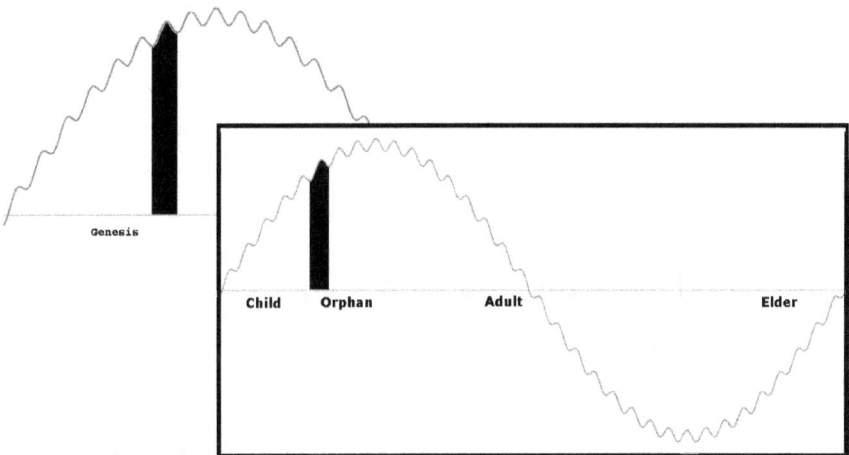

The sine wave representing Luther's life is the smaller sine wave represented on the macrocosm. This places Luther in the sequence of generations and individuals that make up western civilisation. We could then mark the major events in Luther's life on the microcosmic sine wave, and these would now be contextualised against the macrocosmic perspective. For example, Luther's trip to Rome, the confrontation at the Diet of Worms, and his translation of the Bible into German can all be understood much better when we locate them at a specific point in the cycle of western civilisation. We can then think through the collective changes that led to those events and also the changes that resulted from them.

Because our integrated model is valid for both single individuals and generations of individuals, it works for the two major schools of historical thought that battled it out in the realm of ideas beginning around the 19th century. Until that time, historical scholarship had been dominated by what is sometimes called *the great man theory of history*. This is the kind of history most of us still know since it is the dominant way people think of the subject i.e. a sequential list of important people and events. The underlying assumption is that history is created by individuals of greatness who change the course of events through their own willpower. Our new integrated diagram allows us to capture that idea by singling out great individuals like Luther for analysis.

A new conception that became popular in the 19th century was the notion that history is determined by a set of impersonal forces that work through individuals. According to this view, any particular leader is just a conduit for those impersonal forces. If it was not one leader who seized the day and marshalled those forces, it would have been another. Thus, historical scholarship should not concern itself with the individual but with the forces themselves. Here, the idea of generations becomes more relevant since we are concerned more with the zeitgeist and the collective developments that are presumed to drive events. With this change of perspective, we are no longer preoccupied with the events of Luther's life as with the milieu in which he was born. This does capture a number of important facts. For example, the reason Luther was not *neutralised* by the papal authorities was almost certainly because of the support he received from both the general public and the kings of northern Europe. The zeitgeist was on his side. Even though Luther was undoubtedly a heroic character and a *great man*, it's clear that he was also a conduit for the wider social forces that were at play.

These two ways of looking at history are not mutually exclusive, and our model can easily handle both perspectives if we simply assume there is a two-way channel of communication between microcosm and macrocosm.

That is, great leaders are both the conduits for impersonal social forces and have some ability to channel those forces in certain directions.

Nevertheless, it's important to understand that the comparative history that we have built into our integrated model falls into the latter category of historical research. That is, it takes a view of history as a set of impersonal forces that come from within the civilisational cycle itself. According to this way of thinking, the phases of the civilisational cycle impose their own developmental pressure on the civilisation. Just as we all must go through the microcosmic archetypal phases of life, so too must civilisations go through their own archetypal phases. The individuality of a civilisation then becomes a question of how it responds to those challenges, in the same way that each of us uniquely responds to the challenge of what it is to be a human being.

All this follows from our microcosm-macrocosm assumption. We are assuming that civilisation is the same kind of thing as a human individual. To what degree this claim is true is an interesting question. Perhaps civilisations are only like human individuals in the highly abstract sense that they are both cycles with qualitatively distinct segments. Perhaps we can go even further and say that a civilisation has spirit and soul in a theological sense, or conscious and unconscious psyches in a psychological one; perhaps it has a metabolism and an Exoteric identity exemplified by its institutions. In short, perhaps civilisation resonates at all three levels of being in just the same way that human individuals do. That is an idea we will explore more in the rest of this book, especially in Part 4, when we turn our attention to the civilisation that we all know intimately since it is the one we are living in: the modern West.

Of course, in many ways, this is a book that is about western civilisation, since the set of ideas we are attempting to unify into a single model are all taken from the 19th and early 20th centuries, and this is no coincidence because the work of the comparative scholars was predicated on a global cross-cultural comparison that only became possible with the truly international reach of western civilisation. Curiously, it seems that western civilisation was perhaps predestined for just this outcome and this is another point the comparative historians made, which is that the qualities of a civilisation that later mark it as unique are to be found in embryonic form right from the beginning, well before they have come to maturity. Consider that a uniquely western institution is the university, and this was present right from the beginning of modern Europe. The word university comes from the Latin *universitas*, meaning *universal, whole,* or *aggregate.* Western scholars have always been concerned with what can be said in general with the necessarily abstract results that must come from that approach.

The idea of history as a set of impersonal forces follows directly from this preoccupation with the universal, the general, and the abstract. It's also true to say that, when this idea reached maturity in the 19th century, it caused what can really be called an existential crisis. Part of the reason was that it seemed to de-humanise people who were no longer individuals in the fullest sense but carriers of impersonal forces and ideologies. It's true that, even today, some people find the abstractions of archetypal and comparative analysis alienating and degrading. On this point, we may reflect on a philosopher who faced these issues head-on and wrote some of his finest work on the question of the despair that can come from such abstractions, the Danish philosopher Soren Kierkegaard. In Kierkegaard's view, on the other side of the despair caused by the alienation of modern abstractions lay the promise of a more direct connection with God, or what we have called the higher Esoteric. This, too, is a theme that we will return to near the end of the book.

With these considerations, we can wrap up Part 1 by making explicit a point we alluded to earlier. We have now incorporated the macrocosmic and microcosmic sine waves into a single fractal sine wave that resonates at numerous hierarchical levels. We can now add the two additional levels pertaining to the macrocosm to our archetypal table. Once again, we have modified the segments of the macrocosm to fit the 3-part structure we are using.

	Separation	Transition	Incorporation
Civilisational Cycle	Genesis-Growth	Growth - Breakdown	Breakdown - Disintegration
Lifecycle of an Individual or Generation	Child-Orphan	Adult	Elder
Orphan Phase of Life	Initiation	Adolescence	Marriage
Initiation rite of Christianity	Baptism	Confirmation	Communion
Mass	Start of Mass	Body of Mass	Eucharist (Communion)
Communion	Consecration of bread and wine	Movement to altar	Receipt of bread and wine

When we model the macrocosm in this way, we can make an identical observation that we made earlier for the microcosm, which is that civilisation itself can be viewed as a rite of passage or a Hero's Journey. We could further make the claim that the individual archetypes of the macrocosmic cycle are also mini-Hero's Journeys or rites. This is a notion that will become clearer as the book proceeds, and we will provide more solid evidence for this idea in Part 4. For now, we merely note that our table above implies that this is true.

Note also that the extra levels at the top of the table enhance our understanding of the lower levels. For example, in relation to the rite of passage of Holy Communion, what our table allows is to contextualise that rite as we move up the hierarchy. Thus, we know that Holy Communion belongs to the 3-part initiation rite of the Catholic Church; we know that rite belongs to the Initiation phase of the Orphan archetype; and we know where the Orphan archetype fits into the human lifecycle. The addition of the macrocosm allows us now to make clear how the rite of Holy Communion has changed over the course of the civilisational cycle. During the Genesis and Growth phases of western civilisation, we can say that Holy Communion was as good as a universal rite that all people in that civilisation would have taken during the Orphan phase of their lives. Clearly, this is no longer true for modern western society, and the time when that change began was what Toynbee called the Breakdown phase of the cycle. That is no coincidence, because what begins to break down in the third phase of the cycle are the rites of passage linked to tradition.

Thus, our table allows us to place an individual rite of passage within the broader macrocosmic pattern. This movement up and down the hierarchy is a big advantage of our integrated model because it allows us to begin either at the top or the bottom and work from broader trends down to specifics, or from specifics back to the larger context in which they exist. Now, when we select a specific individual or generation from the sequence of generations that make up a civilisation, we can place them within a specific phase of the larger cycle, just as we did earlier with Martin Luther.

With the addition of the two extra levels at the top of the hierarchy, we now have 3^8 or an incredible 6,561 combinations. If we add our three levels of being to the mix, we get 3^9 or 19,683 combinations. Of course, these numbers are not inherently meaningful; they are only a guide to the level of complexity that our model implies. This level of complexity should not be that surprising since we are dealing with social systems and human individuals, two of the most complex objects on the planet. But what we have seen in this part of the book is how the combination of simple concepts that are interrelated quickly leads into mind-bending complexity. Our analysis for the rest of this book can only deal with a fraction of this complexity, and it will be the fraction that is most relevant to us as we apply the integrated model to our own lives and times and our own civilisation.

To end on a poetic note, we might also extend the music metaphor we introduced earlier. If the sine wave of the microcosm is indeed part of the macrocosm, then that would mean that civilisation is not just a rite of passage or a Hero's Journey but also a work of music, and that our lives resonate within that larger composition. Of course, a number of thinkers throughout history have used exactly this metaphor in a very different sense. For them, society and civilisation are not characterised by harmoniousness but by discord and dissonance. Nevertheless, in this metaphor, we may find as good a definition as any for the concept of civilisation: it is the mutual vibration between microcosm and macrocosm that sets the tone of life for individuals and civilisations alike.

Part 2: The Archetypes in Civilisation

The Power of the Story

For the rest of this book, we are going to make extensive use of stories (Hero's Journeys) to assist with our analysis, and so it will be worth our while to spend some time now clarifying our understanding. Stories have a peculiar position in the modern West. Never have there been so many stories. The rise of newspapers, mass pop-culture, audio and visual media, and communications technologies like the internet and social media have meant that it is now possible to broadcast a story from anywhere at any time. Entire industries exist for the creation and promulgation of fictional stories, while stories have also become the main battleground of modern politics, including the never-ending *culture wars*.

By contrast, it's also true that stories have been relegated to second-class status with the rise of modern science. Within the materialist philosophy, to believe a story to be true is an outdated and deficient form of understanding. The paradox of modern science is that its results must be translated into story form for public dissemination. This was the point I made in my book *The Plague Story and Other Essays* which was about how the public debate during the corona event revolved around a battle between two competing stories. Ironically, the story that "won" did so because it was seen to have the backing of the "experts", whose understanding the public assumes should be trusted precisely because it is not based on stories but on "science".

Part of the reason to highlight the underlying structure of stories as we did in Part 1 with our analysis of the Hero's Journey is to show there is a mathematical element to stories, one which could be rendered into more scientific terms through the modern disciplines of cybernetics and systems thinking. Both of those disciplines deal with cyclical processes that transcend to higher logical types, which is exactly what the Hero's Journey is all about. Since logicians of the 19th and 20th centuries wrestled with the seeming contradictions that come from logical typing, and since many myths and stories feature seeming logical contradictions that are resolved once we incorporate hierarchical levels into our analysis, a very strong argument can be made that stories are a precursor to cybernetics and systems thinking and, in fact, embody a level of complexity that modern science is still struggling to grapple with.

It's for these reasons that we are going to use stories to elucidate the integrated model presented in Part 1 rather than come at the problem from the point of view of cybernetics or systems thinking. There is another reason, however, and one which will become more important as we go. In their highest form, art and storytelling are expressions of what we have been calling the Esoteric. It is on this subject that modern science has waged a mini and perhaps covert war against storytelling since stories have always been used by religion to promulgate theology. The materialist philosophy of modern science requires that the Esoteric be downgraded to the realm of epiphenomena. Stories, however, put the Esoteric first and foremost, something that materialists would obviously have a problem with.

In fairness to the sceptical science-minded, it is true that the use to which stories have been put throughout history has some elements that we would find implausible or even outright invalid. In fact, we see the calcified remains of the old ethic in the very words that we have been using repeatedly in this book. The word *history* is nothing more than the word *story* with a *hi-* in front of it: *hi-story*. That is no coincidence. The English word *story* comes from Latin *storia*, which is simply the shortened form of *historia*. The meaning of *historia* in Latin was a narrative of important events or persons from the past that was assumed to be true. Our word *narrative* comes from the Latin *narrare*, meaning to recount an event or sequence of events. Meanwhile, *myth* comes from the Latin and Greek words meaning told by word of mouth. *Legend* comes from *legere,* meaning to select (the right words for the story). Then there is the Latin *fabula,* which became the English *fable* but which comes from *fari,* meaning *to tell.* This is almost identical to the old English word *tale,* which is related to *tell.*

All these words, which have come to have different meanings for us, are derived from basic verbs with the core meaning of recounting a series of events. The difference is which kinds of events and which kinds of beings were involved in the events. Religious tales are about gods. Legends have typically been about Christian saints. Myths are about supernatural beings that aren't gods. In our modern understanding, we make a big differentiation between history and story. The former is about "real" people, and the latter, fictitious ones. We have to understand that this sharp distinction was not shared by the ancients, nor has it been shared by most cultures over time. We think of Julius Caesar as a historical figure. But the Romans proclaimed Caesar a god some years after his death. A story or a history about Caesar was, by our definition, semi-mythological. The distinction between history featuring real people on the one hand and stories or myths featuring imaginary people on the other was far more blurred in the ancient world.

Our modern approach to the difference between story and history is actually much more recent than most people might believe, and a big part of the transition to this modern viewpoint was based on theological debates. The German scholar, Friedrich Schleiermacher, analysed the Bible as part myth and part history. It was then a small step to say that myth no longer represented what was factually true, as the ancients would have believed. Thus came the distinction of history as factual and real, while myth, fable, and legend became unreal or, perhaps, hyper-real. According to this way of thinking, there are numerous elements of the story of Jesus that were in common use in folk tales popular in the lands around the Mediterranean at that time. These are then given a mythological status. But the story of Jesus also takes place *in history.* Pontius Pilate as the authority figure of the Roman Empire is *in history.* The scribes and Pharisees are *in history.* Presumably there was a man who really did get crucified (whether he was called Jesus or not). That man was also *in history*. This combination of myth and history, timelessness and time, is part of the theological paradox of the story of Jesus. How could God, an eternal being, manifest in time? How can God both be in time and also outside of time?

These modern distinctions between story and history form the intellectual backdrop that gave rise to the concept of the Hero's Journey that we looked at in Part 1. Myths, legends, and religious stories are now assumed to take place in an implied world of timelessness. It's for this reason that Jungian scholars like Joseph Campbell found myth to be such a rich source of analytical material. The archetypes are supposed to exist in a timeless place beyond the perceived world, and since myth also takes place in such a world, the archetypal nature of the characters comes through clearer in a myth. It was against this backdrop of the de-sacralisation of myth and legend that we can understand the attraction of the Jungian interpretations of such stories since Jung re-sacralised those stories by noting their importance as the ground for the collective Unconscious in the new and exciting discipline of psychoanalysis. Of course, Jung was not alone in this. The 19th century had already seen a revival of interest in old myths, which became tied in with questions of cultural evolution and then wrapped up in the various nationalist movements that arose in continental Europe. We will investigate the reasons for this in Part 4.

For most cultures, the temporal transition point between history, which is about real people, and myths, legends, and religious stories, which are about gods or demi-gods, is just as blurred as it was for the Romans. There are the people who are alive today; there are the ancestors whose lives are known to some extent. Beyond that, there is the long period of timelessness, which is where the gods and spirits exist. The historian, Oswald Spengler, noted that even the Romans had what we would now consider an incredibly short cultural "memory". That is part of the reason why Julius Caesar could be thought of as a god just a few short years after his actual death.

This leads to an important observation about modern western society: our historical consciousness is far more exacting and precise than perhaps any other civilisation that has yet existed. This historical consciousness even affects our fictional stories. We expect that works of fiction, including films, should represent the historical context of the story accurately. If the story takes place in the Ming dynasty of China, or medieval Europe, or colonial America, we expect the author or film director to accurately represent that era, or at least our generally accepted stereotypes of it. If a modern film or story happens to take place in the timeless world of myth, we assign it to the specific genre of *fantasy*. The default assumption of our storytelling is realism and, particularly, historical realism.

Our historical realism stretches beyond civilisation and into natural history, too, and this has raised a broader question in relation to myths and legends: are myths really timeless, or do they, in fact, refer to the pre-history which is the common inheritance of all humanity? Modern scientific theories about deep time, evolution, and the natural history of mankind have allowed us to see myth as also being *in time* i.e. belonging to a particular phase of human history. Beyond the realm of recorded societal history, we no longer see gods and spirits but the time before humans existed. From our modern vantage point, we see that myth is not wholly timeless.

But it's also true that modern stories are not wholly without timeless, archetypal elements, and this is where the scholarship of Jung and his followers, including Campbell, is relevant and important. Practically all best-selling novels and Hollywood blockbuster movies follow the Hero's Journey structure we outlined in Part 1. So, too, does history and, for that matter, current affairs. The Hero's Journey is the structure that underlies myth, religious text, modern fiction, and, to a very large extent, the general public's understanding of modern science. Science is communicated to the public via stories, and all stories, both modern and ancient, are framed in archetypal terms.

And here we come to a point that we will need to reiterate several times as we go in order to counteract the bias of modern western society. According to the materialist bias, our extensive use of stories in this book may give our analysis a "trivial" or "superficial" connotation, especially because we are going to make use of some popular modern stories and films. The exact reverse is true. We are using stories because they contain more truth, not less. Great works of fiction are distilled truth that resonates across all three levels of being. They resonate with us because we intuit that truth as much subconsciously as consciously.

Freud may have discovered the Oedipus Complex from clinical observation. But his use of a fictitious and mythical character to name that phenomenon proves that Sophocles had already intuited the same truth more than two thousand years ago and put it into a story. As we will see later, all of Shakespeare's greatest stories capture psychologically, anthropologically and historically important truths. Are the works of Sophocles and Shakespeare less "truthful" than Freud's simply because they wrote fictional stories? We argue that they are more true because they not only capture the Oedipal dynamic but much more besides. This allows authors to look for interrelationships and connections between the individual and society, the psychological, anthropological, and even historical domains.

Meanwhile, scientists limit themselves to one or another scholarly discipline and focus on that to the exclusion of everything else. This is a major weakness of the analytical requirement of modern science, which, like the story of Humpty Dumpty, divides the world up but then cannot put it back together again. This was true even of Freud and Jung, whose focus on the psychological realm led them to miss some obvious facts about their patients and therefore to posit psychological "causes" which were really side effects in a larger context. Our integrated model aims to focus on the interrelationships and connections between scholarly disciplines, and that is why we will be making such extensive use of stories since stories have a holistic focus built in.

As a final note, we should remember our point from earlier about the Hero's Journey and the rites of passage. The middle phase of the journey is the descent into the sacred. What was the sacred? It was about un-wholeness and the point of a story and a rite of passage is to go through a period of un-wholeness but to return at the end to wholeness, health and holiness. To divide and analyse is to step into the unknown, just like the hero does in a Hero's Journey. Science really is like a Hero's Journey in that respect. But the hero needs to return to the sacred by integrating what they found there. If science and society cannot do that, then we are trapped in the middle of the journey, stuck in the *sacred* with the implications of unholiness, un-wholeness and unhealthiness that this implies. It is not a coincidence that those adjectives are all very good descriptors of the collective mood of western society in recent years and decades, since we live in a society which knows how to break Humpty Dumpty up but not how to put him together again.

With all this in mind, we are ready to begin our own Hero's Journey down the rabbit hole that leads us to the archetypal analysis of civilisation.

The Microcosmic Perspective

In this section of the book, we are going to be deepening and broadening our understanding of the archetypes of both the microcosm and macrocosm that we introduced in Part 1. We will begin with the microcosm since it represents the firm ground where we have an intuitive understanding of the domain. We'll then turn our attention to the macrocosm, with a particular emphasis on how the movement through the cycle of civilisation modifies and modulates the microcosmic archetypes.

Here we will find a more pragmatic reason to add to the list of reasons just given about why we are relying heavily on stories for our analysis in this book. While there are examples of rites of passage that last for a long period of time, perhaps weeks or even months, in truth, most of rites of passage take less than a day and therefore represent a moment in time, albeit one that can mark a major life change. Hero's Journeys in the form of fictional stories, on the other hand, can be written in such a way as either to cover a long time period in terms of the action within the story or to condense the experiences that normally occur over a long period of time into a dramatic story arc that takes place in a shortened time frame. Either way, we can find stories that provide us with exactly the concentrated information we need to enhance our understanding of the archetypes, and that is what we will now do.

Recall our table of archetypes of the microcosm from earlier:-

Archetype	Level of Being		
	Physical	Exoteric	Esoteric – Dominant Faculty
The Child	Birth - Childhood	Son or daughter	Imagination
The Orphan	Puberty	Student, friend, protégé, initiate	Intellect
The Adult	Adulthood	Husband/wife, parent, citizen, employee/boss, churchgoer	Will
The Elder	Old Age - Death	Retiree, Mentor, Teacher	Soul

We noted earlier that each archetypal phase of life needs to be thought of as a Hero's Journey and we know that a Hero's Journey is made up of three parts: Separation, Initiation and Return. We can think of the three parts of the Hero's Journey as running orthogonal to the three levels of being. What the means is that the Hero's Journey pattern holds at each level of being. Thus, we can analyse the Physical, Exoteric and Esoteric levels of being using the Separation – Initiation – Return categories. Let's think through what this means, using the Child archetype as an example.

At the Physical level of being, the Separation phase of childhood can be thought of as the period from being born up until when we are independently mobile at around three years old. There follows the Initiation phase, which is what we typically think of as the childhood years of energetic play. Puberty can then be thought of as both the Return phase of childhood and the Separation phase of adolescence. It marks the boundary between the two, and we would all agree that it is a qualitative change to a new state.

At this point, it is worth mentioning that there is a significant asymmetry between the sexes at the Physical level of being. If we think through the full life progression of Child, Orphan, Adult and Elder, we can see that both men and women have much the same biological phase changes in childhood and adolescence, with the onset of puberty being a definitive state change, albeit one that takes a number of years to fully develop. For the Adult and Elder phases of life, however, there is no definitive biological marker for men that marks the archetypal change while, for women, childbirth and menopause fulfil these roles, with the former marking the beginning of the Adult phase and menopause marking the beginning of the Elder phase.

Men do not have the same biological challenges that demarcate the archetypal transitions. Even puberty is arguably a much less dramatic transition for men than it is for women. It is surely for this reason that the *puer aeturnus*, or Peter Pan phenomenon, is almost exclusively seen in men, since men are not forced by biology to confront the archetypal changes. It is almost certainly for this reason, too, that it appears to be a universal of human culture that initiation ceremonies for men are far more intensive than for women and often involve significant physical hardships. We might posit that these are there to *even up the score* and provide men with the additional assistance they need to signify the archetypal phase change.

Another important point about the way the archetypal changes manifest at the Physical level of being in women is that they really are discrete and discontinuous changes that come upon women all of a sudden. Menstruation, pregnancy-childbirth and menopause are all direct and decisive changes that must be navigated. Thus, there really is a Separation phase for women that has a clear beginning, which demarcates one phase from another, and which requires the woman to attune herself to a new set of physical circumstances.

This brings us back to a point we made earlier, which is that the transition points between the archetypal phases are the most dramatic and also the riskiest because there is a requirement for us to reshape our perspective on ourselves and our world. This really is a Hero's Journey because we must leave the "old world" that we have mastered and that we know how to navigate through and step into a new world that we do not yet understand. The reason why the levels of being concept is so important is that it helps us to demarcate the exact nature of the challenge that we face because it turns out that the challenges at the Exoteric and Esoteric levels of being are perhaps even more important than those at the Physical.

In this book, we will mostly be concerned with the Exoteric and Esoteric levels of being, and this for two reasons. Firstly, we are concerned with the interrelationships between macrocosm and microcosm, and these almost exclusively take place at the Exoteric and Esoteric levels. The second and related point is that the Physical level of being shows very little change in relation to the macrocosm and certainly far less than the other levels. In other words, our individual progression through the archetypal phases at the biological level shows little variation between, for example, the Genesis and Disintegration phases of the macrocosmic cycle. Biology is far less influenced by the macrocosm than psychology and sociology. Having said that, there are some biological changes that seem to occur as a result of the macrocosm. One example is that the age of puberty has been getting progressively younger in the last hundred or so years in the West. One of the theories why this is the case is because of the increased quality of nutrition in the general population. If that is true, then that would be a prime example of how the macrocosm affects the Physical level of being of the microcosm.

A second example is how what we might generically call *technology* can affect the archetypal phases. The birth control pill and the condom have both provided women with the ability to exert some level of control over when the Physical change of pregnancy-childbirth takes place. In more recent years in the West, we have seen the rollout of puberty blockers as well as surgical interventions, which, in theory at least, allow young people to choose when they go through the archetypal phase change of puberty. All of these are examples of the macrocosm of civilisation modifying or attempting to modify the archetypal phases of the microcosm.

Where we have occasion, we will be referencing the Physical level of being in the analysis which follows, but our focus will be on the Exoteric and Esoteric levels since the former is the most obvious way in which the microcosm and macrocosm are linked and since the Exoteric rites ultimately derive their meaning from the Esoteric realm, which is the repository of the ideas and ideals which form the core of civilisation. At these two other levels of being, we find the same pattern plays out in that the archetypal progression can also be broken up into the three phases of Separation – Initiation – Return.

One way to think about the archetypal phases, and this matches with our characterisation of them as Hero's Journeys, is that they each have a specific mission which needs to be accomplished and then transcended as one moves to the next phase. In relation to the Child phase, for example, we have Freud and Jung's focus on the psychological aspect of fitting into the family structure, captured in perhaps the most famous concept of psychoanalysis, the *Oedipus Complex*. This has both an Exoteric and an Esoteric dimension to it since part of what the child is learning to do is to be a son or a daughter, and that requires socialisation. Learning how to be a son or daughter is the Exoteric mission of the first half of childhood, while learning to be a friend and student is the mission of the second half.

At the Esoteric level, we have listed the dominant faculty of the Child archetype as Imagination, and that should be uncontroversial since every parent and teacher knows that children love to turn everything into play. We can further distinguish between extroverted and introverted forms of Imagination, with play belonging to the former and the latter being what we normally refer to by the word *imagination* as an introverted state. Putting all this together, we can characterise the main mission of the archetype of the Child as both finding a stable place in the family at the Exoteric level of being and developing the Imagination at the Esoteric.

At the Exoteric level of being, the Orphan mission begins when we receive initiation into the institutions of society, where we are expected to begin to fulfil an Adult-like role. It is the beginning of the development of our Adult identity in the four domains of economics, politics, religion and sexuality. Hence, the aforementioned rite of Holy Communion marks the initiate as a full, Adult-like member of the church. A first date and a first kiss normally take place during this period, representing the beginning of a sexual identity. A first job interview and job may occur, as may the first ability to take part in formal political institutions.

We have noted that the Intellect is the primary faculty of the Orphan phase, and this matches the medieval judgement of this time of life as the *age of reason*. Our educational institutions still imply this in the fact that it is only in high school that advanced subjects are offered that require significant reasoning capabilities. In combination with the Exoteric challenges listed above, we can summarise the mission of the Orphan phase of life as learning to use the Intellect and also joining the Exoteric institutions of society for the first time as a member who has some level of rights and responsibilities. We will go into more detail about the Adult and Elder missions later.

Our archetypal table allows us to drill down to the specifics of each archetypal mission, but there are also a few points that we can make about the archetypal phases in general. If we continue with the idea that each archetype has a mission, it's also true that the mission is offered to us during the Separation phase in just the same way that the hero receives a Call to Adventure at the beginning of the Hero's Journey. Here we see the wisdom of the Hero's Journey analysis since it's also true that the archetypal Call to Adventure comes to us from the Unconscious. We do not ask for the mission. The mission is given to us. This is clearly true of the Physical level of being, and puberty serves as the classic example since it comes upon us unbidden. It's also true at the Exoteric, since this represents the rights and responsibilities bestowed upon us by society, that are encompassed in rites of passage that we are expected to go through. The challenge comes at the lower Esoteric in that both the Physical and Exoteric Call to Adventures force us out of our comfort zones and into the unknown with all the heightened emotional and mental states that come with that.

In psychoanalytic terms, the archetypal transformations arise from our Unconscious as a challenge to the ego. The ego can further be seen to represent the equilibrium of the current archetype we are manifesting. If we are comfortable and secure in the Child phase of life, puberty and the Orphan phase come as a challenge to our egos, just as do the archetypal challenges of the latter phases. Since the archetypal challenge forces us into the Esoteric, at least in the form of heightened emotions, there is always a temptation to introvert or dissociate from it. It is this dynamic which Freud and Jung discovered with modern psychoanalysis. The unchanneled energy bubbling up from the Unconscious could not find adequate expression and was channelled inward. From there, it gives rise to various neuroses and psychoses that are expressed in ways completely unrelated to the source of the problem.

It is no coincidence that Freud and Jung's main demographic were young, aristocratic women. In our terms, these were Orphans who were trying and failing to make the transition to the Adult archetype. The reason why aristocratic women were particularly affected in the Victorian era was because, in those days, their only pathway to adulthood was via marriage and childbirth. That had become a problem because the age of marriage for women had been pushed back, which left young aristocratic women without any Exoteric role, unlike their male counterparts. Unable to find an Exoteric outlet for the psychic energy coming up from the unconscious, aristocratic women of the Victorian era channelled the energy inward and developed various neuroses and psychoses.

The key point to understand here is that the problem was not just psychological. It had at least as much to do with the Exoteric and the Physical, if we count sexuality as belonging to that level of being. Therefore, the dynamic needs to be understood in the holistic fashion that our integrated model implies, which is failing to meet the archetypal challenge at all three levels of being.

Even though we need to stress that we must consider both the Physical and Exoteric levels when thinking about the archetypal progressions, we will nevertheless use a concept taken from Jung to describe the failure of those progressions. Jung posited that there was a part of the psyche called the Shadow, which was a kind of blind spot in our understanding of ourselves and which we projected onto the external world. We will refer to the shadow as the parts of being that want to reject the archetypal change. Another way to think about it is that the archetypal transformation represents an energy that comes up from the Unconscious. To the extent that we learn to channel that energy in a positive direction, it contributes to the archetypal transformation. To the extent that it is channelled inward, it is introverted back into the Unconscious part of the psyche, the shadow. The reason we are using the concept of the shadow in this way is not just because it broadly aligns with Jungian psychology and captures the psychological difficulties of the archetypal transformations, but also because the symbolism is used extensively in film and literature, as we will see shortly.

To reiterate, we posit that the archetypal transformations are a kind of energy coming up from the Unconscious that we need to learn to master. That energy is channelled according to the archetypal phase that we are in, and it is heightened during the transition points between archetypes, which is why those are the most risky times of life, and that is why societies construct rites of passage to assist people through them. If the archetypal energy does not get channelled into a productive adaptation to the archetypal phase, it introverts and causes problems at the Esoteric level of being. Since the failure of an archetypal transformation implies excessive attachment to the ego tied to a preceding archetypal phase, we get specific shadow forms for each archetype, as follows:-

Archetype	Level of Being		
	Exoteric	Esoteric	Esoteric (shadow)
The Child	Son or daughter	Imagination	Dissociation
The Orphan	Student, friend, protégé, initiate	Intellect	Ideology
The Adult	Husband/wife, parent, citizen, employee/boss, churchgoer	Will	Hyper-Masculine, Devouring Feminine
The Elder	Retiree, Mentor, Teacher	Soul	The Abyss

The Child who fails to make the transition to Orphan ends up manifesting the shadow form of Imagination, which is Dissociation. This is sometimes called the Peter Pan Complex because the individual ends up trapped in their own Imagination. The Orphan who fails to transcend to adulthood tends to manifest the shadow form of Intellect which is Ideology. The term ideology has been given many meanings over the centuries, but we use it here in a general sense of the power of ideology to control the mind such that all negating phenomena are ignored, discarded, or misinterpreted in line with the ideology.

The Adult faculty of Will needs a little elucidation. In the "real world", we are called upon to act with imperfect information. This means the Intellect, while it can still be of assistance, cannot be relied upon to provide definitive answers to questions of action. That's where Will, determination, and fortitude come into the picture. It is Will that we draw on when we gather up the courage to step into the unknown, and it is Will which allows us to withstand the slings and arrows of outrageous fortune as we see through a course of action to the end. The graduation from Orphan to Adult is, in some sense, the first time we learn to go beyond the excuse-making limitations of the Intellect, and draw on the resources, faculties, and strengths that our mind did not know of. Thus, the transition from Orphan to Adult is largely achieved when we activate the Will.

The shadow forms of the Adult, the hyper-masculine and devouring-feminine, are a reference to the way in which the two sexes tend to go about the fulfilment of their Will. What differentiates the healthy expression of Will from its shadow forms? That is not a psychological and certainly not a biological matter, but rather a moral or spiritual one. Therefore, it belongs to the faculty we have given the name of Soul. It is the failure to transcend to Soul which leads to the deviant form of the Will. The hyper-masculine and devouring-feminine are about the wilful attainment of what is not right. Though it may be wilful, this doesn't entail that it is conscious since the whole point of Will is that it can operate in the realm, beyond what can be known by intellect. (It is the Soul, which allows one to "see" the hyper-masculine and devouring feminine, not the Intellect).

The Elder faculty of Soul also needs some elaboration. In our modern secular age, it might be easiest to reference Carl Jung's concepts of the *anima* and *animus* for this purpose. For Jung, the Soul was feminine (*anima*) in men and masculine (*animus*) in women. The task for the Elder archetype is to confront the Soul. It might sound strange that we need to confront our own Soul but Jung noted that the task is not pleasant and will be actively (although unconsciously) avoided by most people for that reason. Jung also believed that the confrontation with the Soul was the greatest challenge, and this fits our archetypal analysis since the stakes are raised with each subsequent archetypal transition. As Shakespeare so perfectly portrayed in *King Lear*, the Adult who fails the Elder transition risks oblivion. That is why we have named the shadow form of the Elder *The Abyss*.

The Elder transition is perhaps also the most difficult because it comes upon those who have learned to master their Will and turn it to successful enterprise in the world. The Soul implies a kind of resignation that feels like defeat or giving up from the point of view of Will. In modern society, we exacerbate this tendency since old age is accompanied by retirement, which literally means *to withdraw*. We leave the elderly without a socially meaningful role to step into. This leads to two negative outcomes: the person who continues to work and activate the Will until they are forced by physical necessity to stop (which really does feel like defeat) or the person who "gives up" in a spiritual sense and reaches an early grave through an inability to find meaning and purpose in the later years of life.

We should note that the confrontation with Soul need not happen only to the elderly. Another way to think about Soul that I think Jung would have agreed with is that it's about doing what you truly believe to be important and right. The Adult archetype implies taking on responsibilities to our marriage partner, our children and our society. Meeting those responsibilities means that we often have to do what is necessary rather than what is meaningful. Once we have fulfilled those Adult responsibilities, we become *free*. But this freedom can be disorientating to those who have learned the discipline of Will. Both the retreat from meaningful work (retirement) and the desire to carry on regardless, leading to overwork, are denials of the archetypal mission to confront the Soul. The freedom to choose and the freedom to manifest our highest meaning and purpose are dangerous precisely because they leave us naked. We can no longer say we were doing what was necessary to fulfil some ulterior purpose. We realise a new kind of responsibility: the responsibility to do only what is right as the full expression of our being. The difficulty and even terror that this can invoke have been a prime preoccupation of modern existentialism.

All of this may seem very abstract and difficult to follow, and that is precisely why we will make use of Hero's Journeys to elucidate these points since they give us real-life characters that we can understand at the human level. As it turns out, all of the best-known Shakespeare tragedies and many of the comedies are about the archetypal transformations, and this makes some sense because, as we have noted, these are the most dangerous periods of life and therefore make a natural quarry for a great dramatist and writer. Let's take just a few of Shakespeare's most famous stories and show how they fit the archetypal analysis just given.

The Archetypes in Shakespeare

We have said that the Adult archetype's dominant faculty is Will. There is a sub-archetype of the Adult which represents Will most directly and that is the Warrior (other sub-archetypes of the Adult include the Ruler, the Sage and the Fool). Two of Shakespeare's best-known characters represent the Warrior: Macbeth and Othello. Both are tragedies because the two men fail to learn how to sheath their swords and transcend from the Adult-Warrior to the Elder archetype. Macbeth is the Warrior who, having won a battle that has secured the kingdom of his just and noble Ruler, Duncan, is offered the title of Thane. Although the age of Macbeth is not explicitly spelled out in the story, we can surmise that he is in his 40s or 50s. What he is being offered is the chance to take up a role as a societal Elder. That is Macbeth's Call to Adventure and it is a call that requires an archetypal transformation that includes not just a new Exoteric role but, more importantly, a significant personal transition. Macbeth, the great general newly victorious in battle, must temper the faculty of Will and incorporate that of Soul.

Why the story of Macbeth is especially relevant from our archetypal point of view is because he actually receives two Calls to Adventure. One is from his Ruler, Duncan, who represents the positive archetypal transition that awaits Macbeth including an Exoteric role in a just and noble kingdom. The other is the shadow Call to Adventure, which comes from a prime symbol of the Unconscious, the three witches in the foggy wood. Macbeth is called by his king to complete the archetypal transition from Adult to Elder. What do the witches, representing his shadow psyche, promise him? They promise that he will become king. They promise the extension of his Will because Macbeth will need to take the kingship using his own sword, which had previously been turned outward against enemies and will now be turned inwards against friends. All of this is a symbol for Macbeth's own shadow battle, as he fails to channel the archetypal energy to its positive outlet and instead it is diverted to the negative.

Macbeth has risen to the highest Exoteric post that he can rightfully expect in life. After what we can presume is a career of just and noble service, he has been offered a Thaneship. There is no higher post for him to obtain legally. But there is a post that he can obtain illegally. The shadow forces of Macbeth's psyche push him to reject the Elder transition. Instead, he will manifest the hyper-masculine, the shadow form of the male Adult.

Remembering that, within the Jungian paradigm, a man's Soul is represented by the feminine *anima*, what we find in *Macbeth*, and indeed in all Shakespeare stories, is that the hero's Soul is represented symbolically by the female characters. In *Macbeth*, the female characters are the three witches and Lady Macbeth and it can be no coincidence that all four of them are pushing Macbeth to his doom. These are not Macbeth's "real" Soul which would counsel him to temper his ambition and transition to the Thaneship. Rather, they represent the shadow Will which drives Macbeth to his destruction through the unlawful killing of Duncan and other crimes. They represent the failure of Macbeth to embrace his Soul. The tragedy of Macbeth is, therefore, the tragedy of the archetypal Adult who fails the transition to Elder.

Shakespeare gives us a second example of the failure of the Adult – Elder transition in the story of *King Lear*. Macbeth must transition from the Warrior archetype to the Elder. Lear must transition from the Ruler to the Elder. Once again, the opening scene conveys to us the archetypal mission. We see that Lear is in the process of retiring. He is handing over his kingdom to his daughters and their husbands. Nominally, this would indicate that he is on the right track since he is giving up the exercise of Will and, potentially, embracing the Soul. But we see immediately that Lear is not up to the task. Rather than justly apportion his kingdom based on wisdom, something an Elder might do, he states that he will give whichever daughter loves him the most the greatest share, leaving a crucial decision in matters of state up to a spurious exercise that does nothing more than stroke his own ego.

Since Lear is the hero of the story, we know to expect that the female characters will symbolically represent his Jungian *anima*, his Soul. Once again, Shakespeare gives us two pathways for Lear to take, one representing the positive archetypal transition and the other representing the shadow. The positive *anima* is the daughter, Cordelia, who refuses to play Lear's silly game and instead tells him the truth (remember that the Soul represents the highest forms of truth). The other two daughters, Goneril and Regan, represent the shadow *anima*. They flatter the old man with obsequious declarations of affection. Just as Macbeth chose to follow the shadow Call to Adventure offered to him by the three witches, Lear rewards Goneril and Regan while disinheriting Cordelia and banishing her from the kingdom. In his final act as king, Lear rejects the positive version of his Soul, the one that can guide him to the Elder archetype, and embraces the shadow. The rest of the story describes the playing out of this failure, which Lear's fool captures perfectly with the quip to his master, "Thou shouldst not have been old till thou hadst been wise." Wise like an Elder.

The stories of *Julius Caesar* and *Othello* also represent the failure of the Adult – Elder transition, but we will skip these and turn to Shakespeare's other great tragedies, which deal with the second main archetypal transition that we are concerned with in this book: the Orphan to Adult transition.

The stories of *Hamlet* and *Romeo and Juliet* are about Orphan archetypes who need to make the transition to the Adult. Recall that the Orphan phase of life is about beginning to establish an Adult identity in the economic, political, religious, and romantic/sexual senses. We can see that all three Orphan characters are set up to fail right from the start of their stories, which is why they are tragedies. But a crucial point, which is often overlooked because Hero's Journeys foreground the individual, is that Hamlet, Romeo and Juliet are being subverted from their archetypal missions, not just from their own shadow psyche but, arguably, more from the external world. Romeo and Juliet's love is subverted by the feud between the Montagues and Capulets, while Hamlet's rightful claim to the throne is being usurped by his uncle, Claudius. All of these prevent the expression of these characters' Exoteric identities and force them back into introversion, which is where their psychic battle takes place. The implication is that it's the failure on the Exoteric level of being which forces the characters back into the shadow forms of the Esoteric.

This is another way in which Shakespeare represents the shadow archetypal forms because the characters in his tragedies are always tempted by literal shadow figures in the dark. Thus, Hamlet receives his shadow Call to Adventure from the ghost of his father in the middle of the night. Romeo and Juliet, unable to make their love public, must meet clandestinely under the cover of darkness. Macbeth kills Duncan in the middle of the night. King Lear is abandoned by his daughters and thrown out to face the tempest in the dark. Even in *Othello*, we find that Iago's trickery only works because it is hidden from the great general and works in the shadow parts of his psyche. The great warrior used to confronting his enemies directly on the battlefield is brought undone by the invisible parts of himself.

Just as Shakespeare demonstrates the importance of the Exoteric in the formation of the tragedies, he also demonstrates the macrocosmic effects that come from the microcosmic failure. That is why so many of Shakespeare's stories feature royalty and aristocracy, because, in them, the personal failure becomes public. King Lear's failure almost results in the destruction of his kingdom. The same goes for Macbeth. The Hamlet royal family is completely destroyed, and the royal house is taken over by Fortinbras at the end of the play. The Montague and Capulet families are left childless. The failure of the archetypal progressions is as much caused by the macrocosm as the microcosm, and the failure does not just bring ruin to the individuals involved but also to the societies of which they are a part.

We can see that this is true by comparing the tragedies to a couple of Shakespeare's comedies. In *Much Ado About Nothing*, the characters are headed for disaster when the wise friar steps in to save the day. The same is true in *The Taming of the Shrew*, where it is Petruchio who intervenes to set the other characters on the pathway to happiness. In these cases, the crucial factor comes not from a personal psychological battle but from outside assistance from society. The success or failure of the archetypal transitions in Shakespeare takes place as much on the Exoteric level of being as on the Esoteric. Ophelia, Hamlet, Romeo and Juliet are Orphan archetypes who are being blocked in various ways from transcending to an Exoteric role in adulthood. That is their main problem and the cause of their subsequent psychological ones. Meanwhile, Macbeth rejects his rightful Exoteric role as Thane, and King Lear bungles his transition to Elder by failing to make rational arrangements for the handing over of his kingdom. All of these are Exoteric failures, and that is why our archetypal analysis aims to look for the connections and relationships between the levels of being rather than focus on only a few individual aspects in isolation.

With this, we have concluded our initial overview of the archetypal progressions using some famous examples from literature. The key points to reiterate are that the archetypal progressions can be thought of as a kind of energy source which, from the individual's point of view, comes from the Unconscious in the broadest sense of the word, meaning that it is something which comes from outside the conscious mind. Although we certainly allow that there can be purely psychological drivers to the dynamic, we must be clear in stating that both the Physical and Exoteric levels of being play a very large role in the archetypal transformations, and that they both can be seen as working "through" the Unconscious. In fact, Jung often analysed the Unconscious as being the lower part of the psyche that interfaced with the Physical realm directly. But even Exoteric and societal events, such as rites of passage, push our psyche out of equilibrium and into unknown territory. Thus, they can also be seen as causing a descent into the Unconscious as per any Hero's Journey. In short, we must consider all three levels of being and the relations between them in our archetypal analysis.

And that is the primary reason behind our use of literature. Great stories connect all three levels of being. Fictional Hero's Journeys resonate with us because they are a mirror of our own Hero's Journey. When Hamlet fails his Orphan mission or King Lear fails the transition to the Elder role, we can understand these both at the specific level of the archetypal failure of the Orphan and Adult but also at the more general level as a failure to come to grips with the necessarily difficult challenge presented by an archetypal transformation. Our own lives are almost certainly not as dramatic as the stories of Shakespeare but that is mainly because the archetypal transformation is spread out over many years in real life, while Shakespeare, as any great dramatist does, condenses the meaning down to its purest and most concentrated form.

Part of that concentrated form is to show the relationships between the Exoteric and Esoteric levels of being, as the heroes of Shakespeare's stories are not just brought undone by their own inner psychology but as much by their societies. But there is even more to unpack in the archetypal dynamic, and that is because not all relationships are created equal when it comes to the archetypal transformations. The hero's relationship with broader society is important, but their relationships with those closest to them are even more crucial. It is not merely a dramatic or entertaining twist in the story to have the Father archetype try to subvert the mission of the Orphan hero as in *Romeo and Juliet* and *Hamlet* or to have the daughters bring the Father undone, as in *King Lear*. It reveals a deep and important reality that is psychologically, anthropologically, and, as we will see later, historically, of crucial importance.

Although the archetypes stand alone as both an analytical concept and a lived reality, it's also true that there are two fundamental pairings of the archetypes. Let's turn to those now.

The Two Fundamental Pairings

Of the four archetypes we have defined – the Child, the Orphan, the Adult and the Elder – only two are universal and undeniable. Every culture makes a distinction between a child and an adult. Yet we forget the extent to which even these basic categories show significant cultural variation. In the modern West, for example, we define adulthood entirely by bureaucratic methods. In most western nations, 18 is the magic number at which we can legally gamble, drink, drive, vote, and marry, irrespective of our physical, psychological, or spiritual development. Our archetypal approach ideally would not rely on culturally specific criteria to define the archetype, and that is why we have drawn on comparative anthropology, mythology, and history to derive the integrated model of Part 1.

This raises the question: when do the archetypal phases begin? Here we see yet another reason why we need to differentiate the Physical, Exoteric and Esoteric. We have already pointed out that, at least for women, the archetypal phases are clearly demarcated at the Physical level into puberty (menstruation), pregnancy-childbirth and menopause. Each of these represents a significant and unavoidable challenge, especially childbirth, which has, for most of history, been extremely dangerous for both mother and child. What is crucial to understand is that the Exoteric and the Esoteric take place on a different timeline than the Physical. It's for this reason that van Gennep distinguished between what he called *physical puberty* and *social puberty*. The latter refers to what we have been calling the Exoteric level of being. The cultural practices that any society carries out do not need to match up exactly with the Physical developments, although we can say with some certainty that they lag behind the Physical. At some point after puberty, the society will recognise the archetypal transformation of the individual, this is *social puberty*, the Exoteric manifestation of the archetype.

The Esoteric is even less temporally tied to the first two levels of being because we humans can introvert and dissociate from the external world for a surprisingly long time, perhaps an indefinite one. This is more true the more the individual has a certain leeway in the form of wealth and social status. Thus, it has historically been true that psychological problems correlate very closely with wealth and position in the social hierarchy. "Mental illness" is a luxury that only the rich have been able to afford for most of history. But, at least in relation to archetypal development, "mental illness" is just a failure to adapt Esoterically to the archetypal challenges of life. This can occur even though both the Physical and Exoteric manifestations of the archetype have been carried out "successfully", although our review of Shakespeare earlier indicates that it is far more likely to happen when something goes wrong at the Exoteric level.

When we abstract away from these details and ask the question, when does an archetypal phase begin? – We find that there is no fixed answer. Rather, it is a complex process of interactions and relationships across the three levels of being, with the Exoteric being more malleable than the Physical and the Esoteric even more malleable again. Consider that Shakespeare wrote *Romeo and Juliet* sometime in the 1590s. The plot of the story revolves around the proposed marriage of Juliet, who is not even 14 years old. Juliet's mother, speaking in favour of the marriage, points out to Juliet early in the play that girls younger than her were not only married but had already had their first child. This was, indeed, a common age for women of that time to be married, and that places physical and social puberty far more in temporal alignment than in our time, where social puberty can continue even beyond the time when physical puberty has ended.

Having pointed out the complexity of the matter, it's also true that there is a very simple fact staring us in the face, given the definition of our four archetypes. The Child phase of life begins at birth; that much is obvious. But so does the Adult phase of life. This is definitely the case at the Physical level for women, but it is Exoterically true for both parents, and that is why it is a universal of human culture that marriage and childbirth have some of the most extensive rites of passage built around them. It is also a truism that, from the Esoteric point of view, the birth of the child is life-changing for all parents, even those who fail to fulfil their obligations to the child. The act of becoming a parent is the act of taking on Adult responsibilities. The length and seriousness of those responsibilities mean that the relatively carefree and experimental phase of the Orphan archetype goes away forever. The possibility of childhood is replaced with the necessity of adulthood.

In this respect, we also need to recall how recent the relaxation of the institution of marriage in the West has been. It needs to be remembered that most societies throughout history held marriage as a solemn and permanent connection, only to be severed with severe penalties, if at all. This was done precisely because marriage was the institution for raising children and needed to be made strong and lasting since raising children requires a decades-long commitment. Since childbirth was assumed to happen almost immediately after marriage, we can think of marriage and childbirth as combined rites of passage that mark the transition to the Adult archetype.

Thus, with the qualifications that we will get to shortly, we can state that the beginning of the Adult archetype coincides with childbirth, which means that it coincides with the beginning of the Child phase of life in the child of the parents. In other words, the Child – Parent (Adult) archetypes are a pair, and we will call this the first of our fundamental archetypal pairs. We'll label it Child – Adult and Child – Parent interchangeably, as fits the context.

Now, of course, it is also true that our Adult identity is not limited to the family and child rearing. Full Adult membership in society entails an economic, political, religious and a sexual identity. Marriage has traditionally entailed the fusion of all these identities into one institution for the purpose of childrearing, and, thus, our generalisation that the Adult phase begins in tandem with the Child phase of the offspring holds well enough. In the modern West, we have deprecated the institution of marriage at the same time as splitting up the four main categories of Adulthood into a dizzying array of possible identities, with our complex economy, our numerous political parties and sub-parties within parties, the possibility to practice any faith whatsoever, and the freedom to practice any sexual orientation. Why that has happened is partly due to the macrocosmic cycle and partly due to some factors that are unique to the West, which we will address in due course. Despite all this, even in the modern West, we can say that the first of our archetypal pairings of Child – Adult still holds. That brings us to the second pairing.

Orphans and Elders

It's a seeming universal of human society that the Child – Parent relationship dominates for about the first six to seven years of life. Even in communitarian ancient Sparta, male children were only removed from their parents at seven years of age. In the modern West, primary education begins at five or six, which is not the full removal of the child as in Sparta but the first tentative steps towards independence. During the first several years of life, the parents dominate the child's world, and this is why Freud and Jung were able to analyse the psychology of these years entirely with reference to the Child –

Parent pairing.

When we say that the child is "removed" from the parents or that they begin their steps towards a kind of independence, what we really mean is that it is around the age of six that the child first begins to be inducted into the institutions of society. This induction is a mild affair and one that barely constitutes a rite of passage. In the modern West, the first day of primary school is arguably a much bigger deal for the parents than for the child since, for the parents, the event signifies the formal giving over of control to the institutions of society. It is the beginning of the process by which the child will eventually become independent of the parents and a full member of society. It is the beginning of the end of the Child – Parent relationship in the form which existed for the first years of the child's life.

Nevertheless, unless you happen to live in ancient Sparta, where the children were completely removed from their parents at age seven, it's almost certain that the parents will continue to be the dominant influence on the child into the teenage years, and this is one reason that we hold that the Child phase of life lasts all the way until puberty. It's noteworthy in this respect that, even though the ancient Spartans removed the child from its parents at age 7, they still waited until age twelve to formalise the relationship that constitutes our second fundamental archetypal pair. At twelve years of age, the young Spartan boy was paired with an experienced warrior who would become the child's mentor, not just in the martial arts but in introducing and inducting the child into the adult world of Spartan society. In archetypal terms, the warrior was the Elder and the twelve-year-old was the Orphan. This Orphan – Elder relationship is our second fundamental archetypal pairing.

As we saw in our review of the anthropological literature in Part 1, most societies have a rite of passage at around 12 years of age that marks the beginning of the Orphan transition. Religious rites such as Holy Communion or the *bar/bat mitzvah* take place around this age. In hunter-gatherer societies, this was the time when the young person was removed from their parents and given initiation by the wider tribe. It's the beginning of what van Gennep called *social puberty*. The crucial point to understand is that the rites of passage are not given to the Orphan by their parents but by an Elder of the wider society. The mature Spartan warrior, the Christian priest, the tribal leader of a hunter-gatherer initiation - these are all Elders of their respective societies. The initiation of the Orphan is the induction into society by a leader of that society who represents its Exoteric institutions. In most cases, the relationship with the Elder will be ongoing after the initiation, which follows literally since the word *initiate* means *to set in motion*. The Elder's job will be to monitor the Orphan's progress as they work towards becoming a full member of the institution. This is the basis of the Orphan – Elder relationship.

The modern West marks this distinction with the beginning of secondary education, which is almost always a much bigger deal for the child than for the parents. The parents have already begun relaxing their control over the child, beginning with primary school. Secondary school does little to change that. But secondary school corresponds to the beginning of the Orphan archetype and the self-consciousness, which is also the beginning of self-awareness, which comes with it. All of the familiar challenges of the archetype come together at this point: the need to prove oneself, to find friends and a place in the social structure, the beginning of an identity one shapes for oneself rather than receives from one's parents, the beginnings of sexual desire etc. We might be tempted to say that secondary school teachers are the Elders in modern western society, but that is only somewhat true. The main problem with this formulation is that there is no explicit rite of passage in the form of a ceremony which marks the beginning of the relationship between a teacher and a student in the way, for example, that a religious rite does. Furthermore, there is no ongoing mutual obligation between student and teacher as there is with the Orphan – Elder relationship. We will be going into this issue in much more detail later. But, in order to make the case that the Orphan – Elder relationship really does exist, we have to give a basic explanation why it is absent from our culture.

To reiterate, the progression into adulthood can be thought of as achieving full membership in the Exoteric institutions of society in four domains: economic, political, religious, and sexual. We have defined full membership in these as the starting point of the Adult archetype usually signified by the rites of passage of marriage and childbirth. The Orphan archetype marks what we might call the beginning of the attainment of these four identities. It is our first tentative step towards the final goal. In relation to modern society, your first job can be thought of as a rite of passage that will lead to your eventual Adult economic identity. Your first kiss is the beginning of your sexual identity. Your first vote is your entry into the political sphere. Whatever rite is relevant for your religion is your entry into that sphere e.g. Holy Communion.

Both the sexual and political rites in the modern West do not have Elders attached to them, and it would seem very strange to us to even imagine what such rites and Elders might look like. But the anthropological literature shows that the West is perhaps an outlier in this respect. In ancient Sparta and ancient Greece in general, the Orphan – Elder relationship almost always had a sexual element to it while also being a kind of political induction too. The anthropological literature tells us that such arrangements are not uncommon, with some cultures having rites of passage that are explicitly about sexual maturity. Meanwhile, the swearing of allegiance to a local lord in feudal Europe is an example of a rite of passage that begins the Orphan – Elder relationship in the political sphere.

What has happened in the modern West is that we have removed some of the standard Elder roles that exist cross-culturally and we have deprecated the ceremonial aspects of the rites of passage. We still have rites of passage; it's just that we don't think of them in that way. Most people wouldn't think of their first job interview as a rite of passage, yet it has all the formal elements of one. There is a special time set aside for the interview. You will have to wear special clothing, and there are behaviour expectations you will have to meet. There is a relatively formal process where your skills and experience will be put to the test through a series of questions and maybe even exercises. The interviewers for the job are in the role of Elder who determine whether or not you will be inducted into the Exoteric institution, which is the company or organisation who is offering the job. If they do induct you, there is an expectation of an ongoing relationship. All of these are properties of a rite of passage.

Thus, it's not true to say that we have gotten rid of rites of passage in the modern West, but rather that we have deprecated them. In some cases, we have removed rites of passage altogether. In others, we do not make the Orphan – Elder relationship explicit in a way that most other cultures do. All of this is not an accident. It began with the rebellion against the Elders of the Catholic Church during the Reformation, and we will go into much more detail about the ramifications of this later in the book since it is related to several other key points that are required for an understanding of the modern West. For now, we can simply state that the West is unusual in our rejection of the Elder role, and this is why the archetype might be harder to understand than the others on our list.

There are two more potential ambiguities around the Orphan – Elder relationship that we need to clear up. The first is that it may be the parent who actually takes on the Elder role in relation to their own child. A good example of this is ancient Rome where the father of the house was also responsible for carrying out the religious rites, including to his own children. Similarly, a child may be inducted into a family business by a parent, or a parent might be the sports coach who gives training to their own child. These ambiguities can be sorted out by a simple definitional statement: whoever inducts an Orphan into an Exoteric institution of society is an archetypal Elder whatever other commitments or relationships they might have to the person they are inducting. It's precisely because of this clash of responsibilities that parents who become sports coaches to their own children have to manage an extra layer of complexity since they must balance two possibly conflicting roles: Parent and Elder. The same issue holds for family businesses, where the clash of relationships can sometimes lead to the destruction of both.

The final ambiguity in relation to the Orphan – Elder relationship is more general. There is a common metaphor that seems to be a universal across cultures, whereby a person in a position of authority at a societal level is referred to as a parent. *The father of the nation* is a common epithet for an influential political leader, for example. Even the USA has its *founding fathers*. This metaphor is part of a larger nation-as-family metaphor. Consider the use of *fatherland* and *motherland* as examples. The word *king* is etymologically related to the word *kin*. *Clan* is Gaelic for "family". The word *nation* comes from the Latin where it has connotations of familial lineage. *Patriot* comes from the Greek *patria*, meaning family. In the Roman Empire, Caesars were referred to as *pater patriae*, father of the fatherland. The metaphor also works for any kind of authority figure. Thus, *pope* comes from *papa*, meaning father. Many early church leaders were called *patriarchs* from the Greek for "father". Sometimes, an influential thinker is called the father/mother of the discipline e.g. *Freud was the father of psychoanalysis.*

The use of the parental metaphor can also apply to personal relationships, and this is a more direct reference to the Orphan - Elder. A very relevant example for our purposes is the fact that Jung referred to Freud as his "father" in that the latter had taught Jung about the emerging discipline of psychoanalysis. Clearly, fathers teach things to their sons, and the relationship between Freud and Jung may well have had levels of trust or other qualities that exist in a healthy father-son relationship. Still, in the interest of precision, we must insist that the relationship between Freud and Jung was that of Orphan – Elder. Freud inducted Jung into the nascent Exoteric institutions of psychoanalysis, of which Freud was the highest representative. Freud was the Elder, Jung was the Orphan. Crucially, Jung's subsequent break with Freud also fits the Orphan – Elder pattern, which we will investigate in detail later in the book.

The reason the parental metaphor works, of course, is that if we count the family as an Exoteric institution of society, then it is clear that the Parent is the authority figure in the family relative to the Child. In that case, the Orphan – Elder relationship is a reproduction of the Child – Parent relationship only in the new Exoteric institutions in which the Elder is the authority figure. Of course, we may very well reverse the metaphor. Since the parent is literally the elder in the Child – Parent relationship, they could just as well be said to be the Elder of the household. In this respect, it is noteworthy that the word priest comes from the Latin and Greek *presbyter* which literally means "elder". But, of course, the Pope is referred to as the holy *father*.

We cannot expect clear-cut definitions on such matters since they are tied up with the inherently messy world of human beings. Still, we should do our best to define our terms as much as possible, and with that end in mind, we can sum up the two fundamental relationships as follows:-

The Child – Parent (Adult) relationship exists where the prime responsibility is parental care, including shelter, nourishment and love of a Child, who is young enough to have no independent Exoteric identity separate from the family unit.

The Orphan – Elder relationship exists where the prime responsibility is for the Elder to induct the Orphan into an Exoteric institution of society. The Elder's role is to guide the Orphan in the formation of their Exoteric identity independent of the family unit. This almost always involves a period of training and education with the goal of making the Orphan *self-sufficient*, at which point they transition to the Adult archetype with full membership in the institution in question.

The differences between the two fundamental pairings will become clearer as we work through our analysis, but this gives us a starting point. Since the Child – Parent relationship is fundamental and a universal of human experience, we don't need to go into more detail about it. The Orphan – Elder relationship is about the Exoteric institutions of society and, therefore, has a socio-political dynamic which we need to be clear about. Let's now review the types of initiation that are available to the Orphans of society.

Two Types of Initiation

Traditionally, the elites of society have comprised three primary archetypes: the Ruler, the Warrior and the Sage (priest). These archetypes are universals. Even in relatively undifferentiated societies such as small tribes, there will be the medicine man, who represents the Sage archetype, and the chief, who usually represents a combination of the Ruler and the Warrior. The anthropological literature shows that the elites are demarcated from the general public by extensive rites of passage. This is true for religious practitioners, who are usually required to take vows of celibacy, relinquish property rights, and otherwise renounce the economic, political, and sexual identities taken by the average person. A military career usually involves extensive training as well as demarcation from the rest of society. Many societies will perform rites of passage on warriors leaving for and returning from battle, for example. Political leaders also have extensive rites of passage around them. Even in modern democracy, an election campaign is a paradigm example of a rite of passage, with the calling of an election belonging to the Separation phase, the election campaign itself being the Transition phase, and the swearing-in ceremony being the Incorporation phase of the rite.

Once again, we see here that the modern West is unusual, and the changes that mark out the difference begin with the Reformation, which was the rejection of the Sage archetype in the form of the Pope and the hierarchy of Elders of the Catholic Church. Later came the negation of the king as the Elder of the political class, to be replaced by parliament. Finally, there are the Warrior elites, who have also been replaced, to a large extent, by technology. For all these reasons, we can say that the modern West has replaced the traditional archetypes of the elites with new ones, and this also plays a significant role in our problematic relationship with the Elder archetype in general. Nevertheless, the archetypal pattern that we are about to outline still holds in the West.

We know that, for most of history and across cultures, the Adult phase of life begins with the twin rites of marriage-childbirth. That is true for the majority of the population, including the elites who start their own families (religious practitioners being the exception in this respect). In addition to the usual rites shared with other members of the general public, the elite class of society undergoes a second set of rites of passage. These rites of passage serve both to demarcate the elites as a separate group and to provide the more intensive education and training that pertains to elite performance. We can say that the elite rites of passage serve the same archetypal function that marriage and childbirth serve for the general public, but with an additional property. They entail a transition to the Adult archetype with a special status of "elite".

We noted earlier that the initiation of Orphans serves the function of inducting them into the Exoteric institutions of society. Thus, the Holy Communion of the Catholic Church marks the initiate as now a full member of the congregation, after which they will take part in the rites pertaining to that category. The elite initiation fulfils the same function, but the initiate is not just going to be a full member of the institution but, in fact, a leader of that institution. One of the seven sacraments of the Catholic Church is set aside for the initiation and instruction of future priests. That is what we are calling elite initiation, since it sets the individual on a path to a leadership position. We see an identical initiation in the military in the fact that the officer class receives a separate, longer, and more intensive initiation than the general soldiery.

If we give the general name to any rite of passage given to an Orphan who is being inducted into an Exoteric institution for the first time as *initiation*, we can see that the anthropological literature shows us two primary types of initiation: one for the elites and one for the general public. We can further categorise elite initiation with reference to the elite archetypes outlined earlier. There is the initiation given to those joining the religious elite e.g. a priest, anchorite, or nun. There is the initiation given to those joining the military elite (officer training). Then, there is the initiation given to the political elite. What each elite initiation has in common is that it is an intensive exercise which requires the individual to be taken out of mainstream society and to forego the normal burdens and pleasures that everyday life entails. As a general rule, the initiation given to elites is more intensive than that given to the general public.

Again, even small-scale communities like hunter-gatherer tribes also feature an elite initiation. The chief religious figure of such tribes, sometimes called the *medicine man*, has a severe and exacting initiation that goes well beyond the rites given to others. Such an initiation is all the more necessary since the religious rites for which the medicine man is being trained involve significant physical ordeals such as fasting, long periods of solitude, and the use of mind-altering drugs, which bring the practitioner into a state of being where connection with the spirit world is attained. On a purely practical level, such activities require extensive training in order to be carried out safely. But the medicine man is also a powerful figure, and one who must be taught to use that power responsibly. Thus, the extensive nature of elite initiation is also a safeguard against the improper use of power once it is attained.

A famous historical example of elite initiation is the mathematician and philosopher, Pythagoras, who was himself the Elder of a cult (*cult* in the general sense of a group with a shared purpose without the negative connotation the word has taken in our time). There was a four-year initiation and training period if you joined Pythagoras' cult. Initiates were required to remove themselves from general society and live in the compound with the other students. Only once you were inducted as an adept could you expect to train and spar with the man himself.

We could cite more examples from anthropology and history, but this is enough to make the point. There are two types of initiation: one for the general public and one for entry into the elite classes. When we apply our levels of being concept to the two types of initiation, we find that the initiation given to elites is designed to resonate far more at the Esoteric level of being than that given to the general public. This is true even where the initiation involves significant physical ordeals, such as in elite military training, since what is really being trained is the mental fortitude to achieve peak physical conditioning. For this reason, we will call the initiation given to elites *Esoteric initiation*.

For most of history and across most societies, Esoteric initiation has only been given to would-be members of the elite class. By contrast, members of the general public are given a different set of rites, which we will call *Exoteric initiation*. Exoteric initiation requires only that you carry out the prescribed external behaviour. It does not require that you understand that behaviour. If we again take the Christian church as an example, anybody can receive the Eucharist by following along with the rest of the congregation. To understand the meaning of the Eucharist within the tradition of the church in question requires Esoteric understanding. A member of the congregation may achieve some level of Esoteric understanding of the Eucharist, but their membership in the Church is predicated only on carrying out the Exoteric part of the rite. By contrast, a priest is not fit for the role unless they understand the Esoteric meaning of such rites.

Esoteric initiation is designed to facilitate the archetypal transition from Orphan to Adult at the elite level of society. It is not just a break with the old identity of Child but also a break with the identity of the general public, since, while they are in the elite role, the practitioner is not seen to be a member of the public but a separate role. In relation to the experience of Esoteric initiation, William James captured this in broad terms with his distinction between being *once born* versus *twice born* (also known as *born again*). An Esoteric initiation requires one to be born again. The biblical passage we referenced earlier in the book is worth repeating in this respect.

"Jesus answered him, 'Truly, truly, I say to you, unless one is born again he cannot see the kingdom of God.' Nicodemus said to him, 'How can a man be born when he is old? Can he enter a second time into his mother's womb and be born?' Jesus answered, 'Truly, truly, I say to you, unless one is born of water and the Spirit, he cannot enter the kingdom of God. That which is born of the flesh is flesh, and that which is born of the Spirit is spirit. Do not marvel that I said to you, 'You must be born again.'"

The "spirit" which Jesus talks of is what we have been calling the Esoteric. An Esoteric initiation is to be born again in Spirit. This contrasts with what William James called the *once born*. The *once born* conform to the consensus version of reality of their culture. Once born initiation is what we have called Exoteric initiation. It's the initiation given to the majority of people who are not expected to join the elite class and therefore do not require an in depth understanding of the issues involved, whether they be in the religious, military, or political domains. Here we can start to see why these concepts jar against modern Western culture, since our assumption is that everybody is capable of attaining Esoteric initiation if only given the opportunity to do so. The ramifications of that belief and its practical manifestation are crucial to understanding the modern West and we will be going into detail about this in Part 4.

Given that we earlier defined the Elder archetype as the one who will initiate the Orphans of society into the Exoteric institutions, and given that we have just said that the role of Elder is limited to a minority class called the elites, this poses the question of what the Elder role means for those who are not part of the elites. Firstly, we can say that, outside of the elite class, there are gradations of rank based on experience in most areas of life, and thus there is an implied non-elite Elder role that is attained over time for a member of the general public. This is true in the economic sphere, where experienced workers usually take on more responsibilities relative to newcomers, and it's also captured in the military ranks that exist among the general soldiery i.e. private, corporal, sergeant etc.

But it's also true that there is an Elder role within the family, and that is, of course, the grandparents. This leads into the final concept we need to introduce before we once again turn to literary examples to help bring these abstracts concepts to life.

The Generations

We have seen that there are two parallel pathways through the archetypal progression. One pertains to the family unit, and the other to broader societal institutions. We are each born into a family, raised, and then may go on to create families of our own. But we are each also inducted into the institutions of civilisation. This is another way to consider the concept of being *born again*. We are born as Child to Parent on the Physical level of being. We are re-born as Orphan to Elder on the Exoteric and Esoteric levels of being.

The word *generation* comes from the Latin *generatus*, which literally means "to beget". From the same etymology comes the idea of *genes* and hereditary biology. The word *pregnant* is related and means prior to birth: *pre- generatus*. Following the *born again* idea, we can see why the parental metaphor works when referencing societal Elders as parents, because it is the Elder's job to metaphorically beget the next generation at the Exoteric and Esoteric levels of being by inducting them into the Exoteric institutions and Esoteric traditions of civilisation. In short, our two fundamental archetypal pairings are required to beget the generations in a civilisation. We can capture this in diagram form as follows:-

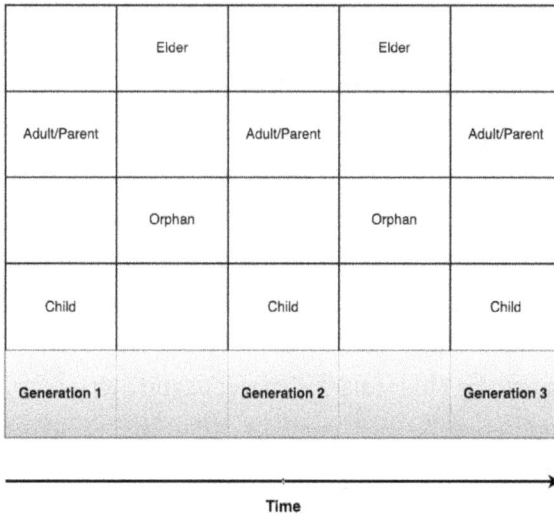

	Elder		Elder	
Adult/Parent		Adult/Parent		Adult/Parent
	Orphan		Orphan	
Child		Child		Child
Generation 1		**Generation 2**		**Generation 3**

Time

The diagonal flow represents the archetypal progression of the individual. Each cell in that progression maps vertically to the archetypal pairing that holds for the phase of life. As children, our main relationship is with our parents. As Orphans, our main relationships will be with Elders. When we become Parents ourselves, the Child is our main archetypal pairing and when we become Elders it is the Orphan relationship that corresponds. What this progression implies is that the attainment of the Elder at the individual level involves the gradual relinquishing of the Adult/Parent role. It means stepping back from a position of direct authority to a position of guidance, oversight, and, hopefully, wisdom. The Elder becomes a guide for the next generation.

The same is true for all the other archetypal progressions. As we noted earlier, it is the transition points between the archetypes which are the most dangerous in both a psychological and social sense because they require not just the acceptance of the new archetypal phase but the letting go of the existing one. What our archetypal pairing concept implies is that there are two sides to the risk because there are two parties involved. Each archetypal progression is not just an individual one but relates also to the other archetypal pair. It's for this reason that the rites of initiation aimed at Orphans often symbolically represent the breaking off of the Child – Parent relationship at the same time. Not only must the Child graduate to the Orphan, the Parent must graduate to the Elder by letting go of their control of the Child. Since the Parent and the Adult go hand-in-hand and since the primary Esoteric faculty of the Adult archetype is Will, this letting go requires a tempering of Will. The Parent rightfully exercises their Will over the Child in the early years of life, and that is healthy. But the transition to Orphan requires the Parent to step back and temper their Will. Thus, the relinquishing of control over the Child also begins the Parent's transition to the Elder role since the Elder role is about Soul and doing what is right. It is right for the Parent to relinquish control so that their Child may become an Orphan, but it requires giving up the dominance of the Will.

Thus, the transition points between the archetypal phases become doubly difficult because there are really two transitions involved. The Child must become an Orphan at the same time the Parent becomes an Elder. The failure of either of these threatens the transition to the other. What happens if the Parent does not temper their Will? They become domineering and force the Child to either acquiesce or actively rebel. We will see the problems with those options shortly when we turn to some literary examples. The most likely scenario in that case is that the Parent fails to transition to the Elder role and the Child fails to transition to the Orphan. Since both are failing the archetypal transition, both will manifest the shadow forms of their current archetype. Recall our table from earlier:-

Archetype	Level of Being		
	Exoteric	**Esoteric**	**Esoteric (shadow)**
The Child	Son or daughter	Imagination	Dissociation
The Orphan	Student, friend, protégé, initiate	Intellect	Ideology
The Adult	Husband/wife, parent, citizen, employee/boss, churchgoer	Will	Hyper-Masculine, Devouring Feminine
The Elder	Retiree, Mentor, Teacher	Soul	The Abyss

The failure of the Parents to relinquish control of their child leads them to manifest the shadow form of the Adult archetype i.e. the hyper-masculine and devouring feminine. Since we are talking about the parental relationship, we can be more specific and label such parents the Tyrannical Father and the Devouring Mother. The child of such parents should be making the transition to the Orphan archetype, but they get stuck in the shadow form of the Child which is Dissociation if they acquiesce to the Parent or Ideology if they rebel against the parent. Again, we will see examples of this as we progress.

We can represent these dysfunctional forms as follows:-

	Elder
Adult/Parent	Tyrannical Father - Devouring Mother
	Orphan
Child	Shadow Child (Peter Pan Complex)
Generation 1	

97

Rather than graduate to the Orphan, the Child gets stuck in the shadow forms of their archetype. The Parents fail to ascend to the Elder archetype and get stuck in the shadow forms of Tyrannical Father and Devouring Mother. Since the archetypal dynamic holds not just at the family but at the societal level, we can also see how such shadow forms can manifest at the collective psychological level. This is what I discovered and described in my book, *The Devouring Mother: The Collective Unconscious in the Time of Corona.*

Of course, life marches on regardless of whether we are ready for it. At the Physical level of being, the transition to Orphan occurs and so, too, does it take place at the Exoteric level of being, except in extreme circumstances. It's for this reason that the relationship between a Tyrannical Father/Devouring Mother and their child almost always takes a psychological form since it is mostly about what happens in private and is therefore Esoteric in nature. In many ways, it's more about what did not happen. The Child did not join a sports club, is not allowed to hang out with friends, is not given the freedom to participate in social activities etc. Meanwhile, the parents fail to allow or encourage such healthy developments. The Esoteric level of being is, by definition, hidden, and so the most common manifestation is psychological introversion.

What the introduction of our two fundamental pairings does is create a kind of archetypal logic from which we can draw conclusions. The presence of a Tyrannical Father/Devouring Mother implies both a failed Elder transition in the Parent and a failed Orphan transition in the Child. Similarly, wherever we find the shadow forms of the Orphan, the Peter Pan Complex or related phenomena, we also expect to find a Tyrannical Father/Devouring Mother.

With these thoughts in mind, let's re-evaluate our earlier analysis of two Shakespeare classics from the point of view of the archetypal pairings.

The Shadow Elder: King Lear

At the beginning of *King Lear*, we can see quite clearly that Lear manifests the Tyrannical Father archetype to a tee. He demands flattery from his daughters and then blows his top when one of them (Cordelia) does not acquiesce. We find that Cordelia had previously been Lear's favourite daughter, and we can infer from this that all three daughters had previously acquiesced to their father's demands, showing him the obedience that his ego requires. While Lear is in the Parent role and his daughters in the Child role, such obedience is right and fitting. But, of course, we are not talking about children here. The three daughters are either married or about to be, and Lear is about to retire. We are well beyond the point where the transition away from the Child – Parent relationship should have happened.

What we see at the beginning of the story, in fact, is the final failure of the archetypal transition. Lear forces the transition through, even though he and his daughters are not ready. The only one who upholds her side of the bargain is Cordelia, who, presumably for the first time, speaks truth to her father and goes against his wishes. In doing so, she exercises her own Will, a fitting thing to do for the Adult archetype and, therefore, evidence that she is making the steps towards the archetypal transformation that she needs to take. If he were a (wise) Elder, Lear would accept both the truth and the will of his daughter, or, at least, her right to speak her mind. Instead, he flies off the handle and completely overreacts, thereby destroying his and Cordelia's final chance at successfully navigating the archetypal transition.

Lear's final act as king shows that he is still the Tyrannical Father and has failed to become the Elder. The actions of Goneril and Regan show them as the Shadow Orphans pandering to their Father for their own benefit. With the final, fateful decision of Lear in the apportioning of his kingdom, he forces the archetypal transformation through, not just for himself but also for his daughters. Goneril and Regan graduate into the Adult role not in the positive form of exerting their own will and speaking their own mind, as does Cordelia, but in the shadow form of the devouring feminine. We now know that this is not merely a character flaw on their part because the archetypal transitions happen in pairs. Goneril and Regan are forced into the shadow form because Lear has not graduated to the Elder role and is still trying to exercise his Will and control over them. All this implies the past failure of all of them to graduate to the Orphan – Elder pairing. Lear should have eased himself out of power and allowed his daughters and their husbands to step into their new roles gradually. He could then have provided counsel and guidance while they learned the ropes. That would have made him the Elder and they the Orphans.

A large part of Lear's tragedy is that he is oblivious to this. A Tyrannical Father rules by power (Will) alone. While the Tyrannical Father holds on to the reins of power, the situation at least has some stability since everybody knows who the boss is. As soon as Lear hands over the reins, he ceases to have actual power. Shakespeare reinforces this reading by having Lear attempt to retain one hundred knights, who form a kind of mini-army for him, but who end up causing no end of trouble for his daughters, who, since they now hold all the power, forcibly remove the last vestiges of Lear's official power. He is left powerless, and we have the dramatic symbolism of the Child exerting a tyrannical Will over the Parent, an inversion of the proper state of things. Had Lear made the transition to Elder, he would have retained a form of power and influence that comes not from Will alone but from wisdom, truth, and justice. Since he has not made the transition to Elder, he ceases to be the Tyrannical Father too. What has he become? Lear's fool gives him the answer: "I am better than thou art now; I am a fool, thou art nothing." Lear finds himself in the shadow form of the Elder: The Abyss.

In *King Lear*, Shakespeare gives us the failure of two archetypal transformations simultaneously. Lear and his daughters have already failed to transcend the Child – Parent pairing into the Orphan – Elder pairing before the story begins. The failure brings ruin on them all, but not before they manifest the shadow forms. Goneril and Regan become the devouring feminine. Lear and Cordelia are relegated to The Abyss (represented symbolically by Cordelia's disinheritance and banishment from the kingdom). Since Cordelia also symbolises Lear's *anima* (Soul) and his positive pathway to the Elder archetype, the story of *King Lear* is still primarily about the tragedy of the man who fails to find his Soul. It is, therefore, fitting that both Lear and Cordelia are relegated to The Abyss since this is what precedes spiritual enlightenment. Many mystical traditions express the idea as *the long night of the soul*. It's for this reason that film and literature very often symbolise The Abyss by the use of a large bridge over a gaping chasm.

In psychological terms, as Carl Jung pointed out, the connection with the Soul is terrifying for precisely the reason that one must risk crossing The Abyss to get there. Most people sense this and do not even try. It is part of what makes King Lear one of the great tragedies that Shakespeare gives us hope towards the end that Lear can make it to the other side. The reunion with Cordelia near the end of the story suggests the promise of a successful archetypal transition for both of them. But this is quashed by nothing more or less than the shadow forms of the Adult driven by the two daughters alongside the hyper-masculine character of Edmund, the bastard son (archetypal Orphan!) of the Earl of Gloucester. It is the combination of the devouring feminine in the form of Goneril and Regan and the hyper-masculine in the form of Edmund which kills Lear's Soul.

Again, we see that all of this fits the archetypal logic, which can only be understood once we have partitioned the four archetypes into their two pairs. We can draw inferences from this logic. The presence of the devouring feminine/hyper masculine implies a failed Elder transition **and** a failed Orphan transition. Edmund, Goneril and Regan have become Adults at the Physical and the Exoteric level. It is at the Esoteric where they have failed the transition, and they failed that transition precisely because Lear himself has failed it. As the ruler of the kingdom, his failure to become the Elder denotes the failure of the kingdom to manifest the highest forms of the Esoteric. The result is a kingdom that runs not on Soul but on force and Will. When Lear relinquishes rule over his kingdom, he has made the transition to Elder at the Physical and Exoteric level but not at the Esoteric.

We can represent the archetypal logic of *King Lear* on our generational diagram from earlier as follows:-

	The Abyss (Lear and Cordelia)
Tyrannical Father (Lear)	Devouring feminine
Shadow Orphan (Goneril, Regan, Cordelia)	
Generation 1	

King Lear is a story about an archetypal progression from two shadow forms to two other shadow forms. We begin the story with Lear as the shadow Adult manifesting the Tyrannical Father. His three daughters are manifesting the shadow Orphan. It is Cordelia who makes the attempt to break out of the shadow form and bring both herself and her father into the relationship of Elder and Orphan. But this is also an inversion of the proper state of things because it means that Cordelia is trying to *initiate* her father. It is the Elder who must initiate the Orphan and not vice versa. Lear's final decisions as Tyrannical Father force the archetypal progression, which precipitates the demise of himself and Cordelia, who are relegated to The Abyss. Meanwhile, Goneril and Regan graduate from the shadow Orphan archetype into the shadow Adult where they manifest the devouring feminine.

The tragedy of Lear is, therefore, not just the tragedy of a single man. It is a tragedy across generations. Nevertheless, the responsibility lies with Lear. Both the Parent and the Elder carry the burden, not just for themselves but for the future generation. Therefore, The Abyss is not merely a personal psychological or spiritual journey but has an Exoteric and societal element as well. The failure of the Elder brings ruin on society. That is what Shakespeare makes clear in all his great tragedies.

The Shadow Orphan: Hamlet

In the modern west, we have become used to an extended adolescence during which we have the luxury of pondering what Adult role we might pursue when the time comes. For most of history, however, a person's role was all but defined at birth. A member of the peasantry might have some choice about which trade to pursue, but, even then, options were limited. The life path for most people was very fixed. The same is true for one of Shakespeare's greatest characters, Hamlet. He is the only son of a king. Therefore, he will become king. Hamlet's Exoteric life path is already defined.

Recall that the Orphan's archetypal mission is to establish themselves on a path to full adulthood in four main areas of life: economic, political, religious, and sexual. The Exoteric role of king incorporates all of these into one. The king has the highest Exoteric role in the land in the economic and political senses, and often in the religious sense as well. A king usually has no problem finding a queen, if not out of love, then out of political calculations. In many ways, then, the life of royalty is the most fixed of all life paths since the whole society has a vested interest in ensuring that the Orphan royal, a prince or princess, goes on to become the king or queen.

It's because of these dynamics that we can see right from the start of the story of *Hamlet* that, to take a famous phrase from the play, something is rotten in the state of Denmark. Hamlet is dissociated from the affairs of court. In the opening scene, we find him brooding at the end of a table, completely disinterested in the discussion going on around him. This is not the behaviour of an enthusiastic prince who should be paying close attention to what is going on so that he can learn the ropes and graduate to the role of king one day. Since Hamlet is manifesting the behaviour of the shadow Orphan, our archetypal logic tells us to expect a Tyrannical Father/Devouring Mother and that is precisely what we find. As the story progresses, we learn that Hamlet's father, the king, had been killed by Hamlet's uncle, Claudius, two months prior to the beginning of the story. We also see in the opening that Hamlet's mother, Gertrude, is behaving in a form indicative of the Devouring Mother, lavishing excessive affection on her adult son and rewarding him for his aloofness when she should be scolding him for it.

It's no coincidence that Freud was interested in the story of Hamlet since there is an obvious Oedipal theme involved. But a purely psychological reading misses the point. Hamlet's real problem is not some leftover psychological baggage from childhood but the fact that he is being blocked from his archetypal transcendence at the Exoteric level of being. At the Physical level of being, Hamlet is already an Adult. But his Exoteric life path has been blocked by the crime of his uncle, who has not only usurped the role of king but taken Hamlet's mother as wife into the bargain. If this had been done in the open, we could rightly define Claudius as the Tyrannical Father and, in that case, Hamlet would have been next on the hit list. History is full of such stories in royal courts. It is the deceptive nature of Claudius' crime that turns the problem into a psychological one for the young prince. Claudius puts on a show of fatherly love towards Hamlet. He is hiding the truth behind a façade of kindness.

But the story of Hamlet is just as much about the Devouring Mother in the form of Gertrude. Again, Shakespeare lays this out for us in the opening scene, as we see Gertrude doting on Hamlet and even kissing him in front of the rest of the court. She is treating him not as an Adult but as a Child. The smothering love of the Devouring Mother is intended to keep her child dependent, and that is exactly where Hamlet finds himself, trapped at home under the faux-care of two Shadow Parents who pretend to have his best interests at heart.

Hamlet's problem is not a psychological one, as Freud believed. He is not acting out repressed psychological drives acquired during childhood. Rather, he is acting out repressed energy from the unfilled Orphan's need to find an Exoteric place in society and Esoteric meaning in life. It is that repressed energy which manifests as Hamlet's desire to kill Claudius and escape his situation. But this would only allow Hamlet to graduate from Shadow Orphan to Shadow Adult by manifesting the hyper masculine. It would make him no better than his uncle. Once again, this highlights the fact that the archetypal transitions must be seen in pairs, but we can also say that the elder of the archetypal pairs plays the dominant role since they set the scene. It is because Claudius and Gertrude have manifested the shadow Parent forms that Hamlet is left to grapple with the problem of how to break out of the Orphan. The story of Hamlet is the story of a man who must find a way out of the archetypal trap that has been set for him.

Gertrude and Claudius are, like Lear, the Adults who are failing the Elder transition. It is exactly their failure which holds Hamlet back by usurping the Exoteric role that is rightly his. Lear vacates his Exoteric role all of a sudden and with no preparation. Claudius and Gertrude refuse to vacate. What options does Hamlet have? He can murder Claudius and take his rightful Exoteric role as king. This would bring him into the Adult archetype in the shadow form of hyper masculine. We know from the famous soliloquy that Hamlet considers suicide (*to be or not to be*). That option represents what we have called The Abyss. Hamlet's other option would be to escape the intolerable situation of the family home and seek a new life elsewhere, but that possibility is shut off right at the start of the story when Claudius forbids Hamlet from returning to university since he wants to keep an eye on him.

All of this represents the repression of Hamlet's identity in the political, economic, and religious spheres. Meanwhile, in the sexual sphere, Hamlet has an obvious romantic partner in the person of Ophelia who is the daughter of one of the king's advisers, Polonius. We see at the beginning of the play that there is mutual interest from both Hamlet and Ophelia and yet, here too, the prince is stifled when any hope of a successful romantic relationship is quashed by another figure who fails in their role as Elder. Polonius should quite literally be an Elder to Hamlet since Hamlet should be king and Polonius his adviser. Instead, he orders his daughter to stay away from Hamlet thereby preventing any hope that the two might marry and make the transition to Adult that way. Ophelia and Hamlet are both shadow Orphans held back by the failure of the Parents to transcend to the Elder role. No surprise, then, that later in the play, Ophelia puts into action what Hamlet only ruminated over and launches herself into The Abyss.

Our integrated model allows us to see the problems of Hamlet and Ophelia by incorporating the three levels of being. From adolescence onward, we should no longer be dominated by our parents. Our Exoteric identity should become far more determined by our connections and interactions with our society and its culture. The Orphan phase of life is the bridge between childhood and adulthood. The failure to cross the chasm leaves the Orphan stuck in infantile psychology and infantile relations with the parents. That is what the story of Hamlet and the sub-story of Ophelia communicate. Both of them are trapped in their family home well beyond the age at which that is healthy. Both are thrown back into psychological introversion at just the time when they should be extroverting themselves into society. The choice for both Hamlet and Ophelia is four-fold. They can acquiesce to their Tyrannical Father; they can murder him; they can try to escape; or they can commit suicide (an alternative form of escape). Ophelia chooses the latter option. Hamlet is eventually forced into murder. Hamlet's murder of Claudius is not that different from Goneril and Regan's almost-murder of their father by throwing him out into the tempest at night. Hamlet murders the Tyrannical Father at the Physical level of being, Goneril and Regan at the Exoteric and Esoteric levels. All of this makes sense when we understand the archetypes as consisting of two fundamental pairings.

We have now covered the main theory around the archetypal progressions and how they need to be viewed as a set of pairs. Let's finish our review of the microcosmic archetypal progressions by turning to a real world example as we re-evaluate Freud's most famous case study using our archetypal framework.

The "Dora" Case Study

Life marches inevitably on through the archetypal progressions at the Physical level of being. We are thrown into the Physical world at birth. Puberty arrives unbidden. Women, at least, have childbirth (although not inevitably) and menopause to surmount. Death is the final event on the Physical plane that awaits us all. The human individual and human society can attempt to ignore these facts, but that merely leads to dissociation from reality. What van Gennep and other anthropologists have shown is that human societies do not ignore these facts. Rather, they save the most important rites of passage for the archetypal transitions as a way to assist the individual through them. In this way, it's common sense that a societal Elder archetype should be in charge of the rites of passage since they are somebody who has been through it all before and can bring their experience to bear for the assistance of those going through it for the first time.

Freud and Jung discovered a variety of pathological psychological adaptations in adolescents, which they diagnosed as having a basis in trauma left over from childhood. Our archetypal approach has implied a different way of looking at these issues. Let's re-evaluate perhaps the most famous example from Freud's work, the case study called "Dora" to see how it looks from our perspective.

Dora's real name was Ida Bauer. Like many of Freud and Jung's patients, she was a young woman, 18 years old, born into an aristocratic household in Victorian-era Vienna. Her brother would later become the foreign minister of Austria. Ida was brought to Freud by her father after an incident involving the father's friend, who made sexual advances towards the young woman while visiting the family home one day. Ida slapped him in the face, causing a scene. Why would this sequence of events lead to Ida being taken to a psychiatrist? Did her father really think she was mentally ill, or was he trying to avoid the social and personal ramifications of the situation he had helped create? The latter explanation seems unlikely, as Ida also had other symptoms that were indicative of mental illness. Of course, it's also true that there is a cultural bias implied by the story. It was a common trope in 19th-century literature for aristocratic women to have "episodes". Usually, this was put down to a strange (and fictional) disease called "brain fever". Prior to the advent of modern psychology, it was always a hapless doctor that was called in to treat the problem, and his prescription often included drugs that are now illegal, such as laudanum and cocaine. It is no coincidence that both Freud and Jung received their initial education in medicine.

Applying our archetypal analysis to the case of Ida Bauer, we can see that, as an unmarried 18-year-old, she belongs to the Orphan category. We know that the healthy development of the Orphan archetype involves being on a pathway towards adulthood through the development of an economic, political, religious and sexual identity. We know that the Orphan should be paired with an Elder who can help them navigate the pathway to adulthood by inducting them into the Exoteric institutions of society. Viewed through our archetypal lens, we can immediately see the problem that young women like Ida Bauer in the Victorian era had: there was no pathway for them into the Exoteric institutions of society; no way for them to begin the formation of an Adult identity.

We saw earlier that Shakespeare's Juliet was not even 14 years old when she was proposed to by Paris. This was not uncommon in Europe at that time, which is why Juliet's parents are in favour of the marriage in the story. But there is an important caveat, which is that it was not uncommon *for aristocratic women*. For other demographics, such a young marriage was far less common, and, in fact, modern Europe, beginning in medieval times, has been anthropologically unusual for the relatively late average age of marriage among the general population. Some historians have speculated that it was the late age of marriage and the proclivity of both men and women to work for a number of years beforehand which allowed capitalism to occur in Europe since there was a ready workforce available.

Aristocratic women in Europe were the exception to the rule. Aristocratic men were expected to prove themselves by taking an Exoteric role in society before getting married, and this included a period of education beforehand. But this was not true for aristocratic women. It was a matter of debate in the learned circles of the medieval era whether it was worthwhile educating women. Treatises written by the scholastic philosophers argued that, even if women did have the intellect to receive a scholarly education, they should be spared the trouble and left to pursue the feminine ideal of beauty and leisure. Whatever the theory, in practice, what happened was that aristocratic women were married off young for economic and political reasons. Whatever else we might want to say about this practice, it was at least an Exoteric pathway by which women were given a role and an identity in society i.e. the family. Marriage *was* the Exoteric role expected of women. Arguably, there was no Orphan period for most aristocratic women of this era. Like Shakespeare's

Juliet, they went from being children to being married. They became Adults all at once, with no preparation required.

If we fast forward from medieval times to the Victorian era, we find that very little had changed for the other demographics of society. Aristocratic men still received an education and found an Exoteric role before marrying. Working class men and women still worked before marriage. The one demographic which had changed was aristocratic women, and one of the main ways that played out was that they had begun marrying later. This was part of a broader trend in 19th century Europe where people from all classes suddenly desired to marry somebody of the same age; which is known as *age homogamy*. Prior to that, it was taken for granted that the groom would be older, perhaps much older, than the bride.

Although educational opportunities were slowly opening up for women in the 19th century, it was still uncommon for even aristocratic women to attend university. With the age of marriage pushed back but no other Exoteric pathway available, the result was that aristocratic women's attainment of an Adult identity had been delayed. Such women ended up hanging around in their parents' house, waiting to be married off. If this sounds familiar, it is the exact scenario that we have just analysed in *Hamlet*. Both Ophelia and Hamlet were fictional precursors to what would happen in the Victorian era. But it was aristocratic women who felt the brunt of the changes. Archetypally speaking, they were Orphans without initiation. Unable to extrovert themselves into the Exoteric institutions of society, they introverted themselves into the psychoses and neuroses that Freud and Jung would later diagnose.

It is no coincidence, therefore, that Ida Bauer's episode should have been triggered by the sexual advances of an older man. Many Victorian aristocratic women developed strange disorders around sexuality. Remember that a sexual identity is one of the four main identities that the Orphan needs to be initiated into. Marriage had traditionally been the beginning of a woman's sexual identity, but, with marriage delayed, aristocratic women found themselves with no socially acceptable way to initiate their sexuality. We have posited that archetypal energy comes from the Unconscious and the sexual energy of the Orphan phase of life is perhaps the most potent form of that energy. If that energy is unable to find a productive outlet, it gets channelled into the shadow parts of the psyche, where it emerges as what Freud called *transference*, what Jung called *projection,* and what we have called Dissociation.

What our archetypal analysis makes clear is that the root cause of episodes such as Ida Bauer experienced was not psychological. More precisely, the psychological response is the effect, not the cause. The cause is the failure of the archetypal Orphan transition. That transition occurs across all three levels of being. Aristocratic women of the Victorian era had their Physical being, their sexuality, denied by society; they had no Exoteric initiation to induct them into meaningful membership in the institutions of society; and they had no Esoteric meaning to life, especially since it was at just this time that Christianity was no longer taken seriously among the upper classes of Europe.

We might put all this together and say that aristocratic women were having an existential crisis, although perhaps a better phrase for us would be an *archetypal crisis.* It's the same archetypal crisis that Shakespeare had already shown through Hamlet and Ophelia. Freud and Jung were surely right in saying that the dissociation seen in such cases is indicative of childlike psychological patterns. But that must be understood against the backdrop of the Exoteric level of being. Why were Hamlet, Ophelia and 19th-century aristocratic women trapped in childlike psychology? It was because they remained under the thumb of their parents. They were stuck in the family home with no way out. They had become trapped in the Child – Parent archetypal pairing, unable to transcend to the Orphan – Elder relationship.

The irony of the Dora case study is that what Freud ended up doing was to become Ida Bauer's Elder. Unlike her parents and other adults of that era, Freud simply listened to Ida without being judgemental. Rather than impose his Will on her as her father had done, Freud listened and offered some semblance of wise counsel in return. He became the Elder that Ida and other aristocratic women of the Victorian era needed.

It is because the archetypal phases of life come upon us, whether we like it or not, that we must become Orphans, Adults and Elders at the Physical level of being. It is the other levels of being that are more flexible and, therefore, more problematic. Ida Bauer was already physically an adult woman. Her problems were at the other levels of being. Exoterically, she was still a child, stuck at home in her parents' house. Esoterically, she was manifesting symptoms of Dissociation. Time marches on at the Physical level of being while the Exoteric and Esoteric may get out of sync. When the levels of being get out of sync, the individual begins to manifest the shadow forms of the Esoteric.

Following Freud and Jung, our society categorises these pathological states as "mental illness". But our archetypal model provides a different analysis. How many of the so-called psychological problems of the elderly in modern society are caused by the fact that we have no Exoteric role for our old people to fulfil? How many drug and alcohol addictions in adults have a similar cause? These are not primarily psychological problems, but social ones. One of the side effects of the psychological lens is to focus on the individual. In doing so, we miss the bigger picture. It is the Exoteric level of being which most obviously provides the link between microcosm and macrocosm, and what we see in Ida Bauer, Hamlet, Ophelia, Romeo and Juliet is a problem of Exoteric identity first leading to problems at the Esoteric.

Summary

With this, we come to the end of our introduction to the archetypes of the microcosm, and since we have yet again covered a lot of space in a short period of time, it is worthwhile taking stock and reflecting on the main points of our analysis.

We have seen that the archetypes and archetypal transitions hold across the three levels of being, and that a big part of the analytical complexity comes from the fact that the archetypal progression does not take place simultaneously across each level. Van Gennep's distinction between physical and social puberty demonstrates the lag between the Physical and Exoteric levels of being from an anthropological point of view, a lag which can take many years or even decades in extreme examples. We know from the work of Freud and Jung that the psychological aspects of the archetypal transformations are even harder to pin down since not only is there more flexibility in the temporal aspect, but an irreducible level of individuality is also introduced into the equation. This comes back to the fact that the Esoteric level of being is the most flexible and personal. The Exoteric may lag behind the Physical, but it usually does so for everybody in the culture. The attainment of the Esoteric elements of each archetypal phase, on the other hand, is inherently personal and may, in fact, never occur for some people. This relates back to a point we made earlier: the highest levels of the Esoteric are inherently individualistic, and this is why theology, literature, and the other arts are primarily concerned with the individual. Our archetypal approach necessarily abstracts away from the individual, and so all we can do is recognise that there is something higher that we are leaving out of our analysis.

The complexity of the archetypal calculus is increased once we understand that the archetypes need to be analysed in terms of the fundamental pairings of Child-Adult and Orphan-Elder. Because of the tight coupling of these pairings, the risk of a failure of the archetypal mission is magnified by the fact that at least two individuals are usually required to make a transformation, even if the mission is simply *letting go*, as in the case of the Adult who must step back and allow their child to become an Orphan with the risk that comes with the independence of that archetype. In fact, this *letting go* is common to all the archetypal transformations, and it is a letting go at all levels of being. We must let go of our old Physical state, our old Exoteric identity, and our old Esoteric equilibrium. This can be summarised psychologically as the *death of the ego*, where the ego is itself a summation of our identity at all levels of being. We are then reborn into a new ego and a new archetypal phase of life.

Thus, another way to think of the archetypal pairings is the interaction of at least two egos, where the failure of one increases the likelihood of the failure of the other, as we see with King Lear's inability to transcend to the Elder, leaving his daughters in the lurch - the same pattern we see with Claudius, Gertrude and Polonius in relation to Hamlet and Ophelia. The shadow archetypal forms can then be defined as a refusal to allow the old ego to die and the new one to be born. We get stuck in the old ego, which is necessarily tied to the archetypal phase that we need to transcend. This gives us the common shadow forms of the archetypes: dissociation, ideology, hyper-masculine and devouring feminine, and the Abyss, which map to the Child, Orphan, Adult and Elder respectively.

In general, we can characterise the archetypal transformations as being a kind of energy that comes up from the Unconscious to challenge the ego of the individual. Our archetypal mission is to channel that energy into a productive adaptation to whichever phase of life we are moving into. Where we fail, the energy is usually directed back into introversion. And yet, this tendency towards introversion is only one potential outcome, and this is a drawback of the individualistic focus of the psychological viewpoint. That is why we need to be clear on the importance of the Exoteric and its role in the process.

We saw in the case of Ida Bauer that many aristocratic young women in the Victorian era had become enmeshed in an archetypal challenge that was, in some sense, the normal mission that faces the Orphan archetype, but which had modified due to macrocosmic trends. Young women of the Victorian age found themselves stuck in the Orphan phase of life, trapped in the parental home. It was because their Exoteric pathway had been blocked that the archetypal energy was channeled to introversion, leading to the various neuroses and psychoses that Freud and Jung found.

But we also know that this was the era of the suffragette movement and the various feminist movements which followed it. This hearkens back to a point we made in Part 1: an imbalance between the Esoteric and Exoteric can sometimes result in the rearrangement of the institutions of society. Just as Luther had demanded a change in the macrocosm to bring it into alignment with the Esoteric experience of a large section of the general public at that time, so too did the feminist movement tap into the Esoteric energy of women like Ida Bauer to cause a similar change in the Exoteric. And here we see yet another temporal lag that adds much analytical complexity. The "archetypal circuit" also includes the macrocosm, and changes in the macrocosm take decades or even centuries to play out. Therefore, we can posit that a great deal of Esoteric energy has been introverted before it finds Exoteric expression at the macrocosmic level.

This implies that there is a two-way channel of communication between the microcosm and macrocosm. Macrocosmic changes affect the individual, causing archetypal pressure to build up, and once enough individuals are affected, the pressure flows back to the macrocosm, where it forces an adaptation in the larger circuit. This is a major difference between the microcosm-macrocosm relationship pertaining to civilisation and the one we began our book with: the rotation of the Earth on its axis and its orbit around the sun. The cycle of the day does not affect the cycle of the year. The microcosm does not influence the macrocosm at the celestial level. But that is not true in relation to civilisation where there is a reciprocal relationship of influence between microcosm and macrocosm.

Although a reciprocal relationship of influence does exist, we know from the work of the comparative historians that there are common patterns in the way in which the macrocosm of civilisation affects the microcosm. Now that we have a solid grounding in the archetypal calculus, we are ready to make sense of what those patterns are. Let's now turn our perspective back to the macrocosm.

The Macrocosmic Perspective

Orphans and Elders as the Engine of Civilisation

It is sometimes said that the great writers are all great psychologists, but when we take the broader view of the archetypes as the link between microcosm and macrocosm, we find in Shakespeare also a compelling sociological and political insight. Almost all of the great tragedies of Shakespeare are not just about the individual characters but the damage done socially by the failure of the protagonists. King Lear and Macbeth almost bring ruin on their lands. The house of Hamlet is destroyed at the end of the play and handed over to its enemies. Othello's failure robs Venice of its great general. Romeo and Juliet's deaths rob Verona of two of its next generation (five when we include the related deaths of Mercutio, Tybalt and Paris). Archetypal failure is as much a macrocosmic problem as a microcosmic one.

Written from an objective, third-person perspective, the story of *Hamlet* sounds like countless footnotes that one might read in a scholarly work of history:

The king's brother assassinated him and took the throne. The king's son sought revenge. Both died in the ensuing battle, and, in the chaos that followed, the kingdom was conquered by its neighbour.

If we were to translate the story into our archetypal analysis, we might get something like the following:

The arrival of the Tyrannical Father signified both the failure of the Elder and Orphan transitions in the general culture. The next generation was left with the choice of either suicide/dissociation or violent rebellion against the Father. Since both of these signify a breakdown in the propagation of the culture, the destruction of the culture was imminent.

This might sound fanciful, and yet it is little more than a translation of the analysis of the comparative historians into archetypal terminology. Recall that Toynbee divided the cycle of civilisation into two halves. The first was governed by the Creative Minority and the second by the Dominant Minority. The Dominant Minority rules not through organic bonds but through force. What is that, if not the Tyrannical Father? And what are "organic bonds" if not the ordering of the archetypal relations with the Elder's practice of governance through wisdom as the guiding principle? As we are about to see, the other trends which Toynbee identifies in the historical cycle also fit our archetypal analysis. In short, the archetypal calculus is just as valid for the macrocosm as it is for the microcosm.

We have noted that the Elder archetype has the responsibility to initiate the Orphans of society into the Exoteric institutions of the culture. We have also noted that there are two types of initiation. Esoteric initiation is given to would-be members of the elite class, and Exoteric initiation is given to the general public. These distinctions are central to the propagation of a culture, so it should be little surprise that Toynbee builds them right into the heart of his account of civilisation. Consider the following quote:-

"The leader's task is to make his fellows his followers; and the only means by which mankind in the mass can be set in motion towards a goal beyond itself is by enlisting the primitive and universal faculty of mimesis."

Swap the word *leader* for *Elder*, the word *fellow* for *Orphan* and the word *mimesis* for *Exoteric initiation*, and this sentence is an exact match for our description of archetypal initiation. Exoteric initiation is mimicry. It does not require any deeper understanding, only the carrying out of the prescribed actions that can be gleaned from copying the behaviour of others. It is the Elders who must model that behaviour, and this implies that they must receive a different, higher form of initiation in order that they may then induct the general public by Exoteric methods. We have already identified this as Esoteric initiation and have shown that Esoteric initiation appears to be a universal of human society where a select group of individuals is given an intensive rite of passage designed to prepare them for leadership roles in the political, economic, military, and religious institutions of society. What's more, we should remember that all of this is backed up by the anthropological literature on the subject, which fits with both the historical and cross-cultural scholarship.

What this means, of course, is that the societal Elders must always be a small minority relative to the general population. At the macrocosmic level, not everyone can become an Elder, only those who have gone through Esoteric initiation. Since this jars against the political sensibilities of modern society, we should remember that Elders include more than just political figures. We recognise brain surgeons and rocket scientists as having a degree of knowledge that far surpasses that of the average person. Since both brain surgeons and rocket scientists are assumed to require a long period of education and training (Esoteric initiation) to get the position, they are one group of Elders in our society. Thus, from an anthropological point of view, we have our Elders, we just don't think about them in that way. Rather, we call them *elites*.

We can diagram these distinctions as follows, showing how the differentiation into elite and general public (Majority) categories works out over the archetypal phases:-

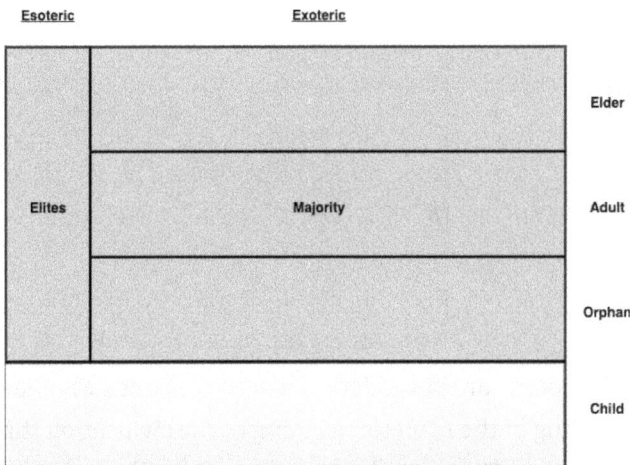

From the macrocosmic point of view, children are not expected to play any productive role in the Exoteric institutions of society or to have a great deal of conscious Esoteric understanding of the culture. It is during the Orphan phase that the sorting process begins, with those who may become part of the elite receiving an Esoteric initiation, while those who will become part of the general public receive an Exoteric one. The Elders of the elite class will take up leadership positions at the top of the institutions of society, while the Elders among the general public have family- and community-based roles. When we model life as a progression "upwards" through the archetypes, we can see that it is at the Orphan phase of life that it will almost certainly be determined whether we join the elite class or not. This is true even in the egalitarian modern West with membership in the deep state, business sector, or technocracy.

If we now rotate our diagram, we capture the elite – majority dynamic as it has been practiced throughout the history of civilisation:-

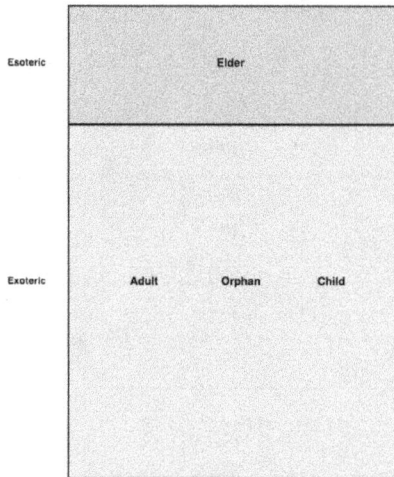

Toynbee's "leaders" are our Elders. They are the ones who have attained an understanding of the Esoteric meaning of the civilisation through their extended initiation. They are also the ones who will conduct the Exoteric rites of passage for the rest of society. For example, the Christian priest (Sage archetype) conducts the funeral rites for the departed Elder, the wedding ceremony for Adults, the Holy Communion for Orphans and the baptism for Children. In this way, the religious Elder administers Exoteric rites for the general public. In the political realm, a king or other powerful Ruler is the archetypal Elder who governs the rites. The Elders of the Warrior class conduct and manage the rites pertaining to war.

We can see, therefore, that the Orphan – Elder relationship at the macro-cosmic level is another way to characterise the hierarchical structure of society. Traditional institutions like the church, the army, and politics all have a chain of command, meaning there are Elders (leaders) with differing levels of responsibility and differing degrees of importance. At the top may be a king, a general, or a Pope. After initiation into adulthood, an Orphan of the general public becomes a citizen to the king, a soldier to the general and a believer to the Pope. The Exoteric rites of passage formalise these transitions. The same is true of the modern West with our Technocracy and the Exoteric education system that feeds into it. The general public receives an education that allows them to work in jobs, and most jobs are, within our framework, Exoteric. Only the positions at the top of the hierarchy require an Esoteric understanding.

In Toynbee, as in many other thinkers, there is a necessary power imbalance at play since the majority do not attain the Esoteric understanding of the culture. It's noteworthy in this respect that the anthropological literature suggests that most, if not all, societies have specific rites of passage that facilitate the interaction of societal Elders with the general public. These are for the protection of both parties since the power of the Elders makes them a risk to the general public and makes the general public a risk to them through feelings of resentment. It's also for this reason that the Elders are located in *sacred* buildings separated from the general run of society e.g. churches, palaces, government buildings, and military installations.

If we accept all this as true, then we also accept that the Orphan – Elder relationship is fundamental to the structure of civilisation and also to its propagation. Toynbee analyses the breakdown of the civilisation as the breakdown of this Orphan – Elder relationship, although, of course, he doesn't put it in those terms and so we need to do a little translation to make this clear. Toynbee's Creative Minority are the Elders during the first phase of civilisation, which Toynbee gave the names Genesis and Growth, while the Dominant Minority rules during the Breakdown and Disintegration phases. We might be tempted to say that the first set of Elders are good and the latter bad, since that's what the terms imply. In one sense, that is true since Toynbee's definition of Breakdown is the time when the Elders are no longer able to solve the problems faced by society, and this leads the culture into terminal decline.

But things are more complicated than that, as can be seen by the fact that a civilisation typically achieves the peak of its political and economic powers in the Disintegration phase. Most of the properties we attribute to civilisation like military power and law and order, belong to this phase of the cycle, which sounds counterintuitive since this is the phase given the rather gruesome name of Disintegration and run by the almost as unpleasantly named Dominant Minority. If we take a more neutral attitude, we can see that the change between Creative Minority and Dominant Minority is as much a qualitative change as anything. It represents a modulation in civilisation away from the Esoteric level of being and towards the Physical. This modulation is reflected in the fact that a different group of Elders comes to the fore during each period. The Creative Minority of the first half are the Sage archetypes, while the Dominant Minority of the second half are the Warriors. It makes sense that the Warriors should dominate in the latter phase since that is also the time when the civilisation expands outward via military conquest.

The outward expansion of a society during the Dominant Minority phase goes hand-in-hand with the centralisation and homogenisation of the culture. The reverse is true for the Creative Minority which governs over small, local, decentralised societies. Let's take medieval Europe with its feudal system as an example of the relationship between a Creative Minority and the general public.

A peasant in the feudal age of Europe had two primary Elders: the local priest and the local lord. The priest was the Elder of the Exoteric institution headed by the Pope and the lord was the Elder of the Exoteric institution headed by the King. The former was responsible for the religious identity of the public, and the latter for the political and economic identity. Nevertheless, the local peasant's relationships and responsibilities were not to Pope and King. The peasant had a direct relationship with his local Elders and, at least in the case of the vassal – lord relationship, he was only obligated to his lord and not to anybody higher up the chain. As a result, the peasant in feudal times was initiated by an Elder to whom he or she would have an ongoing relationship in the locality where they both lived. That relationship was based on shared interests, since the labour of the peasant funded both the manor and the local church. This gave the peasant some amount of power and resulted in the creation of mutual obligations. In addition, feudal peasants also had responsibility and some authority in the governance of the manor, such as policing and law enforcement. For these reasons, the peasant class is usually not the bottom rung of the social hierarchy in a feudal society. That honour typically goes to merchants, musicians, and actors.

None of this is meant to glamorise the feudal era. Many of the criticisms made of it are justified. But what we are concerned with is the Orphan – Elder relationship and the feudal era provides an example of the situation early in the cycle of civilisation when that relationship is localised and personalised. It is based far less on written law than on local, unwritten customs. That is why we can classify it as Esoteric. Bonds of allegiance are organic, and the rites of passage are taken seriously as initiation into the rights and responsibilities of adulthood. Perhaps the most important quality of the early phase of the civilisational cycle is the way in which it orients itself to the past. The rites of passage through which Orphans are initiated into society are based on the authority of tradition stretching backwards to the ancestors. Beyond the ancestors are the gods or spirits, and this is why we can associate the Creative Minority with the Esoteric level of being in a theological sense. The Creative Minority receives the justification for its authority at least partly by upholding the tradition going back to the ancestors.

We can capture this dynamic by expanding on our diagram from earlier: -

		The gods/spirits		
Ancestor		Ancestor		Ancestor
	Elder		Elder	
Adult/Parent		Adult/Parent		Adult/Parent
	Orphan		Orphan	
Child		Child		Child
Generation 1		**Generation 2**		**Generation 3**

Time

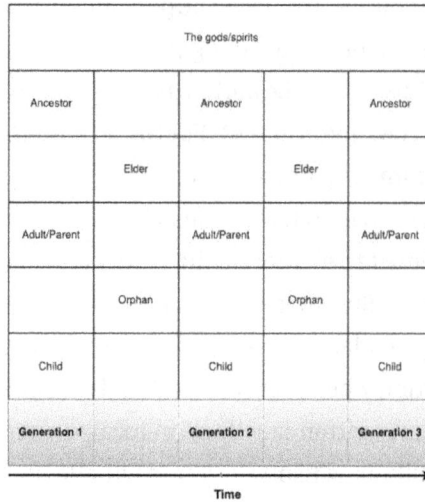

As Elders die, they join the ancestors. Beyond the ancestors are the gods and spirits. But we can also read this the other way around. That is, the Orphans are initiated into a culture by the Elders who are conduits for the authority granted by tradition that stretches back beyond the ancestors to the gods and spirits. This is the theological, or Esoteric, basis for the culture in the first half of the civilisational cycle. To take just one example, Romulus, the founder of ancient Rome, was said to have been conceived of the god, Mars, and the virgin, Rhea Silvia. To be a member of Roman culture was to be part of a tradition stretching back to the gods.

This is the dynamic which holds during the reign of the Creative Minority. The archetypal Orphans initiated into the Exoteric institutions of society during this time feel an innate Esoteric connection to tradition. Although we have characterised that initiation as Exoteric, it is also true that it has an inherent Esoteric element which we might call *faith.* This faith is facilitated by the direct relationship the Orphan has with the local Elders. To be initiated is to become a living part of the tradition.

The change to the Dominant Minority in the second half of the civilisational cycle involves the breakdown of this tradition and its re-orientation away from the past and towards the future. Toynbee puts it this way:-

"But when 'the cake of custom' is broken, the faculty of mimesis, hitherto directed backward towards elders or ancestors as incarnations of an unchanging social tradition, is reoriented towards creative personalities bent upon leading their fellows with them towards a promised land."

Note here that the "creative personalities" are the same Elders or elites of society that exist in the first half of the cycle. There is still an Orphan – Elder dynamic which is captured in Exoteric initiation (mimesis). What has changed is the orientation. The Elders no longer claim authority from a tradition looking backwards to the ancestors and gods but forwards towards the future. But this re-orientation does not come out of nowhere. What precedes the arrival of these new Elders is the drying up of the Esoteric component of the old rites and traditions. The reason people go looking for a new source of meaning is because the old source has gone away.

One way to understand this is to use the definition of religion that van Gennep worked with: religion = metaphysics + magic. The metaphysics of a culture is what we have been referring to as the *higher esoteric*. It refers to the core assumptions of the culture about what constitutes reality. Meanwhile, magic refers to the rites of passage of the culture and the extent to which they have an effect in line with the metaphysical assumptions. The philosopher, Nietzsche, noted that metaphysics only gets called into question when the magic dries up. Philosophy is the doctor who arrives on the scene to find the patient already dead. The patient are the rites of passage. When the rites of passage no longer work, when they no longer produce the magic, then and only then are the metaphysical assumptions challenged. Since the Elders are the upholders of the metaphysics of the society and since they are seen to represent the ancestors and gods, a religious crisis manifests in the breakdown of the old Orphan – Elder relationship.

Historians can and do try to find specific causes for such breakdowns. For example, the Black Death is often cited as an example of a disaster which broke the bonds of allegiance within the society of medieval Europe in multiple ways. What Toynbee showed, however, is that the specific reasons are unimportant. Every civilisation seems to follow the same pattern. At around the midpoint of the cycle, the break with the past occurs, and with it, the inherent respect due to tradition. It's highly likely that one of the main drivers behind the phenomenon is the increasing success of society. As economic, military, and political power increases, the attention of the elites is turned away from the Esoteric and towards the Physical. This causes anger among some members of the elites, who demand that the Esoteric traditions be upheld. We can cite another great Shakespeare work to highlight this dynamic since it is the attitude of Brutus in *Julius Caesar*. Brutus sees in Caesar exactly the kind of "creative personality" that Toynbee identified with the Dominant Minority. This led him to believe that Caesar had become a threat to the republican tradition of Rome. This example is highly accurate from a historical standpoint since Julius Caesar really did represent the transition to the Dominant Minority in Rome.

The arrival of the Dominant Minority causes a schism between those still wanting to uphold the traditions of the past and those looking forward to the possibilities of the future. The deaths of Brutus and thousands of other Roman aristocrats in the civil wars represented the victory of the Dominant Minority. But this victory comes at a great cost, including a great opportunity cost. With the movement towards the Dominant Minority, the elite class of society fails to incorporate the new members who are needed to bring fresh Esoteric energy to the enterprise. During the Growth phase of a civilisation, the geniuses and other creative personalities are incorporated into the tradition and become part of it. We see a diversification and complexification indicative of growth. Breakdown occurs when the creative personalities are no longer brought into the mainstream tradition but are also powerful enough that they cannot be shut down. By definition, these creative personalities become opponents of the institutions of society, just as Brutus became the opponent of Caesar. This puts an end to the diversification and complexification of society i.e. the growth phase.

The Exoteric institutions of society become controlled by what now becomes the Dominant Minority. The Elders of the Dominant Minority harden in response to the challenge that comes from without. Deprived of the Esoteric energy they should have received from new members who challenge the status quo and help them adapt to changing social conditions, the Exoteric institutions become empty shells lacking the Esoteric drive that fuelled the civilisation in its Growth phase. Unable to lead by Esoteric example, the Dominant Minority begins to rule by force instead. The society shifts its focus ever more into the Physical level of being. At an archetypal level, we can see that this is the shift away from governance by the Elder archetype to governance by the Tyrannical Father.

None of this happens at once. Neither does it happen to everybody in society. These are general social trends that play out over centuries. At the beginning of the Breakdown phase, many Orphans will still be initiated into the old ways by Elders faithful to the tradition. The general public is still given Exoteric initiation just as it always had. What increasingly dries up is the magic (the Esoteric). This is true among the ruling class and among the general public. The mainstream culture atrophies. People are just going through the motions. Toynbee puts it this way:-

"It would be easy to indicate many points of resemblance between the subjects of Diocletian and the people of that Celestial Empire where, during many centuries, nothing has been learned or unlearned; where government, where education, where the whole system of life, is a ceremony;"

The mainstream culture hardens and stagnates in the second half of the cycle. What Esoteric energy exists now flows to the rival Elders who have detached from the mainstream. This attracts them a following from the Orphans of society who are looking for something meaningful to believe in. What we see, therefore, in the second half of civilisation are two groups of Elders. The Dominant Minority are the Elders of the mainstream culture, which has now become fixated on the Physical level of being and pursues military and economic power almost exclusively. Meanwhile, new groups of Elders arrive who offer the promise of the Esoteric to their followers. Some of these may offer a return to the "traditional" ways and a reconnection with the authority of the past. But even this is an admission that the connection with the past has been lost.

Since the new group of Elders is usually in direct conflict with the main-stream culture, we will call them Rebel Elders. These Rebel Elders can be further categorised into Rebel Commanders, who manifest the Ruler and Warrior archetypes, and Rebel Priests, who manifest the Sage. The Rebel Commanders lead military insurgencies against the Dominant Minority while the Rebel Priests enunciate new theologies and philosophies. We can diagram this dynamic as follows. Note that we represent it as a straight line for clarity's sake, but, really, this is the cyclical progression of civilisation that we showed earlier:-

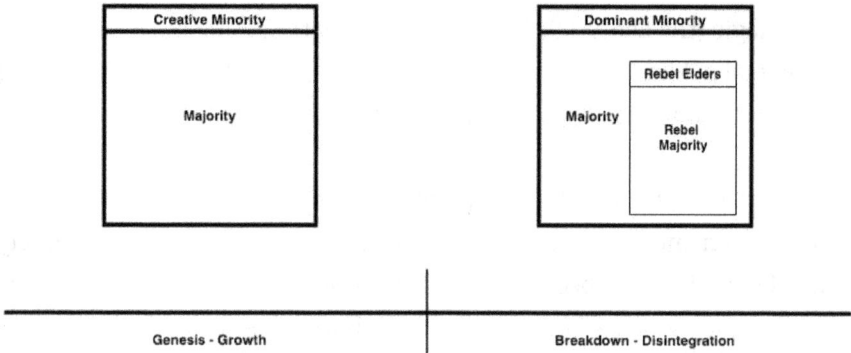

During the Genesis - Growth phase, the nascent civilisation is united behind the Elders of the Creative Minority who successfully solve the challenges faced by society. The Orphans of society are initiated into the Exoteric institutions, while those Orphans who are deemed capable will be given Esoteric initiation and will go on to join the Creative Minority. The process is not perfect. Even in the early phases, there is always some level of rebellion by people who deserved to be incorporated into the Creative Minority but were denied. The Creative Minority are also not perfect little angels who float above worldly matters. They will use the force necessary to ensure those who cannot be incorporated will be neutralised, and this works well enough to keep the culture unified.

The turning point into the Breakdown – Disintegration phase begins with the breakdown of the Orphan – Elder relationship at the Esoteric level of being. The rites of passage no longer produce their Esoteric (magic) effect. Martin Luther and the Reformation serve as a prototypical example here since Luther's rebellion was intellectual and spiritual. The corruption of the church had been obvious to all for a long time, leading up to the Reformation. The failure of the church to incorporate people like Luther who wanted to reform it created a schism. But the truth was that the Catholic Church had lost the faith of its adherents at the Esoteric level of being first, and only later did the schism manifest at the Exoteric and Physical levels. Once the Elders of the Creative Minority have lost the organic bonds of allegiance, they begin to govern through physical, political, and economic force. At that point, they become the Dominant Minority. This creates a split between those willing to follow along in a mainstream culture that becomes increasingly devoid of the Esoteric and those who search for it elsewhere. Toynbee called this the process of *proletarianisation.*

In the Breakdown phase, an Internal Proletariat is formed. Marx and Engels considered this to be primarily an economic development. For Toynbee, the defining feature of the proletarian mindset is Esoteric. It rests in a feeling of no longer having a historical connection to mainstream culture. As Toynbee puts it:

"The true hall-mark of the proletarian is neither poverty nor humble birth but a consciousness - and the resentment that this consciousness inspires - of being disinherited from his ancestral place in society."

Marx and Engels were themselves prime examples of the proletarian mindset since they both came from wealthy, property-owning families. What drove them to rebel was not economic circumstance but the feeling that something was not right in society. They turned away from membership in the Dominant Minority to become Rebel Elders who provided an alternative source of meaning in opposition to the stale status quo of 19th-century Europe.

The real unifying force of the proletariat is not shared class interest, as Marx and Engels believed, but the shared feeling of disinheritance. Of course, it's true that the feeling of disinheritance does not just come out of nowhere, and its arrival is accompanied by economic developments. Early civilisation is characterised by self-sufficient peasants who have a direct relationship with local Elders. Economic surpluses are small and based on agrarian production, which means that the overall civilisation is neither wealthy nor powerful. For this reason, the Elders at the top of the hierarchy are themselves politically and economically weak, both in relation to external powers and, perhaps more importantly, in relation to their own subjects. That is why political power is decentralised.

The increasing centralisation of power that occurs in the second half of the cycle is achieved at the cost of local bonds of allegiance and the traditions which uphold the self-sufficient peasantry. This breakdown correlates with the arrival of mass agriculture. In ancient Rome, there was the establishment of the *latifundia*, a precursor to modern industrial agriculture that was powered by mass indentured slavery. This had the effect of destroying the economic livelihoods of the small-holding peasants, while the cruelty of the practice left a moral stain on those who supported it. We see an almost identical development in modern European civilisation with the enclosure acts in England, the highland clearances in Scotland, and the use of indentured slavery in colonial America and other places.

The peasantry is forced off its ancestral land and into the cities, whose populations swell. These become the seats of political and economic power. This centralisation means that the Elders at the top of the social hierarchy come increasingly to dominate as all the money and power eventually get sucked up and away from local communities and into the cities. In an archetypal sense, the transition of power and authority is away from local Elders who had a direct relationship with local Orphans and towards the Elders at the top of the pyramid, who do not have such a direct relationship. Local initiations become moribund, while initiations carried on in the cities have a scale which is alienating. The overall result is that many rites are done away with altogether, while what rites still exist are devoid of Esoteric meaning.

To sum up, the progression from Creative to Dominant Minority correlates with an increasing centralisation of power, as evidenced by the rise of the mega-cities, which become the focal point of the culture in the second half of the cycle. This contrasts with the first half, where decentralisation ensures that power is pushed down to the local level. The first half of the cycle sees direct relationships between Orphans and local Elders while the second half sees the rise of cults of personality for both the Dominant Minority and the Rebel Elders. Such cults of personality entail an increased social distance between the Orphans of society and the Elders.

Local Elders who claim authority from local tradition disappear and are replaced by larger-than-life Elders who rule from the top of the social hierarchy in the mega-cities. Just as money and power concentrate at the top of the social pyramid, so too does the Esoteric energy, which is now focused on Elders far removed from the average person. The Dominant Minority does not just rule by force. Rather, it learns to channel all the Esoteric energy of society onto itself. Both Julius Caesar and Octavian were adept at propaganda for this exact purpose. The cult of Caesar which began with Julius speaks to the Esoteric energy concentrated in the mega-city, which comes to be focused on individuals whose perceived power and status are elevated to magnificent heights.

Of course, this power also exists on the Physical level of being. Julius Caesar was not primarily a propagandist but a great general. The transition to the Dominant Minority sees the Warrior archetype become the dominant Elder of the civilisation. It is this concentration of power which allows the Warriors of the civilisation to rule over their external enemies. But the flipside is that the state can also turn that power against internal opponents. The historical record shows that the Rebel Commanders, those who lead military insurgencies against the Dominant Minority, do not have much success. This makes sense since the late civilisation is held together both externally and internally by the projection of military power. The one area where the civilisation is still advancing in the late stages is military prowess and technology. Accordingly, the Dominant Minority has little problem seeing off challenges from Rebel Commanders given the huge power imbalance that exists.

It is the Rebel Priests of the proletariat who have more success, and this for two main reasons. Firstly, the late civilisation has little interest in Esoteric matters and doesn't see theological and philosophical movements as a threat to the established order. Second, even if the Dominant Minority decides to strike against the Rebel Priests, this only turns them into martyrs and ends up advancing their cause. The execution of St Paul and St Peter are two prime examples that we know from our own historical tradition, but the subsequent persecution of the Christians in general only appears to have advanced the cause of that religion until it eventually was merged into the Roman state. It is for this reason that what Toynbee called the Universal Church is born out of the proletariat of the late stages of civilisation. It is the "victory" of the Rebel Priests and the failure of the Rebel Commanders that creates this dynamic.

The Tyrannical Father and the Rise of the Hyper-Masculine

Although we have thus far taken a neutral tone in describing the transition from Creative to Dominant Minority, it is also true that the transition to the late stages of empire shows a distinct pattern when seen through the lens of our archetypal analysis and one that points in a negative direction. We have included the Warrior class as a member of the Elders of a civilisation and yet, as far back as Plato, the dangers of allowing the Warrior class to exercise power have been known. For most wise men through the ages, the Warrior class must be subordinate to at least the governing class (the Ruler archetype) if not also the priestly one (the Sage archetype). When the Warrior class takes power, there is nothing to stop them using that power for their own ends and not for the public good.

We have a paradigm example of this in the Roman Empire. It had become customary for each new Caesar to make payments to the praetorian guard and the army when they came to power. The size of those payments had already become a major burden on society by the early days of the empire.

That was bad enough. But the Warrior class over time began to exercise its power in more obviously corrupt ways, including in the murder of Caesars and, in one case, the auctioning off of the Caesarship to the highest bidder. Corruption turned to outright slaughter when various Caesars came to power through the ranks of the army itself, perhaps most notably in the case of Maximinus Thrax, who was the first barbarian to become Caesar in a literal sense and who proceeded to live up to the name via a reign of violence and terror.

We noted earlier the four Esoteric faculties, which correspond to the four archetypes of Child, Orphan, Adult and Elder. These four faculties were Imagination, Intellect, Will and Soul. With little modification, it is these properties which Plato assigned to the different classes of society. Will quite obviously belongs to the Warrior class, at least in its martial manifestation. Intellect belongs to the philosophers, Soul to the priests and Imagination to the artists. We can put this in tabular form as follows:-

Archetype	Level of Being		
	Societal Archetype	Esoteric	Esoteric (shadow)
The Child	Artist	Imagination	~~Dissociation~~
The Orphan	Philosopher	Intellect	~~Ideology~~
The Adult	Warrior/Ruler	Will	~~Hyper-Masculine, Devouring Feminine~~
The Elder	Sage	Soul	~~The Abyss~~

What we see in ancient Rome is the ascension and dominance of the Warrior class which means that Will has taken over from the other faculties. The Romans sacrificed all else in the service of money and power. What Toynbee and the other comparative historians have shown is that this trend is common to the second half of all civilisations and is called the Dominant Minority.

It follows that the Creative Minority would map to the Elder archetype, which serves to keep the other archetypal forces in balance and, thereby, to keep the shadow forces in check. Note that this does not imply any particular governance structure. When we say that the archetype of the Elder should be dominant in a well-ordered society, this can be achieved outside of formal governance structures. In fact, it may very well be that the Elder rules to the extent that governance structures are not seen as being political. As we saw earlier in our description of the phase of civilisation governed by the Creative Minority, it's the absence of power in the governing structures that seems to facilitate the ascendance of the Elder archetype at the collective level. It is the commitment of society to the pursuit of the Esoteric rather than the pursuit of power which makes it possible for Elders to lead without governing explicitly.

The arrival of the Dominant Minority signals that society is going to be thrown out of balance. One of the main ways this occurs is the aforementioned destruction of the self-sufficient peasantry with the arrival of mass agriculture, which serves to concentrate wealth into the hands of the few with the associated transfer of power to the cities. The pursuit of power for its own sake signals the arrival of the hyper-masculine. The Elder archetype no longer rules. Instead, the Warrior has taken over. Archetypally speaking, we see the predominance of the shadow forms over their positive manifestation which we can summarise as follows:-

Archetype	Level of Being		
	Exoteric	Esoteric	Esoteric (shadow)
The Child	Artist (propagandist)	Imagination	Dissociation
The Orphan	Philosopher (ideologue)	Intellect	Ideology
The Adult	Warrior (Dominant Minority)	Will	Hyper-Masculine, Devouring Feminine
The Elder	Sage	Soul	The Abyss

The hyper-masculine is raised to the heights of power, which it pursues unfettered by any higher considerations. Intellect turns to ideology, which is also in the service of power. Art turns into either propaganda or entertainment designed to divert the attention of the masses (Dissociation). We also see the arrival of the theological and spiritual manifestations of The Abyss in the apocalyptic visions and fantasies of millenarian cults. It's important to understand that both the positive and shadow forms of the archetypes are present in humanity at all times. In any era, we can find manifestations of the hyper-masculine, of ideology, of dissociation, and of spiritual terror. The difference is one of balance. The Creative Minority are the ones who keep the ledger on the positive side, while the Dominant Minority are the ones who allow the shadow forms to predominate. That is why Toynbee called the latter stages Breakdown and Disintegration.

Once the shadow forms are allowed to predominate over a long period of time, society spirals down to its destruction. The peculiar fact is that, viewed from a material point of view, that destruction seems needless and even deliberate. It is precisely because the late stages are when a civilisation is at its most rich and powerful on the Physical level of being that its destruction is so mystifying since the cause of the failure cannot be due to a lack of political and economic resources. It is at the Esoteric level and, to a lesser extent, the Exoteric, where civilisations breakdown.

Let's now walk through the main elements of the civilisational breakdown phase using our archetypal analysis.

The first and most obvious is the arrival of the Tyrannical Father at the macrocosmic level. It is the Tyrannical Father who finally establishes what Toynbee called the Universal State. This happens around the beginning of the Disintegration phase of the cycle, and it follows a period of warfare called the Warring States Period. The Warring States Period is itself a label given to Chinese history just before the beginning of the Qin dynasty, which was established by the emperor Qin Shi Huang.

To understand the arrival of the Tyrannical Father, we must first understand that the breakdown of the Orphan – Elder relationship occurs long before. As Toynbee noted, the "creative personalities" who appear in the aftermath of the breakdown are often demagogues and commercial exploiters. In other words, they are the hyper masculine, and this is in line with our archetypal logic, which says that, when the Elder transition breaks down, the hyper masculine appears on the scene. The Tyrannical Father is, in fact, the end of a long period where the outbreak of hyper masculine has led to commercial and military conflict within the civilisation itself. Only once all rivals are exhausted or destroyed can one competitor ascend to supremacy. That competitor becomes the Tyrannical Father. The arrival of the Tyrannical Father already implies the failure of the archetypal Elder transition at the macrocosmic level. But this failure implies the failure of the Orphan transition too. If the Elders are gone and replaced by the Tyrannical Father, we expect the Orphans to become Shadow Orphans. What behaviours do we expect from Shadow Orphans? We know from our analysis of the microcosmic level that we should expect to see dissociation, ideology, and various forms of The Abyss (suicide, apocalyptic fantasy).

This raises the question: what evidence do we find in the general culture of the Disintegration phase of the civilisational cycle that would point to the arrival of archetypal Shadow Orphans?

Let's consider the case of Rome. Julius Caesar set the path for his nephew Octavian to walk. Although Octavian took steps to keep up the appearance of the old forms of governance, in fact, he became a military dictator and took on the roles of commander-in-chief, tribune, censor, and even *pontifex maximus* (Pope). In archetypal terms, Octavian was the Ruler, the Warrior and the Sage (Pope). Why did the Romans, a people with a proud republican tradition, accept this tyranny?

What we find is that there was a collective religious movement that coincided with the political change to military dictatorship. It was called the *cult of Caesar*. Most historians will point out that both Julius Caesar and Octavian propagated the cult of Caesar since it was in their political interests to do so. That is certainly true. Nevertheless, the widespread adoption of the cult seems to have been a genuine grassroots movement. We might call it, in the phrasing of Jung and modern psychoanalysis, a psychological event that manifests from the collective Unconscious. The Romans embraced the Tyrannical Father in its Esoteric form of the cult of Caesar.

Why were the Romans looking for a father figure? Yes, Roman society was in turmoil, but it was not just a turmoil caused by civil war. It was what we might call a spiritual (Esoteric) turmoil precipitated by the breakdown of the Orphan – Elder relationship over a period of centuries with the emotional, economic and political insecurity that breakdown caused. With organic, local bonds of allegiance and shared culture severed, the people navigated towards

134

the cities where the collective psychological conditions emerged that led to the eventual desire for a "father" to save the day. Julius Caesar and then Octavian stepped into this role.

Our archetypal logic predicts this outcome, and we have already seen the manifestations of it in the Shakespeare stories we analysed. There appear to be two main ways for somebody trapped in an archetypal phase to behave. They can try to force their way out, or they can acquiesce and try to get by. Hamlet is an example of a rebellious Orphan who intuits their situation and tries to force their way out. Lear's three daughters are examples of acquiescent Orphans, since we can assume that they have been happy to play along under their Tyrannical Father for many years before the story begins. What's more, history shows that acquiescence is the normal state of affairs, and rebellion is the exception to the rule.

Thus, perhaps the main manifestation of the shadow Orphan dynamic is in this acquiescence, while political and spiritual rebellion are the rare exceptions. For that reason, we can deduce that the arrival of the Tyrannical Father at the macrocosmic level will be accompanied by some level of rebellion, but the majority of the population will acquiesce. That certainly explains why proud republican Romans suddenly accepted a political transition to a military dictatorship. Archetypally, what forms thereafter is an equilibrium where the Tyrannical Father (Shadow Adult) rules over a population of shadow Orphans. That state of affairs can last a very long time. In Rome, it lasted many centuries. The reason it can last so long is because the general public becomes dependent on the state just as a child is dependent on its parents.

The bread-and-circuses dynamic of the Roman empire is proof that the general public had become dependent. The state had to step in to ensure the daily bread of the people, just as the mother and father are expected to provide food for their children. The manifestation of the Tyrannical Father in Rome occurred, therefore, across all levels of being. At the Physical level of being, there were the bread-and-circuses. At the Esoteric level of being, there was the cult of Caesar. The Tyrannical Father manifested at the Exoteric with formal rites owed to the Caesar and, more symbolically but no less importantly, the Caesars began taking on the title of *pater patriae* which means "father of the fatherland". This began at the time of Julius Caesar and lasted for centuries afterward. Our use of the archetype concept in this book has been predicated on its integration across all three levels of being. We can see that this is exactly what happened at the macrocosmic level in Rome. Across the board, we see the arrival of the (Tyrannical) Father.

Toynbee notes that other civilisations show a similar pattern whereby religious changes, which we could call in secular terms *collective psychological events*, mirror political ones.

"Thus a number of previously parochial divinities assume the insignia of the newly established terrestrial monarch and then compete with one another for the sole and exclusive dominion which these insignia imply, until at length one of the competitors annihilates his rivals and establishes his title to be worshipped as the One True God."

If the gods also compete for supremacy, just like the hyper-masculine warriors of the Dominant Minority, can we also see evidence of the Child – Parent archetypal dynamic in the religious developments of late civilisation? We do. Can it be a coincidence that we find many of the identical tropes around the Father in Christianity, a religion where the Father – Son dynamic is central to the entire theology? Can it be a further coincidence that Christianity would eventually replace the cult of Caesar as the official religion of the Roman state? This would match Toynbee's concepts of the internal and external proletariat. Archetypally, we see the desire for the Father in both groups expressed in the contrasting religious forms of two different cultural traditions: the cult of Caesar for the Romans and the Christian Father among the Syriac tradition.

St Paul then forms the bridge between these two traditions, and it can be no coincidence that we find him also referring to the Father in his efforts to build up the nascent religion. Consider these lines from his letter to the Galatians 4:6-7:

"Because you are his sons, God sent the Spirit of his Son into our hearts, the Spirit who calls out, "*Abba*, Father." So you are no longer a slave, but God's child; and since you are his child, God has made you also an heir."

Recall that disinheritance was one of the main features Toynbee ascribed to the proletariat in the second half of the civilisational cycle. Here, St Paul invokes a metaphor that implies such disinheritance with the promise of a spiritual re-inheritance via the archetypal Father. What is being offered is the Child – Parent relationship at the spiritual level. Paul assumes that his readers already feel disinherited and detached from the Father. But that is almost the literal definition of an orphan. It appears that the cult of Caesar and the nascent Christian religion were tapping into the same underlying archetypal dynamic, one that implies the archetypal Orphan. Viewed this way, the eventual ascendance of the Christian church after the cult of Caesar had lost its potency makes a lot of sense since it was fulfilling the same underlying need.

We can summarise these developments in tabular form as follows:-

	Genesis - Growth Phase	Breakdown - Disintegration Phase
Archetype of the Creative Minority	Elder	
Archetype of the Majority	Initiated Orphans (Adults)	
Archetype of the Dominant Minority		Tyrannical Father (Shadow Adult)
Archetype of the Proletariat		Uninitiated Orphans (Shadow Orphans): acquiescent or rebellious

There are a few final manifestations of the archetypal dynamic that are worth touching on. We noted that the shadow form of the Orphan's dominant Esoteric faculty of Intellect is Ideology. The problem with Ideology is that it narrows and limits one's perception of the world. The world is no longer seen as a thing becoming, but a thing become, with everything governed according to fixed rules established by Intellect. Once again, we can see that this mirrors the political reality of late civilisation. The Tyrannical Father's word is law, and he has the power to enforce it. Citizens are relegated to the role of children, who must simply be obedient. This becomes the normal state of affairs in society in general, but also finds more philosophical expression. As Toynbee puts it:

"And in a world of men that is governed on this plan the Universe as a whole is likely to be pictured on a corresponding pattern. If the human ruler of the universal state is at once so powerful and so beneficent that his subjects are easily persuaded to worship him as a god incarnate..."

This god-like worship is very much like the way in which a child views their parents, the father in particular. It is one aspect of Freud's Oedipus Complex and, therefore, one more piece of evidence that later civilisation sees a return to a Child – Parent archetypal pairing at the macrocosmic level.

We should also note that the arrival of the philosopher is also an indication of the Orphan archetype's prevalence since Intellect is the dominant faculty of the Orphan. Remembering that Will is the faculty of the Adult and that Will requires one to move beyond the known and deal with what is unknown, the arrival of the philosophers signals a failure of Will and, therefore, also a failure of the archetypal transition. Nietzsche's criticism here was valid. The philosophers are only concerned with what is past and, therefore, what has already become. In this way, they are also fitted to a world where nothing becomes anymore because the growth phase of civilisation is gone. All generative capacity in the culture has ceased, and, to use Toynbee's phrase, life has become little more than a ceremony.

Moreover, as Toynbee noted, the philosopher's highest goal is detachment. This withdrawal from life is nothing more than a spiritualised form of the acquiescent Orphan for whom there is no possibility of making anything of themselves in the real world by exercising their Will. It is here that we see the perceptive genius of Shakespeare at work because it is Hamlet who is his most philosophical character, and, as we have already analysed, Hamlet is the Orphan struggling to find a way to grow up in a world that wants to stifle him. Hamlet's soliloquy is the detachment of the philosopher who has withdrawn from the Exoteric into the Esoteric. Hamlet is detached from the world around him. Sitting alone at night, musing to himself, what do his thoughts turn to? Suicide. Suicide is the logical endpoint for the detachment of the Orphan of late civilisation. It reaches its most spiritualised form in the religion of Buddhism, although there are also tendencies towards it in the Christian religion too, and among the Greek philosophers.

In *Hamlet*, we see the microcosm to the macrocosm that occurs in late civilisation. Hamlet can attempt violent rebellion like the Rebel Commanders; he can withdraw into introversion like the philosophers; he can acquiesce and play along with the game, which is what Claudius and Gertrude want him to do. The other option we identified earlier was for Hamlet to escape by fleeing the parental home and trying to start a new life somewhere else. Toynbee also identified this pattern at the macrocosmic level in what he called *truancy*. There is a spiritualised form of truancy in those who *drop out* of mainstream society, which we see in the schools of the Stoics and especially the Cynics of ancient Greece. An alternative form of truancy are those who physically leave and try their luck elsewhere. Toynbee noted that this migration of people is especially pronounced in *the time of troubles*.

In *Hamlet*, therefore, we see all the options available to the Orphans of late civilisation who find themselves under the thumb of the archetypal Tyrannical Father. Hamlet can acquiesce. That is what Claudius and Gertrude want. They will provide him all the things he needs to live (bread and circuses), and in return, they simply ask that he not demand what is his Orphan's inheritance: an Exoteric and Esoteric place in society. We must reiterate that this pathway is the most commonly taken in the late phase of civilisation and it is so because the fate of Hamlet is the fate which awaits those who try to stand up to the Tyrannical Father.

Therein lies the second option: violent rebellion. That is the path Hamlet takes, and it corresponds to what we have called the Rebel Commander at the macrocosmic level, who takes the fight directly to the Dominant

Minority. The third option is detachment and philosophising and these are, in this sense, an extension of acquiescence. If Hamlet were to hang around in his parent's home and not take up an Exoteric role, presumably he might continue with his philosophical soliloquies. Whether we think that's a problem is largely a matter of perspective. For Aristotle, the detached life of the philosopher was the pinnacle of existence and brought the individual nearest to the gods. Our archetypal analysis, therefore, is not without its moral assumptions. By rating Will and Soul above Intellect, we contradict philosophers such as Aristotle who have a different table of values.

Hamlet's final two options are suicide and to attempt to flee for somewhere else and start a new life there. The latter of these options also fits with the macrocosmic trends of late civilisation since we see colonisation and the movement of peoples, whether official or unofficial, mostly during what Toynbee called *the time of troubles.* It is not an exaggeration to see, therefore, that the story of Hamlet encompasses the major macrocosmic trends of the Disintegration phase of civilisation all of which are predicated on an earlier breakdown of the Orphan – Elder relationship. Hamlet is the stranded Orphan. He represents all the Orphans who find themselves under the domination of the Tyrannical Father.

The Age of the Orphan

We noted earlier in the book that all of the archetypal states are present in any given society at all times. Societies are made up of individuals, and there will always be some individuals who, due to personal circumstances, find themselves struggling with the various archetypal transitions and getting caught up in the shadow forms of dissociation, ideology, excessive dominance over others, the spiritual terror that comes from the confrontation with the Soul or other variations. What we have implied in the last section and now make explicit is that the collective archetypal developments we have described are the product of a kind of archetypal demographic change as the culture manifests now one and now another predominant archetype. That is what Toynbee's analysis implied, and which we made explicit by translating it into archetypal terms.

When we say that the late-stage civilisation is like Hamlet, what we mean is that the dominant dynamic reflects the same archetypal calculus that faces the prince of Denmark. Obviously, that does not mean that everybody becomes a prince and lives under the thumb of an uncle who has murdered their father. It means that the Orphan archetype has come to the fore as the primary pattern that a large section of the population experiences. What that means in practice is that a large number of people find themselves, like Hamlet, with no proper Adult Exoteric role to step into. This failure at the Exoteric level of being then has follow-on effects at the Esoteric level of being, which manifest in various ways, including the collective psychological patterns that I identified in my book *The Devouring Mother: The Collective Unconscious in the Time of Corona*.

In Shakespeare's story, we can place the blame firmly on Claudius and believe that the solution to the problem is to bring Claudius to justice, or at least to hold him morally accountable in some abstract form. But what happens when no single individual is responsible? What happens when we are talking about a general social trend that sees the Exoteric roles available to the Orphans of society dry up? We may place the blame on a class of individuals who, just like Claudius, usurp the Exoteric positions that the Orphans of society should have taken and can, in an abstract sense, be said to have "caused" the problem. We may then find a "solution" in some other abstract course of action which will theoretically resolve matters. Perhaps one day, humans will learn to master the civilisational cycle itself and to address such macrocosmic issues before they become problems. But what Toynbee and the comparative historians suggest is that such problems happen irrespective of the particular circumstances, as if they were a force of nature.

What happens in late-stage civilisation is that both the Exoteric and Esoteric pathways for the Orphans of society get blocked in the same way that Hamlet and Ophelia's get blocked in Shakespeare's great play. The Orphans of the second half of the civilisational cycle have a decision between two incomplete initiations. They can acquiesce to the Dominant Minority which is run through cults of personality around leaders with whom each individual Orphan will never have a personal relationship. Alternatively, they can join the Rebel Elders. The Rebel Elders offer a meaningful Esoteric initiation, but one which is in direct conflict with mainstream culture. Therefore, the initiation does not offer an official Exoteric role in society, and the people who take it must become outsiders to mainstream culture rather than contributors to it. The Orphans of late civilisation can choose between Exoteric rites devoid of the Esoteric or Esoteric rites separated from the Exoteric institutions of society. Neither of these is a "full initiation" that resonates at the Exoteric and Esoteric levels and puts the Orphan on a pathway to Adulthood.

To reiterate, these are general trends. There will still exist pathways that offer a full initiation, but only for a relatively small proportion of the public. It's the majority of Orphans who must make the decision between the two partial initiations. All this is predicated on the breakdown of the Orphan – Elder relationship, which begins earlier in the cycle. Since that relationship is what we have called the engine of civilisation, it makes sense to label these phases of the cycle as Toynbee did and call them Breakdown and Disintegration. The breakdown at the microcosmic level mirrors the breakdown at the macrocosmic. All this happens while the civilisation itself achieves its maximum power in political, economic, and military terms because the late civilisation is concerned with the Physical level of being over the Exoteric and the Esoteric. Viewed another way, it sacrifices the Exoteric and the Esoteric for the Physical. That is a deliberate, although not necessarily conscious, decision.

It is for these reasons that we can label the Disintegration phase of the civilisational cycle in archetypal terms as the *Age of the Orphan*.

By this, we mean that the dominant archetype of this time among the general population is the Orphan and we expect to see the various shadow forms of that archetype manifest in the general culture, as we described in the last section. Our archetypal logic tells us that, where we find the shadow Orphan, we can also expect to find the Tyrannical Father and that is precisely what the elites of society become in the late phase of civilisation as the hyper-masculine arrives on the scene.

Logically, we might just as well call it the *Age of the Tyrannical Father*. That is what all of history shows us, and yet it is a crucial fact of importance that the modern West has bucked the trend. What both Toynbee and Spengler could see from their analyses in the early 20th century was that the West was clearly manifesting the parts of the cycle that led to the formation of what Toynbee called the Universal State, which belongs to the Disintegration part of the cycle. Both men could see that the world wars were indicative of the warring states period that predates the Universal State, and both men made predictions on what they expected to happen next. Both got it wrong. We have the benefit of hindsight, of course, and so it is no great credit to us if we can identify how they got it wrong.

What is noteworthy is that because the post-war period of the 20th century turned out very differently from the predictions of even the expert scholars who had made historical research their life work, some people have concluded that we must be at the *end of history*. From an archetypal point of view, all of history says we should now be in the phase of the Tyrannical Father. But we are not. Nevertheless, we are in an Age of the Orphan and so, in this respect at least, we are manifesting the historical pattern. Now that we have a solid grounding in the archetypal logic at both the microcosmic and macrocosmic levels, we are ready to resolve this seeming paradox and see how our integrated model can account for what has happened in the decades following World War 2.

Since the Orphan archetype is going to be crucial to making our case, we are going to take the time to investigate it in more detail, and it should come as no surprise that we will do so through the medium of storytelling. In Part 3 of the book, we will do a deep dive into the Hero's Journey featuring the Orphan archetype. We will see that modern film and literature, including some of the most popular stories of recent times, have already prefigured the archetypal analysis that will allow us to make sense of our time. This will prepare us for the fourth and final part of the book, where we will return to the "real world" and examine our own era from the point of view of the archetypes.

Part 3: The Orphan Story

The Microcosmic Perspective

It is an unwritten rule of Hero's Journeys that there can only be one hero per story. This rule can be stretched in a number of different ways. For example, there can be epic narratives or cleverly edited films which weave several different Hero's Journeys into the same story. In such cases, however, there are simply multiple Hero's Journeys in the same story, and each Hero's Journey would still have only one hero.

Just as Hero's Journeys almost always follow the underlying pattern we identified earlier in the book, it's also true that the hero of each Hero's Journey almost always falls into one of the archetypal categories we have identified. Thus, there are heroes who fulfil the Child, Orphan and Elder archetypes as well as the several different variations of the Adult archetype such as the Ruler, the Warrior, the Sage and the Fool. This means that we can categorise stories according to the archetype of the hero, and we would expect such stories to share not just the underlying structure of the Hero's Journey but also the common themes that belong to the phase of life that the archetype represents. That has been the basis of our use of literary examples so far to elucidate the archetypal analysis of this book, and it will be especially the basis of this section of the book where we are going to look at one particular category of Hero's Journey that we will call the Orphan Story. It's the collection of stories featuring the Orphan as hero.

We have already analysed one of the great Orphan Stories in Shakespeare's

Hamlet. We will now go into much more detail about the underlying structure and themes of the Orphan Story, using a wider variety of stories for comparison. What we will find is that modern stories elucidate not just the microcosmic viewpoint but also the macrocosmic view with a surprising degree of accuracy. This follows from an observation we made earlier in the book that modern storytelling is expected to have a degree of realism that follows from the historical consciousness of modern western civilisation. What we are about to find, however, is that this historical precision goes beyond the superficial details of various cultures and time periods and matches the archetypal history of the macrocosm that we have outlined in Part 2. This is a surprising fact and one that points to the idea that the historical consciousness of western culture really is deeply ingrained and, mostly, unconscious.

There is one potential source of confusion we should clear up at the beginning, and it has to do with the very name of the archetype, the Orphan. The Child and the Adult are uncontroversial names for archetypes. They have a rock solid grounding in biology and are universals of human culture and language. Elder is also uncontroversial since it literally means *older person,* and, although archetypal Elders don't need to be elderly as such, they do need to be experienced, and that amounts to the same thing since they are more experienced than the Orphans they must initiate. Even though modern western culture has little respect for Elders, we still understand the concept.

All our other archetypal names are uncontroversial, but Orphan has a literal meaning that can be the source of confusion. An orphan is a child without parents. We have been using the term in a symbolic sense rather than a literal one up until now, but we must note that stories will often represent symbols in literal form, which was the cornerstone of Joseph Campbell's analysis. Thus, it's very common to find literal orphans in stories, but not all literal orphans are archetypal Orphans. Learning to tell the difference is a big part of what it means to be able to read symbolism. Sometimes, a snake is just a snake. Sometimes, it's a symbol of the Unconscious. The symbolic meaning does not negate or cancel out the literal meaning. On the contrary, it deepens and enriches it.

The Orphan is a complex symbol that points not just to psychological but also biological, social, spiritual, and historical realities. Orphan Stories in literature and film are an exploration of the meaning of that symbol. It is that set of meanings which we are now going to unpack.

Theme 1: Coming of Age and Becoming an Adult

We begin by differentiating the Orphan Story from what we can call the Child Story. In a Child Story, the hero is a Child archetype who needs to remain a Child. This refers to the Jungian concept of the *puer aeturnus* or eternal child. The clearest indication that a story is a Child Story is that the protagonist is still a child at the end of the story. The archetypal Child's mission is to remain in the safety of childhood. Coming-of-age stories are about the transition from the Child archetypal phase to the Orphan and we include these in our definition of the Orphan Story. In an Orphan Story, the hero's mission is to leave the safety of childhood and face the wider world.

Some well-known characters who are literal orphans but archetypal Children include Frodo Baggins, Huck Finn, Tom Sawyer, Heidi, Pollyanna and Oliver Twist. The first Harry Potter story, probably the most famous literal orphan character of modern times, is not actually an Orphan Story even though it mixes in a number of the elements of that story. The first Harry Potter book is a Child Story. We know that because Harry is still a Child at the end.

The Child archetype needs to remain a child. The Orphan archetype needs to grow up and begin the journey towards adulthood. Thus, the Orphan Story corresponds to both physical puberty and what van Gennep called *social puberty*. Since social puberty in the modern West has been extended perhaps more than in any other civilisation, many of our Orphan Stories feature heroes in their late teens and early 20s. Once a person is much beyond their late 20s, the story can no longer be a proper Orphan Story. The Hollywood movie *The 40-year-old Virgin* is one example which inverts the archetype for comedic effect by imagining a man in early middle age who has yet to make one of the more important transitions into adulthood: that of sexual maturity.

There is one final thing to make clear about the nature of the stories we will be examining, and this relates back to a point we made earlier in the book about how the archetypal transition points of life are the most dangerous and, therefore, the most dramatic. Most of the stories we will be looking at feature a hero who is leaving the Orphan archetype and transitioning into the Adult. These stories condense and concentrate the Orphan journey, which may takes years in real life, into one story. This works to create great drama, but we must remember that the Orphan transition in "real life" usually takes much longer and doesn't need to happen all at once.

Thus, for our purposes, what we are calling the Orphan Story, including stories where the Orphan fails the archetypal mission, such as *Hamlet*, can and usually does include the Orphan's final transcendence to the Adult archetype.

Theme 2: Cruel Parents (usually step-parents or adoptive)

We have already seen a prime example of the cruel step-parent trope in the story of *Hamlet*, whose uncle Claudius has stolen the throne, married Gertrude and become Hamlet's step-father. The cruel step-parent is a very common character in the Orphan Story. We see it in Rapunzel, Snow White, Cinderella, Heidi, Pollyanna, Pippi Longstocking, almost all the Roald Dahl children's stories, Jane Eyre, Oliver Twist, Harry Potter and many more.

The symbolism of the cruel step-parent trope is based on the fact that the Orphan must leave the comfort of the family home and venture into the world. Since a loving home is a place of safety and most children will not willingly leave that environment, they need to be forced out through *tough love*. From the Orphan's point of view, that tough love appears as neglect or even abuse - in short, as cruelty. We see this dynamic elsewhere in the animal kingdom. Here in Australia, the sound of young magpies who have been kicked out of the nest can be heard all over the country from late spring. This is a "cruel" but necessary move by the parent magpies, who would otherwise be supporting their child indefinitely.

More generally, the cruel step-parent trope relates to the fact that most of the tasks the Orphan faces are difficult. First job interview, first job, first date, first kiss, anything we do for the first time we are not good at since we have no experience in the matter. Teenagers are not just moody due to hormonal swings; they are moody because they are having for the first time to prove themselves against the "real world" and they are dealing with the emotional difficulties that come from failure.

Faced with the challenges of the real world, Orphans will be tempted to seek solace in the comfort and safety of the family home. The "cruelty" of the parents may be little more than refusing to allow the child to give up and pressuring them to continue the struggles that are an inevitable part of coming-of-age. Since this is also emotionally difficult for the parents, they are tempted to avoid it. That path leads to the Devouring Mother phenomenon: the parent who wants to "protect" her child from pain. But this amounts to not letting go and allowing the child to come-of-age. Again, *Hamlet* provides an archetypal example of this in the form of Hamlet's mother, Gertrude.

Since parents must err on the side of "cruelty", it is symbolically fitting that Orphan Stories represent this cruelty via a step-parent or surrogate parent since this preserves the fundamental pairing of Child – Parent as a loving and supportive bond. But it is this bond which must be (symbolically) broken in order to allow the Orphan – Elder pairing to emerge.

Theme 3: Victimhood

The process of growing up is painful; hence the phrase *growing pains*. It's not wholly inaccurate to say that the Orphan is a victim. Nobody asks for puberty, or social puberty, to happen. They just do. The Orphan's archetypal mission is forced on them, and that mission is necessarily traumatic as they must leave the safety and security of the parental home with its (ideally) unconditional love and venture into the wider world. Some cultures symbolise the trauma by having initiation rituals that leave a permanent scar on the body. We see the same thing in Harry Potter, who has a mark on his forehead caused by Voldemort, the man who killed Harry's parents. The journey out of childhood can leave scars, if not physically, then psychologically.

Once again, we see that Orphan Stories often represent these things literally. The Orphan is a victim of fate, having lost their parents. They are the victim of the cruelty of their step-parents. They get ripped off, abused and manipulated by the people they meet in wider society. This sets up one of the primary dynamics of the Orphan archetype. The Orphan must overcome their victimhood and not use it as an excuse to avoid the work required to transition into adulthood. It is for this reason that playing the victim and related forms of emotional manipulation are the primary weaknesses of the Orphan and one of the main hurdles that must be overcome to successfully initiate into adulthood.

Theme 4: The Knowledge of Good and Evil

The evil Queen dressed up as a friendly old lady offering the poisoned apple to Snow White is perhaps the ultimate symbol of the Devouring Mother seducing the Orphan. Snow White's suffering is caused by her naivete. She still has a childlike trust in adults. She must transcend that naivete by understanding the motivations of others, including and especially those who would do her harm. Understanding that there is evil in the world and that adults and others in positions of power do not always have good intentions is a key to breaking away from childhood.

This raises a second potential pitfall for the Orphan which is the risk of wallowing in cynicism. The loss of innocence required to break away from the Child archetype can often swing too far in the other direction with the belief that everything in the world is irredeemably corrupt. This belief is often projected onto individuals, especially those in positions of power, who go from being exemplars of perfect goodness and authority to paragons of unadulterated evil.

To avoid this trap, the Orphan must also come to learn that much of their pain is not caused by others but by their own actions and mistakes.

This sorting out of responsibility between self and other is a key part of the coming-of-age process. In Ursula Le Guin's *A Wizard of Earthsea*, the apprentice-wizard Ged brings a shadow into the world through his own hubris. The shadow hurts himself and those whom Ged cares about. The evil in the world is of Ged's own making and his archetypal mission is to face that fact.

The self-knowledge of the Orphan that they are capable of good and evil must be balanced by the understanding that other people are neither entirely good nor entirely bad. This is also why playing the victim is the main weakness of the Orphan. It prevents the understanding that we are just as capable of evil as other people.

Theme 5: The Elder

Earlier in the book, we spent a great deal of time making the case for the existence of the Elder archetype since this has been largely removed from modern western culture for reasons we will examine in detail in Part 4. Given that modern western society is almost devoid of the Elder, it perhaps comes as a surprise to find it almost universally present in our Orphan Stories. Our film and literature could not be clearer on the fact that the Elder archetype is real or that the Orphan – Elder relationship requires the deprecation of the Child – Parent one.

The Orphan's parents are a hindrance and not a help to the Orphan's archetypal mission. That is the symbolic meaning of the cruel step-parent trope. But the Orphan Story also shows that the Orphan will not be alone in their journey. Having left the safety of the parental house, they will meet the Elder who becomes their mentor. Obi-wan Kenobi, Yoda, Dumbledore, Gandalf, Morpheus, Ogion and Heidi's grandfather are just some of the better-known Elders in modern film and literature. Almost without exception, stories featuring literal orphan characters where the Elder is not present are not Orphan Stories e.g. Huck Finn, Tom Sawyer, Pippi Longstocking, Pollyanna.

Crucially for our earlier analysis, there are Orphan Stories that feature what we can call the Shadow Elder i.e. a character who has the outward appearance of an Elder, the Physical and Exoteric qualities, but not the Esoteric. We know from our archetypal logic that we should expect such a character to manifest the shadow form of the Adult: the hyper masculine and the devouring feminine. Again, *Hamlet* provides us with two prime examples in the characters of Claudius (Tyrannical Father) and Gertrude (Devouring Mother). King Lear should be an Elder but is too busy being the Tyrannical Father at the start of his tragedy.

Examples of the Shadow Elder in film and literature include J's grandmother in the movie *Animal Kingdom*. J's mother dies, and his father is already out of the picture. This gives us a classic Orphan Story setup. But the grandmother is not a friendly Elder but a shadow Elder who inducts J into a world of drugs and crime. Another classic example is the evil Queen in Snow White who dresses as a friendly Elder character but represents the devouring feminine.

Probably the most famous example of the Shadow Elder who manifests the Tyrannical Father from recent decades is a character from the story we will go into detail about a little later: Star Wars. Darth Vader is both the Shadow Elder and the Shadow Father literally trying to lure Luke Skywalker to *the dark side*. Vader is the hyper-masculine Tyrannical Father *par excellence*. He aims to entrap his son in a dysfunctional Shadow Orphan – Shadow Adult pairing. Unlike Hamlet, Luke Skywalker has positive Elder figures in the form of Obi-wan and Yoda to guide him away from the shadow path.

Again, we see that it is the presence of the Elder who completes the Orphan – Elder pairing while the absence or corruption of the Elder facilitates the Shadow Orphan – Shadow Adult pairing.

Theme 6: New Friends

Alongside the Elder, the Orphan will meet others and make friends and enemies once they have ventured into the world outside the home. This is part of finding an Exoteric place in society, but it also raises potential pitfalls which the Orphan must navigate: they can be led off track if they come into contact with the wrong crowd. Oliver Twist gets in with a group of criminals, as does J in *Animal Kingdom*. In *The Lion King*, Simba falls in with friends who, while not really criminals, nevertheless hold him back from his archetypal mission. In *The Matrix*, Neo meets a group of new friends, one of whom (Cipher) will betray him.

Part of the Orphan's mission is to figure out who are the good guys and the bad guys, both among their own peer group and those in positions of power and authority - another factor in their deepening understanding of what it is to be human.

Theme 7: The Need to go it Alone

Most Orphan Stories show the process by which the Orphan meets their Elder and then their new peer group. Usually, the Elder is the one in charge of the group or institution which the Orphan will join. Thus, Luke Skywalker joins Obi-wan and the other rebels in *Star Wars*. Morpheus is the Elder leading the crew of the Nebuchadnezzar, who will become Neo's peer group in *The Matrix*. Dumbledore is the principal of the school where Harry Potter will meet his new friends.

All of this locates the Orphan in an Exoteric institution with a specific orientation and mission. However, the highest form of the Orphan Story is at the Esoteric level of being, and this is invariably a personal mission. The Orphan needs to be guided by an Elder and inducted into an Exoteric institution, but the fulfilment of the Esoteric is to find what we might call existential meaning. The Orphan must learn what they truly believe in. That is the highest form of the Esoteric.

This implies that the final transition at the Esoteric level of being can only be done alone. Orphan Stories normally represent this fact in symbolic terms. Luke Skywalker faces Vader alone at the end of *The Empire Strikes Back* and *Return of the Jedi*. Neo faces Agent Smith alone at the end of *The Matrix*. J acts alone to free himself at the end of *Animal Kingdom*. Harry Potter faces Voldemort alone in the first book of the series (even though that book is not technically an Orphan Story). In Batman, we have the vigilante Orphan who alone battles the forces that killed his parents. Ged confronts his shadow alone in *A Wizard of Earthsea*.

The Orphan first is separated from his or her natural parents, then from his or her adoptive parents, then their new friends and finally even from the wise Elder who may only lead the Orphan to the path. "I can only show you the door. You're the one who has to walk through it," says Morpheus to Neo in *The Matrix*.

Just as the death of the natural parents symbolises the transition from childhood to Orphanhood, Orphan Stories will often symbolise the transcendence from Orphanhood to Adulthood with the death of the Elder. Obi-wan is already dead when Yoda dies at the end of *Return of the Jedi*. In Dostoevsky's great novel, *The Brothers Karamazov*, it is the Elder Zosima's death that triggers the Orphan Alyosha's transcendence to adulthood. Morpheus is incapacitated when Neo fights his final battle against Agent Smith.

Again, we have to understand the death of the Elder in symbolic terms. It represents the fact that the Orphan's final transcendence to adulthood must be done alone since adulthood implies a level of responsibility and self-sufficiency. In real life, of course, we keep our relationships with our parents and hopefully also our Elders, but we are no longer dependent on them. That is what the death of the Elder signifies.

Theme 8: Integrating the Shadow

Joseph Campbell analysed the *Initiation* phase of the Hero's Journey as a descent into the Jungian Unconscious. In myth, that often takes the form of supernatural happenings. In modern storytelling, this descent often has a more direct psychological symbolism, including the use of the concept of the shadow.

The shadow side of the Orphan is the beliefs and character traits that are holding him or her back from achieving the archetypal mission. One of these is the aforementioned trap of playing the victim and using other forms of emotional manipulation. Another is a lack of self-belief, which comes from the fact that, no matter how well prepared one tries to be, ultimately, the only way to overcome Orphanhood and transcend into adulthood is to make a leap of faith into the unknown.

In Jungian terms, the Orphan's transcendence is an individuation process that implies a confrontation with and overcoming of the shadow traits holding the Orphan back. There is one modern Orphan story which symbolises these shadow elements literally and that is *A Wizard of Earthsea* by Ursula Le Guin.

The protagonist of the book, Sparrowhawk, is almost literally an orphan. His mother died when he was young. His brothers have moved away. His father is missing in action. He lives in a village, roaming around doing what he wants, while receiving minimal care from his aunt, who only begins to show real interest in him when his magical powers are revealed. After teaching him briefly, she introduces him to the magician, Ogion, who becomes his Elder, teaching him the ways of magic and giving him his true name of Ged.

So far, so good. This is much like a more sophisticated version of Harry Potter. But what happens next is far closer to the psychological reality of the Orphan. Ged's magical powers are as much a burden as a blessing for both himself and his Elder. He unleashes a shadow into the world, and Ogion must use all his magical strength to subdue it. This shows that the Elder's job is also not easy. Keeping the Orphan on track takes work and personal risk.

Ged, manifesting the shadow traits of the Orphan, shows little remorse for the pain he has caused and no desire to take responsibility. He goes off to wizard school, where his great power will cause more trouble and even the death of one of his teachers. Eventually, he graduates from school and is nominally a fully certified wizard.

Here we see a variation on the Orphan Story we mentioned in Scenario 5 above, where the Orphan has attained an Exoteric place in society but has not yet completed the journey on the Esoteric level of being. At the Exoteric level of being, Ged is an Adult. It is at the Esoteric level where he has not completed his initiation. This is symbolised by the fact that Ged's shadow is now chasing him. He must leave his Exoteric role and spend the second half of the book confronting the Esoteric in order to complete his Orphan mission.

The battle is done alone out on the open seas, with civilisation nowhere to be found - quite literally beyond the edge of the Earthsea world. In this, Le Guin symbolises the fact that the confrontation with the shadow, the Jungian individuation process that the Orphan must go through, does not happen in society or civilisation. It does not happen at the Physical or Exoteric levels of being, but at the Esoteric. The ultimate battle for the Orphan is a personal, psychological, and spiritual one. Being a battle against one's own shadow, it is the battle for the understanding that one is capable of evil. Ged must face the evil he has unleashed into the world. He must integrate the parts of himself that he would rather not acknowledge.

In *A Wizard of Earthsea*, Ged had already achieved an Exoteric role in society. He could have kept his day job and gone on being a wizard in the usual fashion, helping out the villagers and enjoying the social status that came with the position. The same can be said for the hero of another famous Orphan Story, Neo in *The Matrix*, who could have kept his well-paying and high status job at the corporation. But the highest level of initiation for the Orphan is at the Esoteric.

A Wizard of Earthsea strips back the symbolism of the Orphan story and presents it in an austere psychological light. Ged's pain is mostly caused not by others but by himself. That's what makes individuation so difficult. Jung himself noted that integrating the shadow is one of the more painful things anybody can do, and most people will avoid the task at all costs because it involves understanding that you are at fault for most of your problems. Incidentally, this is why it is a Hero's Journey because it really does take heroic effort to push through the individuation process at the Esoteric level of being.

The highest task of the Orphan maps to the Esoteric initiation that we discussed earlier. It is necessarily "above" the Exoteric because the very existence of the Exoteric gives the Orphan an easy way out. All you have to do is keep the job, show up to work, do what you're told. Society will reward you for your Exoteric compliance. You can live a whole life that way, but your shadow will always be there. You either confront it or let it control you. The Orphan must choose. The Elder's job is to present The Orphan with the choice. As Morpheus says to Neo in *The Matrix*, "I offer you the truth. Nothing more."

Theme 9: Metamorphosis

At the end of the Orphan Story, the hero has metamorphised. They are no longer an Orphan, but have transcended into an Adult. It's symbolically fitting that in many Orphan Stories, the archetype the protagonist transcends into is the Magician (aka Mage/Sage). Thus, Neo at the end of *The Matrix* re-enters the matrix as the master. He understands both the rules of the game and how to transcend them. Ged becomes a magician (and later an Elder) in the Earthsea stories, as does Luke Skywalker (Jedi).

Other famous examples of Orphans transcending to a different archetype at the end of their Hero's Journey include Jane Eyre, who gets married at the end of the book, thereby manifesting the Lover archetype. In *Animal Kingdom*, J transcends into the Warrior in shadow form, echoing his cousins and providing the final, chilling twist to the story. Batman, both a literal and archetypal Orphan, has already gone through an implied metamorphosis to become the Warrior while Simba becomes the Ruler at the end of *The Lion King*.

The mission of the Orphan is to swap the endless possibilities of eternal childhood, where you can pretend to be anything you want, for the *real world*. The real world is not pretend. In the real world, actions have consequences. The Orphan must face them. The Orphan swaps infinite possibility for a finite life path. The spiritual danger in this transition is that the Orphan overcompensates and swaps infinite possibility for its opposite: infinite necessity. This leads to cynicism or even nihilism. It hardens the spirit and creates a heartless and stifling world that becomes little more than a machine (e.g. "the matrix" that Neo is stuck in). The Cipher character in *The Matrix* represents the Orphan who willingly chooses infinite necessity to escape from the difficulties of the Orphan mission.

The danger faced by the Orphan is a danger for both the individual and for society. We saw in our analysis of the historical cycle that the late civilisation has lost the Esoteric. The Exoteric institutions of society continue to turn, but without any meaning or feeling. This is the world of the Shadow Orphans, who have embraced infinite necessity where all possibility gets snuffed out. The failure of the Orphan to fulfil its mission is therefore both a personal and collective failure that coincides with the absence of Elders.

Recalling our diagram of the Hero's Journey from earlier in the book, we can plot the main themes of the Orphan Story onto it as follows:-

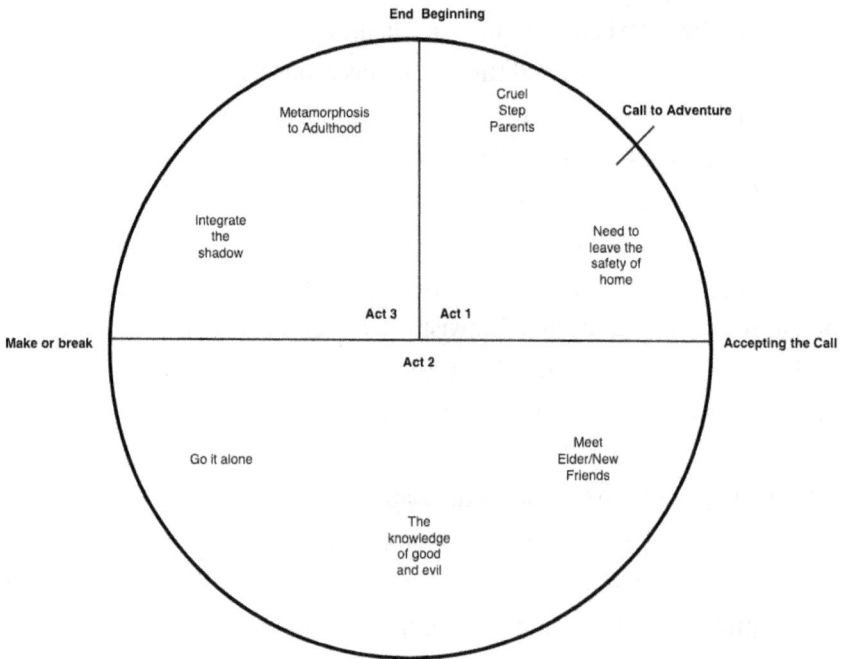

We can also use the three phases of the Hero's Journey: Departure – Initiation – Return, and the three levels of being to aid our understanding.

The onset of puberty takes place at the Physical level of being. It is a *Departure* from your old body - a child's body. Puberty itself is the *Initiation* phase, which takes place over a period of several years as the body gradually changes into its adult form. *Return* is the end of the process when the body has completed the transition.

Few actual Orphan Stories focus on the Physical level of being, and the ones that do are invariably comedies since physical humour is a mainstay of comedy. For example, the well-known Hollywood film, *American Pie*, is an Orphan Story comedy that focuses on the sexual difficulties of the Orphan journey. Most Orphan Stories, however, are about social puberty, and this takes place at the Exoteric level of being.

Social puberty is all about finding your place in society in a sexual, economic, political, and religious sense. The *Departure* phase of social puberty begins when the Orphan's family and wider society no longer treat them as a child. This will mostly match up with the onset of physical puberty, whether explicitly in the form of rites of passage or implicitly in general behaviour.

The *Initiation* phase of social puberty involves the gradual assumption of adult Exoteric roles. This is where Elders and new friends enter the picture, since these imply that the Orphan has joined an Exoteric institution of some kind. In *A Wizard of Earthsea*, Ged joins the wizard school. In *The Matrix*, Neo joins the crew of the Nebuchadnezzar led by Morpheus. In *Star Wars*, Luke Skywalker joins the rebel alliance. The Elder in each case initiates the Orphan into the Exoteric institution where they meet their new friends.

The *Return* phase of social puberty is finished when you are now treated as an Adult. That implies that you have found an economic place in society (a career, your own home), a political place (a citizen), a religious place (full membership in a religious organisation) and a romantic or sexual place (marriage/love).

At the Esoteric level of being, we have identified a lower and a higher Esoteric where the former relates mostly to the emotions and the Unconscious while the latter is about meaning and purpose. Both physical and social puberty put us in situations that evoke Esoteric pressures that everybody is familiar with. Awkwardness, embarrassment, anxiety, and self-doubt are just some of the emotions we stereotypically associate with adolescence. But alongside these is the awakening of the higher Esoteric in the search for meaning and purpose.

Most cultures throughout history have had an Exoteric role which denotes a person who is pursuing the Esoteric as a life path. Anchorites, hermits, ascetics, monks, mystics, nuns, and priests are some of the names given to such a life path. Such people strive to live what we might call the *pure Esoteric* aka connecting with God. The Esoteric is an experience, not a dogma. Mystical spiritual experiences are about a connection with the ineffable thing that is called God. The Exoteric structure of the religion, including its dogma, is ideally there to facilitate this connection and the feeling that comes with it.

We can also connect with the higher Esoteric in the more mundane areas of life. It's possible to fulfil an Exoteric role without experiencing the Esoteric. You can go to church once a week, work a job, be in a marriage and vote in an election. Those are all Exoteric in nature. It's only when you feel a connection with the religion, feel love for your marriage partner, feel stimulated by a job, or passionate about a political issue that you experience the Esoteric level of being. The Orphan story is fulfilled at the higher Esoteric when the Orphan discovers meaning and purpose in the Exoteric institutions they have joined, but also when they experience an Esoteric that seems to go beyond the Exoteric altogether.

Three Orphan Stories in depth

Let's now bring all these considerations together and go into detail on three popular Orphan Stories from the last few decades. The first two are ones that almost everybody will be familiar with: the Hollywood blockbuster movies *Star Wars* and *The Matrix*. The third is less well-known but is one of the best-told Orphan Stories and avoids the Hollywood necessity for action and violence: Ursula Le Guin's fantasy novel *A Wizard of Earthsea*. We'll group our analysis by the now familiar segments of the Hero's Journey: Departure – Initiation – Return.

Departure

Remembering back to our archetypal table from earlier in the book:-

Archetype	Level of Being		
	Physical	Exoteric	Esoteric – Dominant Faculty
The Child	Birth - Childhood	Son or daughter	Imagination
The Orphan	Puberty	Student, friend, protégé, initiate	Intellect
The Adult	Adulthood	Husband/wife, parent, citizen, employee/boss, churchgoer	Will
The Elder	Old Age - Death	Retiree, Mentor, Teacher	Soul

What we find in each of the Orphan Stories we are going to look at is that each of the heroes of the stories has already made the transition to Adult at both the Physical and Exoteric levels of being. In *The Matrix*, Neo works as a software developer for a corporation. In *A Wizard of Earthsea*, we see the process by which Ged becomes a fully certified wizard, having gone through wizard school to attain that role. In *Star Wars*, Luke Skywalker works on a farm with his aunt and uncle and, initially, denies the offer from Obi-wan to leave that position. The economic and political identity of all three young men is already established, although, of course, none of them are married or seem to have any prospects in that area. Neither are they involved in religion.

What all three young men are lacking is what we have broadly called the Esoteric. *The Matrix* presents this in a form we can identify with since that movie takes place in the modern world. We can see that Neo is not particularly interested in his corporate job. Neither does he seem to have much going on in his life outside of work. He seems to have no family or friends, is dissociated from society, and is not married or in a romantic relationship. In short, he is stuck in an Exoteric role that has no Esoteric meaning for him. His life has become machine-like, an empty ceremony. The matrix is a metaphor for both Neo's specific predicament and for the general state of affairs that any of us can fall into in our lives where the Exoteric and the Esoteric get out of balance and we are *stuck in a rut.*

We mentioned earlier in the book that one of the main risks of the Orphan transition is that we trade in the infinite possibility of childhood for its opposite: infinite necessity. The matrix is the perfect metaphor for infinite necessity. It is the Exoteric that has become completely devoid of the Esoteric and those who take up lives within it, such as Neo has, find themselves in a world without meaning. What Neo lacks is the Esoteric, and we see that he has taken some steps to try and find it. He is quite literally looking for the matrix, which is the symbol of his problem. In addition, he has begun to carve out a separate identity, one that he has been developing in secret. His official daytime name is Mr Anderson. Neo is his hidden, Esoteric, name, and it ties in with a shadowy identity that involves being a digital drug dealer who hangs around with shady characters in dingy nightclubs.

In *Star Wars*, the characters who represent infinite necessity are the stormtroopers, and this is symbolised by their identical uniforms, which remove all individuality in much the same way that the identically-spaced cubicles in Neo's office do. The stormtroopers are just pawns doing someone else's bidding, just as Neo is a pawn in the corporate machine. It is symbolically fitting, therefore, that it is the stormtroopers who destroy the farm belonging to Luke Skywalker's aunt and uncle and, thereby, destroy his Exoteric identity. Neo, on the other hand, must choose to destroy his own Exoteric identity. That is the Call to Adventure he receives from Morpheus. It's the same Call to Adventure that Ged receives in *A Wizard of Earthsea.* Ged has achieved the Exoteric role of wizard and has secured a recognised position in society, but is called to the Esoteric by the shadow that pursues him.

The Call to Adventure that all three young men receive is the call to leave behind an established, Adult, Exoteric identity and pursue the Esoteric. Who is the one who gives the Call? It should come as no surprise to us that it is none other than the archetypal Elder in the form of Obi-wan and Morpheus. (The wizard, Ogion, had earlier provided Ged with his initial Call to Adventure in *A Wizard of Earthsea.)* It is because all three heroes have already attained the Exoteric that the Call to Adventure in these stories takes on a specifically Esoteric nature. It is the Esoteric which will break the spell of infinite necessity. Luke Skywalker's is offered initiation into *the Force*. Morpheus offers Neo "the truth" about the matrix. Ged must confront the strange and intangible entity known as the shadow. Thus, in the very beginning stages of all three Orphan Stories, we find the formation of the Orphan-Elder pairing.

Since all three of our Orphan heroes have an established Exoteric identity, it follows that all three stories are about Esoteric initiation. Neo, Luke Skywalker and Ged are called to be *born-again* in spirit. *The Matrix* gives us one of the most memorable examples of the *born-again* concept in film, as we see Neo being pulled out of the womb-like capsule of the matrix into "the real world". Who is the first person he sees in the real world following his "rebirth"? It is not his mother or father, but his Elder, Morpheus. In the archetypal progression of our lives, the first birth creates the Child – Parent pairing. The second birth creates the Orphan – Elder.

More generally, the need to forego the Exoteric to pursue the Esoteric is a common theme throughout religious history, and thus all three Orphan Stories present a historically accurate version of Esoteric Initiation. Many of the best-known spiritual leaders in history had an established Exoteric place in society, which they abandoned in order to walk the path of the pure Esoteric. Jesus was a carpenter before becoming a prophet. Mohammed was a cow herd. Buddha and St Francis of Assisi were princelings. The Orphan Stories of Neo, Luke Skywalker and Ged all contain the core archetypal elements associated with the founders of the world's great religions.

Initiation

The *Initiation* phase of the Orphan Story is where the Orphan has accepted the call to make the journey to adulthood and now must face the Esoteric challenges that we all face when we step into the unknown. To assist them, the Orphan has their Elder, their new friends, and a new Exoteric role that exists to facilitate their transition. Thus, Luke Skywalker becomes a member of the Rebel Alliance and is striving towards an Exoteric role as a Jedi Knight. His new friends are Han Solo, Wookie and Princess Leia. Neo joins the crew of the Nebuchadnezzar and is striving towards a role as *The One*. Ged goes to school and is striving to become a wizard.

The Orphan phase of life implies a period of education and training, and, once again, *The Matrix* has a very memorable example of that with the simulation training that Neo receives, firstly in an automated fashion, and then when he receives direct instruction from Morpheus. In the second and third movies of the Star Wars trilogy, we see Luke Skywalker being trained by another famous Elder character, Yoda. Ged receives informal instruction from Ogion in *A Wizard of Earthsea* before going on to the formal training that sets up his Exoteric role by attending wizard school.

Earlier in the book, we formulated the concept of the shadow forms of the archetypes and the more general principle that the shadow emerges from the failure to channel the archetypal energy towards a productive adaptation to the mission. We also noted how common it was for literature to use symbolism directly related to the shadow and provided examples of this from Shakespeare. It should come as little surprise, then, that we find the shadow represented in our three Orphan Stories. *Star Wars* has one of the most memorable instantiations of the shadow with its concept of *the dark side*, which is the negative correlate to *the Force*. Who is tempting Luke Skywalker to the dark side? Here we see our archetypal logic in action, because it is none other than his own father, just as it was the ghost of Hamlet's father who tempted the prince of Denmark to his own version of the dark side. What is being offered in both cases is the shadow relationship of Orphan-Parent.

A Wizard of Earthsea uses the concept of the shadow directly since it is Ged's shadow which is pursuing him and which he must leave his Exoteric role to confront. This gives the book a more Jungian vibe, and it's fascinating to note that Ursula Le Guin said she had not read Jung before writing the story, which is further evidence for the shadow's place among the archetypes of the Unconscious.

The Matrix represents the shadow in the form of the Judas character Cipher. Cipher is the Orphan who, when faced with the challenges of the archetypal

164

transformation, chooses the safe and easy path of infinite necessity. The stormtroopers represent the shadow form of infinite necessity in *Star Wars*, and it is no coincidence that they are led by Darth Vader, who embodies that life path. In *The Matrix*, it is the people who live in the matrix who are living in infinite necessity since they are just a part of the machine. Most of them are unaware of that fact, but Cipher does not have that excuse. He knowingly gives up on the Orphan mission, and he does so by choosing to embrace infinite necessity. It's the same choice given to Luke Skywalker at the end of *Return of the Jedi*, when Palpatine urges him to take his father's place in the dark side.

To reiterate, the Orphan has a mission to fulfil. All the emotions, temptations, and excuses of the Orphan are based on the desire to avoid their archetypal mission. To go to *the dark side* is to give in to the shadow and fail to transcend to true adulthood. The shadow traits of the Orphan are victimhood, cynicism, and self-doubt, which tempt the individual to acquiesce to a greater power that demands obedience rather than offers enlightenment. It is in the *Initiation* phase of the story that the Orphan must work through these issues and avoid the temptation to take the easy way out.

Note that we also see the primary elements of the Orphan Story in the biblical passages relating to the Temptation of Christ, which can be read as Jesus' Esoteric initiation. Jesus is removed from Exoteric society to the solitude of the desert for 40 days. Satan (the dark side/the shadow) tempts Jesus with food and promises of power and immortality. He is the Tyrannical Father trying to induct Jesus into the hyper-masculine in just the same way that Darth Vader and Palpatine tempt Luke Skywalker. It is not a coincidence that it is food and promises of power and immortality that Agent Smith offers to Cipher to secure his betrayal of Neo and Morpheus in *The Matrix*. The Exoteric institutions of society confer power and wealth. The Orphan can take those and live a materially prosperous life, but they will have sacrificed something. That something is the higher Esoteric. That is what the three Orphans in our stories are pursuing and that is what is earned in the Return phase of the story.

Return

If the *Departure* severs the Orphan from their old Exoteric world and the *Initiation* inducts them into a new one, the *Return* phase of the Orphan Story is the final confrontation with the unknown, where the Orphan proves once and for all that they belong in the new world to which their journey leads. The old world will go away forever, and the new one, which the Orphan still does not fully comprehend, will manifest. It is because it is not possible to fully understand the new world until you are in it that the process requires a leap of faith, which signals a discontinuous transition to a new state. This final leap of faith takes place at the Esoteric level of being. It is a necessarily personal and subjective experience of transcendence that maps to what, in religious mysticism, is the connection with God (the pure Esoteric) or what Jung called Individuation. Since all three of our Orphan Stories are about Esoteric initiation, all three represent this personal experience of transcendence.

The Matrix represents the Esoteric nature of this transcendence in memorable form. The final showdown between Neo and Agent Smith shows Neo metamorphosing into *The One*. But the metaphysics of the story make it clear that the metamorphosis takes place at the Esoteric level of being because we know that Neo's physical body is outside the matrix, as is his new Exoteric role. Therefore, the Physical and Exoteric levels of being remain unchanged throughout the final battle. What does change is something *inside* Neo. In the words of Morpheus, Neo "believes". He has taken the leap of faith to become *The One*. Here we have yet another piece of symbolism that relates back to our earlier analysis of the rites of passage, since the Incorporation phase of the rite is the end of the period of sacredness and implies a return to wholeness and holiness. That is what the phrase *The One* implies. Similarly, Ged tells his friend, Vetch, that he is now *whole* after his own transcendence at the end of *A Wizard of Earthsea*. The final phase of the Orphan Story is the return to wholeness, holiness, and consciousness.

We find an interesting variation on the symbol of transcendence in *Return of the Jedi*, where Luke Skywalker's Esoteric leap of faith during his battle against Vader is represented as an act of submission. Skywalker "gives up" (refuses to kill his father). We know that this perfectly fits our archetypal logic since the refusal to kill the Father prevents a shadow form of transcendence, which would see Skywalker manifest the hyper-masculine. But the act of submission can also be interpreted as a *letting go,* and we know that what Skywalker is letting go of is his old archetype. Only by allowing his old identity to fall away can Skywalker be ready to step into the new. In Jungian terms, he gives up the Ego and wins the *Self.* In our archetypal terms, he gives up the Orphan and wins the Adult. But we also know from our earlier analysis that the archetypes come in pairs, and we see a simultaneous archetypal transition at the end of *Return of the Jedi* because Darth Vader also lets go of his old identity as the Tyrannical Father and steps into the Elder role. The symbol of his return to the positive archetypal form is the removal of his helmet - the restoration of his humanity. (Note that Vader then immediately goes from Elder to Ancestor as represented by his death and subsequent appearance as a spirit alongside Yoda and Obi-wan).

We have said that the final transcendence occurs at the Esoteric level of being and makes the hero *whole.* But wholeness applies to all three levels of being. Because all three of our Orphans have already made the transition to Adult at the Physical level of being, there is no need to emphasise that in the stories. But we see a definite Exoteric transition. Neo becomes *The One.* Skywalker becomes a Jedi. Ged becomes a true wizard. The Orphan's new Exoteric identity is sanctified and confirmed in the Return phase of the cycle. The hero both believes themselves to be what they have become, and so does their society.

At the end of the Orphan Story, the hero is no longer an Orphan. They are an Adult and will be treated as such by friends and the wider society. The hero's Esoteric, Exoteric and Physical existence have been brought into alignment and made whole. More importantly, the Orphan "feels" themselves to be initiated. That is the Esoteric component of transcendence. There is no more doubt, cynicism, or victimhood because the Orphan has experienced their metamorphosis. It is no longer a theory or a promise, but a lived reality. At the end of the Orphan story, the period of "illness" is over. Health and wholeness are returned. The Orphan is ready for the next phase of life.

Summary

Although we have made the argument several times in this book in favour of using stories to explicate our analysis, we nevertheless must admit that stories can become hyper-real to the extent that any connection with lived reality becomes tenuous. This is especially a problem with films, and more especially with modern Hollywood films, which are in a kind of hyper-real arms race. Both *Star Wars* and *The Matrix* suffer from this problem, especially the latter with its gratuitous ultra-violence. For these reasons, it's worth reiterating in summary that the themes from the stories we have just examined really do match up to the lived reality of archetypal transformations and, especially, the Orphan transcendence to adulthood.

The first thing to note is that they are historically correct representations of the born-again religious experience. St Paul had his *road to Damascus* moment. St Francis of Assissi had a vision which led to him renouncing his life of luxury. Muhammed had a vision of the angel Gabriel. Whether we believe in the veracity of such stories or write them off as psychological illusions, they still represent sudden breaks in the lives of the individuals in question. A variation on these are near-death experiences. Martin Luther had one such experience with a lightning strike that nearly killed him. The great Russian writer, Dostoevsky, was sentenced to death and led in front of a firing squad before being pardoned at the last minute. Both events changed the lives of the then-young men. Both can be interpreted as Orphan metamorphoses.

We might be tempted to say that such metamorphoses are specific to the world of religious mysticism or to extreme and unusual events. But that is also not really true. Even at the Physical and Exoteric levels of being, the archetypal transitions are difficult because of their suddenness. Consider physical puberty. It brings on a series of new experiences, situations, and physical symptoms that the Orphan must learn to navigate. This includes the mood swings that come from hormonal adjustments, the onset of sexual thoughts and expressions, and the emotional difficulties of new responsibilities and expectations. From the individual's point of view, these come out of nowhere and all of a sudden. They impose themselves on us as something that must be dealt with and cannot be avoided.

The same is true at the Exoteric level. The major rites of passage for most cultures represent an abrupt transition to a different way of life. This is even true of our rites of passage around our economic identity since the transition to a new job is also a relatively sudden one that brings about an immediate state change that we must navigate through. The same is true of becoming engaged, getting married, pregnancy, and childbirth and the death of a loved one. All of these come upon us suddenly and cause a break with normal, everyday reality. Thus, the representation of dramatic transcendence that we see in literature and film is, in fact, an accurate reflection of lived reality.

This idea of sudden metamorphosis lends weight to the notion we introduced earlier in the book that the archetypal phases of life are mini-lives and that the transitions between them are mini-deaths. That is why the *born-again* motif is not fanciful or exaggerated. Orphan Stories usually represent the danger of this "death" in a literal fashion. Neo is killed and then rises from the dead in the dramatic finale of *The Matrix*. Luke Skywalker is almost killed by Palpatine at the end of *Return of the Jedi*. Ged is threatened with death from his shadow several times in *A Wizard of Earthsea*. Even in the first Harry Potter book, we see Harry rendered unconscious near the end of the story. In archetypal terms, death itself is not the problem but rather the failure to accept that death, and this is why the *letting go* motif and its psychoanalytic form of ego-death are valid also in our own lives, where we must allow the ego that is attached to our former archetypal phase to "die".

It is because the archetypal wheel turns only in one direction that there is another way in which the death motif of the finale of the Orphan Story is valid, and that relates to the Elder. The final transition of the Orphan into adulthood implies a breaking of the Orphan–Elder relationship just as the transition to adolescence implies a breaking of the Child–Parent. The Elder has shown the Orphan the path, and the Orphan has now walked the path. The role of the Elder must now change into something new, but it's also possible that the relationship between the two individuals comes to an end. We see examples of this in the intellectual sphere in Jung's break with Freud,

Nietzsche's break with Wagner (and, more Esoterically, Schopenhauer) or even the implied Elder relationship in the Bible between John the Baptist and Jesus.

In our three Orphan Stories, we see that Ogion's break with Ged comes with the latter's final, solo transcendence. Yoda, Obi-wan and Vader all die, thereby facilitating Luke Skywalker's transcendence to the Adult. Meanwhile, *The Matrix* makes it clear that Neo has surpassed Morpheus at the end of the story, and the closing scene of the movie features Neo alone.

The death of the Elder also represents the successful propagation of the culture, since the Orphan–Elder relationship is what we have called the engine of civilisation. The Elder departs the scene, leaving the new blood to carry the tradition. Conversely, the failure of the initiation process, if repeated often enough, amounts to the failure of the culture to survive. If two Adults fail to produce offspring, this can lead to the end of the family line. If Elders fail in their role as "cultural parents", that can bring the cultural line to an end too.

With that, we have the perfect segue to the next section of our discussion. We have just analysed the Orphan Stories from the microcosmic viewpoint, but recall our earlier statement that the advantage of modern Orphan Stories is that they are also highly accurate in relation to the macrocosmic context that they portray. It is now time to once again flip our perspective around and view the Orphan Story from the civilisational point of view.

The Macrocosmic Perspective

We have seen that Toynbee's work of comparative history can be translated into archetypal terms as the slow breakdown of the Orphan – Elder dynamic into what we have called the Shadow Orphan – Shadow Adult pairing. If the first half of the civilisational cycle features healthy Orphan – Elder relationships that produce fully initiated Adults, the second half sees the demise of that relationship and its replacement with the shadow forms. At the societal level, this manifests as the rise of the Tyrannical Father archetype as the collective "parent" ruling over a general public of Shadow Orphans.

Our choice of the three modern Orphan Stories we have looked at in depth has not been arbitrary. Not only is each of these stories a prime example of an Esoteric initiation and therefore supremely useful to further our understanding of the subjective experience of the Orphan's rite of passage, each story also takes place against the backdrop of a very specific location on the cycle of civilisation. Therefore, we can use each of the three stories to also deepen our understanding of the archetypal changes that occur over the civilisational cycle, with a specific focus on how the Orphan – Elder relationship changes. That is what we will do in this section.

To refresh our memories, here is the cycle of civilisation in sine wave form:-

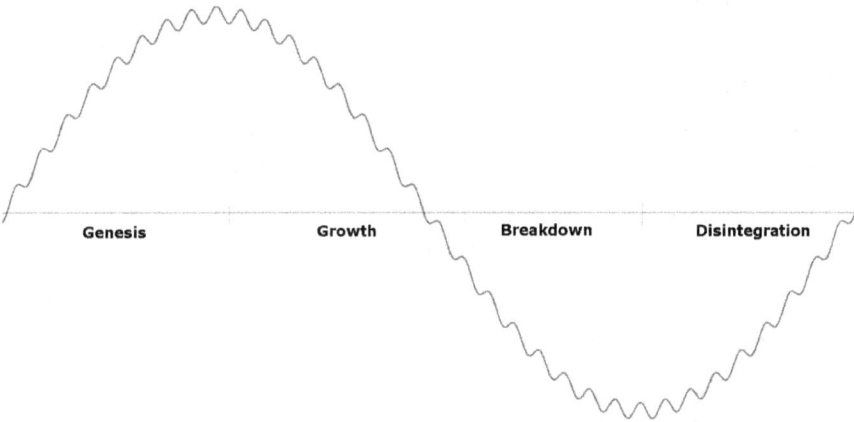

Genesis   Growth   Breakdown   Disintegration

Recall that the first half of the cycle is governed by the Creative Minority which is a decentralised and localised group of Elders (elites) who lead society via organic bonds of authority and allegiance. Such Elders are seen as the carriers of tradition, which stretches back to the ancestors and ultimately back to the founding theological assumptions of the society e.g. gods, spirits. Orphans and Elders in this era typically have a direct and ongoing relationship with each other, symbolised by rites of passage carried out and maintained within a locality.

The second half of the cycle sees the transition to the Dominant Minority. The success of the society begins to translate into physical scale, which is further bolstered by economic, military and political power. The seat of power drains away from localities and into the mega-cities. The direct relationships between Orphans and Elders at the local level are severed, and with them the feeling of a tradition linking backwards in time. Instead of a direct relationship with a local Elder, the Orphans of society growing up in the cities are offered cults of personality to great figures whose fame provides the simulacrum of an Orphan – Elder relationship. The rites of passage, which previously held so much meaning, now become ceremonial and devoid of the Esoteric.

Meanwhile, some members of society become dissatisfied with the new state of affairs and seek to rediscover Esoteric meaning in new ways of understanding the world. There arises what we have called Rebel Elders of which the Rebel Priests provide new philosophical and theological ways of understanding while the Rebel Commanders mount attacks against the perceived injustices of the Dominant Minority. We see a split in society between the Majority who remain faithful to the Dominant Minority and a variety of breakaway groups led by Rebel Elders who provide the Orphans in their charge with an Esoteric initiation of sorts. Overall, this leaves the Orphans of society with two partial initiatory pathways. They may join the Majority and take up a stable Exoteric existence or they may join the Rebel Elders and mark themselves as, at best, outsiders, at worst, direct enemies of the state.

Although we have translated much of this analysis into our archetypal language, we should recall that it is based on the extensive historical scholarship of comparative historians, of which Toynbee has been our main point of reference. This fact is worth reiterating since we are about to see just how well our three Orphan Stories, three different works of fiction written by different people in different decades, fit into the historical framework.

Let's begin with the story which takes place during the beginning of the civilisational cycle: *A Wizard of Earthsea*.

The Beginning of the Cycle

We can use our split diagram of the integrated model to characterise each of our Orphan Stories and their place in the cycle of civilisation as follows:-

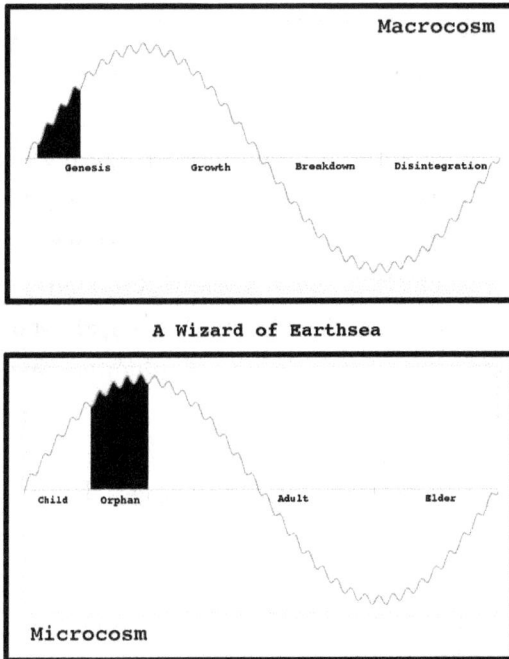

A Wizard of Earthsea

A *Wizard of Earthsea* features a hero in the Orphan phase of life, living during the Genesis phase of the civilisational cycle. We can see this latter fact in that the Earthsea world is decentralised and features a heterogenous mix of cultures, languages, and peoples who have trading relationships with each other and may also share cultural similarities but who are distinct and unique. Although there are presumably political institutions in the Earthsea world, the book itself is focused almost entirely on Esoteric matters, which is also fitting for the early phases of the civilisational cycle where political institutions are weak and the Esoteric dominates.

In the early phases of the civilisational cycle, the relationship between

Orphans and Elders is direct and local. That is exactly what we see in *A Wizard of Earthsea.* Ged is just a local boy living in a village. Having shown magical ability, he is introduced to the local Elder, Ogion, and receives his initial magical training from him. Later, he will attend a wizard school, which is a kind of peak institution that takes students from the various localities. This is quite a similar situation to the early days of modern Europe where the Christian church functioned as the institution that united the various kingdoms and domains of Europe together in a shared Esoteric understanding.

Ged's Esoteric initiation occurs mostly outside the teachings of the wizard school and even of his Elder, Ogion. He must *go it alone.* We might view this as an entirely personal event, and yet Toynbee made the claim that civilisation is driven by individuals who go through exactly this kind of process. He called it *Withdrawal and Return.* For Toynbee, the individuals who drive civilisation forward withdraw to receive some kind of enlightenment and then return to share that enlightenment with the rest of the civilisation. Note that this is identical to the point that Campbell made about the Hero's Journey and van Gennep about the rites of passage. Such events are not simply a personal experience but one of potentially civilisational significance. A prime example of *Withdrawal and Return* is Jesus' 40 days alone in the desert, part of a Hero's Journey which has been of enormous civilisational importance.

The first of the Earthsea books shows Ged's *Withdrawal* while the sequels show his *Return.* Ged becomes a societal Elder who guides the next generation of Orphans through initiation. Therefore, Ged is a paradigm example of what Toynbee meant by the Creative Minority. These are individuals whose *Withdrawal and Return* is creative and adds to the development of the civilisation. It does so in this case because Ged goes on to pass his knowledge directly to the next group of Orphans in the same way that his Elder, Ogion, passed it to him. In this sequence of initiations (Orphan – Elder relationships) the culture is propagated. We might say that every Orphan initiation is a mini-*Withdrawal and Return.* The Orphan must withdraw to face the Esoteric challenge. They return as an Adult.

Putting all this together, we see that the world of *A Wizard of Earthsea* is decentralised, localised, concerned with the Esoteric over the Physical and features Creative Minorities not just conducting Esoteric initiation of the Orphans of society but facilitating the advancement of society through the incorporation of the lessons learned during a *Withdrawal and Return*. The advancement of society is not a military or political question but one of spirituality. For all these reasons, we can say that *A Wizard of Earthsea* takes place during the Genesis phase of civilisation.

The Turning Point

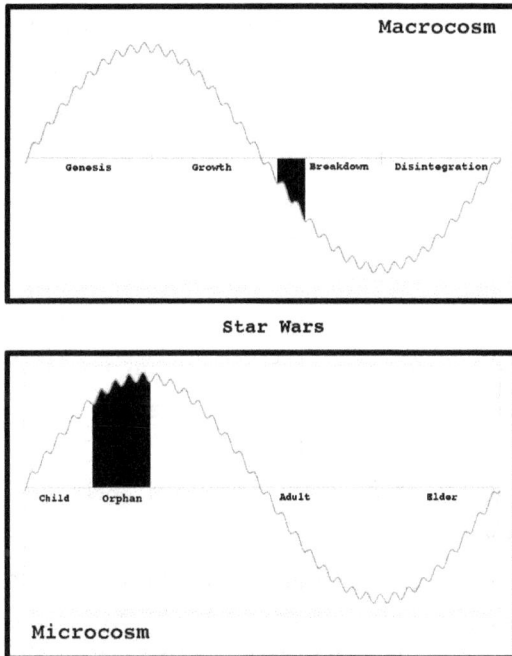

Star Wars features a hero in the Orphan phase of life, living at the midpoint of the civilisational cycle at the transition between the Creative and Dominant Minorities. In the *Star Wars* universe, there still exists the cultural hetero-geneity of the early phase of the cycle. Consider the bar scene in the first movie where Luke and Obi-Wan meet Hans Solo and Wookie for the first time. It is full of weird and diverse characters. Multiple languages are spoken, and even Hans Solo is multi-lingual. The wider *Star Wars* galaxy features a variety of peoples, with localised architectural and fashion styles etc. In short, there is variation and decentralisation.

What differentiates the world of *Star Wars* from the world of *A Wizard of Earthsea* is that it shows us the emergence of the Dominant Minority in the form of the galactic empire led by Palpatine and Darth Vader. The Empire aims to usurp all power for itself by getting rid of the heterogeneous communities and cultures of the galaxy. It does so through the use of force. Crucially for our analysis, *Star Wars* also shows us the emergence of the Rebel Elders who push back against the Dominant Minority. It does this quite literally, since we see the political institution called the Rebel Alliance. Yoda and Obi-wan are a combination of Rebel Priest and Rebel Commander. In any case, they are Rebel Elders.

Star Wars also gives us a glimpse into the motivations of the rebels. Luke Skywalker was not looking to overthrow the system. He was thrown into that world when his old life was destroyed due to the actions of the empire i.e. the stormtroopers killing his aunt and uncle. This matches the historical analysis of Toynbee where the Dominant Minority severs the organic bonds of large segments of the population in its pursuit of wealth and power. What happens to Luke Skywalker happens to numerous others, and this creates what Toynbee called the Internal Proletariat.

Star Wars shows us civilisation once it has split into the Dominant Minority and the various Rebel groups that challenge it both militarily and Esoterically. *Star Wars* does a historically accurate job of portraying the Dominant Minority. We can see the advantages of the Tyrannical Father archetype in the great works of organisation and military technology. We also see that Vader governs not through any organic bonds of allegiance but by a discipline based on cruelty. Obedience and compliance are what he demands.

Not only is Vader one of the great examples of the Tyrannical Father archetype, the stormtroopers are a fine example of the general public of the second half of the civilisational cycle which acquiesces to the Dominant

Minority. The discipline and hard work of the late stages of civilisation come at the cost of individuality. Only by supressing one's individuality can one become an efficient cog in the machine. This is what it means to say that the general public of late civilisation has chosen an Exoteric existence that is devoid of the Esoteric. The Stormtroopers represent the Shadow Orphans of the general public who acquiesce to the Tyrannical Father.

The stormtroopers have no direct personal connection with their Elder in the form of Vader. The concentration of power at the top of an increasingly steep social hierarchy, which occurs in the second half of civilisation means that the initiation of the general public is also Exoteric in the sense that it requires allegiance not to an individual that one knows and interacts with on a day-to-day basis but to a distant figure. The Tyrannical Father in the form of Vader demands nothing more than blind allegiance, and the Exoteric initiation received by the Orphans of the general public is there to inculcate that allegiance.

We can see, therefore, that *Star Wars* fulfils all the main macrocosmic trends that we have earlier identified based on the scholarly research of comparative history. There is one big problem with it, however. The story has a *happy ending* (if we consider *Return of the Jedi* to be the ending). Luke Skywalker chooses Esoteric initiation via the Elders of the story (Obi-wan and Yoda) and rejects the offer of the dark side from his father. At the microcosmic level, he receives an Esoteric initiation and graduates to the Adult archetype. At the macrocosmic level, the Creative Minority defeats the Dominant Minority. Therefore, Luke has been initiated into the Creative Minority which is now in charge again.

This happy ending works for a Hollywood movie, and, since *Star Wars* takes place at the turning point of the historical cycle, there may even be some historical examples where the Creative Minority does win some temporary victories against the emergent Dominant Minority. But the key word is "temporary". The historical scholarship shows that the Dominant Minority always wins in the end, and that is where the third of our Orphan Stories comes into the picture.

The End of the Cycle

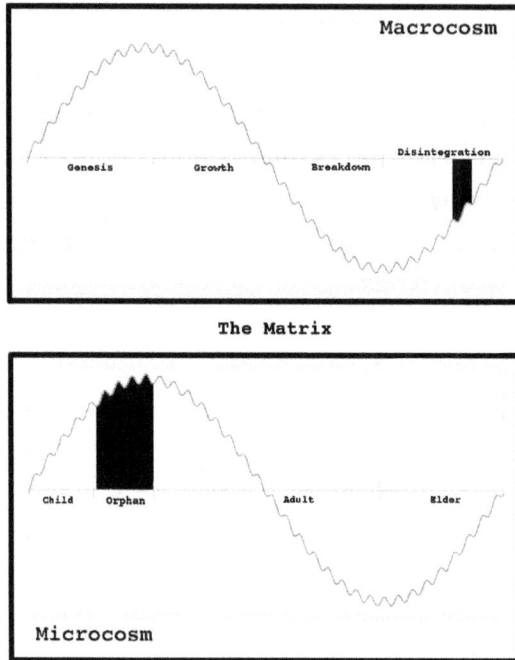

If *Star Wars* shows us the emergence of the Dominant Minority near the midway point of the civilisational cycle, *The Matrix* shows us a world where the Dominant Minority has achieved supremacy. Humans have been reduced to nothing more than bodies which power a giant machine. All heterogeneity is gone. There is no real culture at all, but only a fantasy world built to distract the Majority and keep them fulfilling the role required of them to keep the civilisation going (bread and circuses). The world of the matrix has been ordered entirely in the service of power. Things are run according to rules determined by the Dominant Minority.

Just like Luke Skywalker, Neo is given a choice between acquiescence to the Dominant Minority and rebellion against it. Also like Skywalker, Neo is being offered initiation into the Dominant Minority not as a leader of a military dictatorship but in its modern western form as a member of the technocracy. In fact, Neo has already been inducted and is a reluctant but presumably productive member of the Exoteric institutions of society. The main difference between Skywalker and Neo is that the former is forced into the proletariat through the actions of the stormtroopers, while Neo has a comfortable life ahead of him if he chooses. But he yearns for something more. He is seeking the Esoteric. That is where we find him at the beginning of the story.

The political context of *The Matrix* late in the civilisational cycle maps to the period of stability which Toynbee called the Universal State. The Universal State is almost always a time of empire, which occurs after the Warring States Period, where one of the contenders for supremacy has become all-powerful. The Tyrannical Father of empire keeps both the internal and external proletariat in line through the use of power. Accordingly, major political and economic disputes no longer occur, and we see a long period of peace and material prosperity, such as occurred in the Roman Empire. The cost of this is that life has lost its Esoteric spark. Stability leads to stagnation.

We mentioned earlier that the matrix was a symbol of Neo's microcosmic stagnation in that he had found himself stuck in a rut with an Exoteric identity that had no corresponding Esoteric aspect. But the symbol of the matrix also works perfectly at the macrocosmic level in reference to the late stage of civilisation where, to use Toynbee's phrase, life has become a ceremony. The stability of the Universal State is, in some sense, its advantage, but it leads to a mechanical existence that is devoid of the Esoteric. That is what the matrix symbolises.

Another historically accurate difference between the worlds of *Star Wars* and *The Matrix* is the kind of Rebel Priest that we see. In *Star Wars*, Obi-wan is a member of the old Creative Minority who offers an initiation that links Skywalker back to the past via his own father. That is the old world, which is gradually slipping away. Once the Dominant Minority has governed for long enough, however, the bonds to the old world are broken, and the Creative Minority disappears. The Rebel Priests no longer offer a link to the past but come from outside the civilisation altogether. This is a fact which Toynbee noted. What he called the Universal Church originates from influences outside the civilisation.

We see this accurately represented in *The Matrix* in the character of Morpheus. He and his band of rebels exist literally outside of the matrix and therefore outside of the civilisation that Neo belongs to, which is in its Universal State ruled over by the agents. Morpheus does not offer Neo a link back to the past but an initiation into a completely different metaphysics. This is exactly what occurred during the Roman Empire with a multitude of underground religious cults, of which Christianity was just one. Most of these cults originated from the civilisation which Toynbee called the Syrian.

In the late stages of civilisation, the rebel faction comes from outside the system. Thus, Neo's initiation removes him from the civilisation he was born into and places him in a completely different one. He receives an Esoteric initiation but the cost is that he must become an outsider from the world he knows. Neo makes that choice and, in doing so, faces persecution by the Dominant Minority. That, too, is historically accurate.

Just like *Star Wars*, however, the need for *The Matrix* to have a classic Hollywood happy ending does cause some distortion in the story from a historical point of view. Neo and Morpheus' victory at the end of the story represents the arrival of Toynbee's Universal Church and this is broadly correct. We can find a direct parallel to this in the case of the Roman Empire which, after attempting to persecute the Rebel Priests of nascent Christianity, eventually made Christianity the state church. In that way, the Rebel Priests of the Classical civilisation did eventually "win" but only after centuries of persecution.

The analogy with Christianity here seems quite intentional on the part of the writers of *The Matrix*. Neo corresponds to Jesus, while Morpheus maps more accurately to St Paul. Neo, like Jesus, is a member of the proletariat of late-stage civilisation who is already on an Exoteric life path but breaks with this to pursue the Esoteric. Morpheus, although we don't really know his backstory in *The Matrix*, is like St Paul in that he is an educated man who knows in great detail how the civilisation works and who attempts to translate a new metaphysics into the terms of that civilisation. But the Rebel

Priests of late civilisation do not win personal victories. Jesus, St Paul and St Peter were all killed by the Roman authorities. As individuals, they did not live to see the "victory" of the church that they founded. Still, the overall symbolism is correct. The Universal Church does arise after the Universal State. That is the order of events that Toynbee identified across civilisations.

The Matrix is also accurate in showing us a pathway trodden by many Orphans of late-stage civilisation who seek the Esoteric outside mainstream culture, as does Neo. The seeming paradox is that this happens against a backdrop of peace and prosperity, where the easy pathway is to acquiesce to the Universal State run by the Dominant Minority. At the Physical and Exoteric levels of being, the late-stage civilisation provides all that is needed. But, to use Jesus' words from the Bible, some people do not live by bread alone. They *need* the Esoteric. Once we strip away all of the glitz, glamour and violence of *The Matrix*, we see that the story of Neo is the story of one such person.

We have now covered in broad terms both the microcosmic and macrocosmic aspects of the three Orphan Stories we have looked at in depth, and it is worth reiterating how surprising it should be that each so accurately portrays a distinct part of the macrocosmic cycle of civilisation. Of course, it is only surprising to us in the modern West since we have told ourselves that stories are just for entertainment and not something to be taken seriously as a source of truth. Our analysis has shown otherwise and proves the point made earlier in the book that stories contain more truth rather than less.

We are about to now take that insight to another level and reveal a further ulterior motive behind the choice of our three Orphan Stories. Two of them go beyond a mere correspondence to the macrocosmic cycle to capture some fundamental truths about the civilisation that we live in: the modern West. This shouldn't be that surprising since they are two of the most popular films of all time. In them, we will find the symbolic keys to understanding our modern world, and they, therefore, provide a fitting end to this part of the book and an introduction to Part 4, where we will turn our analysis to our own civilisation. Let's now investigate how *Star Wars* and *The Matrix* represent the primary archetypes of the Dominant Minority.

The Tyrannical Father

We have already seen the parallels between the Orphan Story of Luke Skywalker and that of Hamlet, especially that both young men are given a Call to Adventure which is explicitly an invitation to the shadow form of Orphan transcendence. The ghost of Hamlet's father appears to him in the dark of the night to order him to murder his shadow Father, Claudius. In the dramatic climax of *Return of the Jedi*, Palpatine will instruct Luke Skywalker to do the same by killing his own father, Darth Vader, with an explicit call to come to *the dark side*. Since the story of *Hamlet* takes place in the royal court and since the consequences of Hamlet choosing to murder his shadow Father bring the destruction of that royal court, it is true that Shakespeare connected the microcosm to the macrocosm in his play. He had shown in *Hamlet* and many of his other works how the failure of microcosmic transcendence can wreak havoc at the societal level.

What differentiates *Star Wars* in this respect is the explicit way in which it builds into the macrocosmic context of the story a civilisational battle between the Creative and Dominant Minority. It is important to note that George Lucas apparently took inspiration from the Nazis in portraying both Vader and the empire itself as a military dictatorship. But more broadly, what *Star Wars* shows us is the exact form which the Universal State takes during what Toynbee called the Disintegration period of the civilisational cycle. It is the stereotypical way in which the Dominant Minority has historically exerted itself. It can be no coincidence, therefore, that both the Nazis and the fascists in Italy, as well as Napoleon before them, had all couched their imperial ambitions in reference to history. Napoleon and Mussolini both made explicit references to ancient Rome, while the Nazis drew parallels between the Reich they hoped to create and the Holy Roman Empire.

All of this is, of course, a result of the historical consciousness which has been such a prominent feature of modern European civilisation, and we should point out in this regard that the threat of tyranny and its historical manifestation have been well-known in Europe for centuries and were actually foundational in the creation of the United States. Many people in the 18th century believed Europe was already heading back down the path to tyranny, and the United States became home to those who were trying to flee from that perceived tyranny. That is why an American movie such as *Star Wars* can portray tyranny with a great deal of historical precision, and why a mass audience can appreciate it.

To a very large extent, America was founded on a rejection of both the Tyrannical Father as an archetype and the historical understanding that the arrival of the archetype was indicative of the downfall of a civilisation. This is historically accurate since what comparative history shows us is that it really is the Tyrannical Father who leads the creation of the Universal State of a civilisation. The difference is that for most of history, the people who lived during the Universal State didn't see it this way. The Romans embraced Julius Caesar and then Octavian in much the same way that large segments of the European public embraced Napoleon and, later, Hitler and Mussolini. The Dominant Minority has not historically been seen as a problem by the people living under it, at least as far as we know from the historical records, which are, of course, written by the victors.

It is perhaps only modern European civilisation and its offshoots in places like the United States which have seen the Tyrannical Father as a problem, and especially as a problem linked to history. It is partly this which explains the popularity of a movie like *Star Wars* which is not just a perfectly observed Orphan Story at the microcosmic level but also at the macrocosmic. The genius stroke that George Lucas pulled off was to place the macrocosmic battle right at the heart of the microcosmic one. This creates a brilliant double meaning, one that fits with our archetypal logic. Darth Vader is not just a member of the Dominant Minority, he is Luke Skywalker's father. Because the story comes at the midpoint of the civilisational cycle, Vader represents both the shadow microcosmic and macrocosmic Father offering Luke Skywalker as a microcosmic and macrocosmic Orphan a shadow Call to Adventure.

We have already seen that the *dark side* represents the call of the shadow, which tempts the Orphan not to fulfil their archetypal mission. As Sky-walker's father, Vader represents the microcosmic dark side, inviting the Orphan to transcend into a Shadow Orphan–Shadow Parent pairing. As the leader of the Dominant Minority, Vader represents the macrocosmic dark side, inviting the societal Orphans into acquiescence to a Tyrannical Father. Luke Skywalker is both the microcosmic and macrocosmic Orphan. The difference between him and Hamlet is that Skywalker has an alternative Call to Adventure in the form of Elders offering him an Esoteric initiation. At the macrocosmic level, they are what we have called the Rebel Elders, since they are in battle with the newly emergent Dominant Minority.

Putting all this together, we get the following breakdown of the archetypal calculus that faces Luke Skywalker:-

Luke Skywalker	Microcosmic	Macrocosmic
Esoteric Initiation	Elder (Obi-wan, Yoda)	Creative Minority
Shadow Initiation (the dark side)	Shadow Orphan - Shadow Parent (Vader)	Dominant Minority (Tyrannical Father)

Since we know that the Rebel Alliance wins in the end and that they represent the Creative Minority, there is a symmetry between the two choices available to Skywalker. He can choose Esoteric Initiation through the Elders Obi-wan and Yoda and rise to a leadership position in the Creative Minority as the Sage archetype. Alternatively, he can choose to give in to the shadow forms of the Orphan, which means joining his Shadow Father in a leadership position in the Dominant Minority. The implication, of course, is that Skywalker will become his father and manifest the hyper-masculine himself, just as Hamlet does in Shakespeare's play.

The reason all this works and almost certainly why *Star Wars* became such a huge hit in the United States is not just because it matches the historical scholarship in an abstract sense or that it matches our archetypal logic, but because it matches the popular understanding of history on which the United States was founded. We will be going into more detail about this in Part 4, but almost everybody knows the short version, since it is baked into the

Declaration of Independence and all of the grievances against George III, who was portrayed as a tyrant just like many of the other kings of Europe. The reality was, in many ways, very different. But the story in the popular imagination revolves around a rejection of the Father that is part of the longer tradition leading back to the Reformation, with the denial of another societal Father archetype, the Pope. In short, the rejection of the Tyrannical Father archetype and his political manifestation are part of the origin myth of the United States. Luke Skywalker is not just the perfect microcosmic and macrocosmic Orphan; he is the archetypal Orphan of America who founded a nation based on a rejection of tyranny.

All of this fits the fact that many of those who migrated to America really were the archetypal Orphans of Europe, and that they really were fleeing what they perceived to be tyranny. What's more, the foundation of the United States even comes at the right point in the historical cycle because the US was born out of a form of imperialism, albeit a different kind of imperialism that we will investigate more in Part 4. Thus, the story of Star Wars is archetypally accurate, not just in abstract microcosmic and macrocosmic considerations but in terms of the actual history of the United States.

What all of this implies is that the archetype of Tyrannical Father already had a dual resonance in the minds of western civilisation long before George Lucas made *Star Wars*. The Tyrannical Father is synonymous with civilisational decline. That is what the archetype means for us, and this meaning is especially pronounced in the United States since it really was baked into the foundational myth of that nation (using "myth" here in a literal and non-derogatory sense). The fact that *Star Wars* is one of the most popular movies ever and that Darth Vader is one of the most memorable characters in movie history is because we know what the macrocosmic Tyrannical Father looks like. We "know" it deep down at the archetypal level. This is a crucial point to remember as we now turn to our second movie, which has a very different take on the archetype of the Dominant Minority.

The Devouring Mother

We said earlier that *The Matrix* takes place during the Disintegration phase of the civilisational cycle. All of history tells us exactly what *Star Wars* told us, which is that it is the Tyrannical Father who comes to power during this phase. He creates what Toynbee called the Universal State, which takes the form of an empire run through military dominance. If *The Matrix* does, indeed, take place during the Disintegration phase of the cycle, we would expect to see somebody like Darth Vader running the show. But the curious fact about *The Matrix* - the mystery that we must now attempt to solve - is that it does not feature a Tyrannical Father.

Star Wars presents us with a picture-perfect example of the archetypal logic we have been developing in this book, especially as it relates to the shared structure of the microcosm and macrocosm. As an archetypal Orphan, Luke Skywalker must separate from his parents and form a relationship with an Elder. To join Vader represents a dual failure of his archetypal mission and would bring him into a Shadow Orphan–Shadow Parent relationship at both the microcosmic and macrocosmic levels at the same time. There are two extra points that we touched on in the last section that we must now bring to the centre of our attention.

We said that *Star Wars* represents, in an abstract sense related to the findings of comparative history, the turning point of the civilisational cycle. This is the transition point between the Creative Minority ruling in a decentralised and localised fashion and the Dominant Minority which aims to rule through force over a homogenised mass of people living in the large cities. Obi-wan and Yoda are the Creative Minority. Darth Vader and Palpatine are the Dominant Minority. But we also said that *Star Wars* represented the actual history of the United States, at least the one in the popular imagination. The United States was founded on a rejection of the Tyrannical Father in the form of George III, and, crucially, Europe was seen by many at that time as going down the path towards tyranny.

In our terminology, what that means is that it was believed that Europe was already manifesting what we have called the Dominant Minority around the time when the United States was founded. Many of the people who migrated to the United States did so to avoid that perceived tyranny. Although nobody would have used our terminology, we could say that the people who founded the United States were making the exact choice that Luke Skywalker has to make, which is between the Creative Minority (the USA) and the Dominant Minority (the kings of Europe). All of this fits with what the comparative historians saw too, since the foundation of the United States does appear to come around the middle of the cycle of western civilisation.

If that is true, the fact that *The Matrix* is set in the modern world, albeit some time in the future, means we are faced with the fascinating prospect that *The Matrix* is a symbolic description of the Universal State of western civilisation, and that we are living through it. Again, this fits with the analysis of the comparative historians, Toynbee and Spengler, who analysed the two world wars as the formative events that would lead to the Universal State of the West. It is noteworthy in this respect that the two world wars really did see the arrival of the Tyrannical Father in the form of military dictators trying to establish empires. That's why George Lucas could draw inspiration for his movie from that era. This will be the topic of our analysis in Part 4, but, for now, we can simply note that the Tyrannical Fathers did not win the wars. If we are in the Universal State, it is not a Universal State run by the Tyrannical Father. Let's interrogate the symbolism of *The Matrix* to see if we find any clues about the archetypal dynamic that has occurred instead.

That *The Matrix* symbolically represents the manifestation of the Universal State of the West is evidenced by the fact that the world in which Neo lives, the world of the matrix, implies total control by the Dominant Minority over the public. Yet, we find no trace of a Tyrannical Father in *The Matrix* at either the microcosmic or macrocosmic level. In fact, this is one of the few ways in which *The Matrix*, an otherwise perfect Orphan Story, breaks the archetypal pattern. Recall Theme 2 from our analysis of the Orphan Story earlier, where we pointed out that making sense of the break with the parents is a central issue of the story, which follows from the archetypal logic that dictates that the Child-Parent relationship must give way to allow the Orphan-Elder to develop. This is exactly why George Lucas could make

Vader the father of Luke Skywalker later in the *Star Wars* trilogy. It's a perfect fit with the archetypal logic.

In *The Matrix*, however, Neo's parents are completely absent from the microcosmic aspect of the story. This is unusual, but we can perhaps write it off as an oversight or maybe even creative licence on the part of the writers. The archetypal patterns are not rules after all, and, even if they were, rules are made to be broken. But when combined with the fact that there is no Tyrannical Father at the macrocosmic level, the absence of the Parent archetype in general becomes very problematic. In *The Matrix* we have a perfectly told Orphan Story that we know occurs during the Disintegration phase of the civilisational cycle, yet the Parent archetype is absent in the exact two places where we expect to find it: the microcosm and macrocosm. This cannot be a coincidence.

The question then arises: what archetype is representing the Dominant Minority in the universe of *The Matrix?* All of history tells us to expect the Tyrannical Father. Instead, we have the agents led by Agent Smith, and whatever else we want to say about the agents, they are not Tyrannical Father archetypes. The macrocosmic Tyrannical Father is exactly like Darth Vader. He is the leader of a regime that rules through brute force. He requires rules, hierarchies, uniforms, and weaponry, all of which manifest at the Exoteric level through the institution of the armed forces. The Tyrannical Father sits at the top of the hierarchy as the visible and overt embodiment of its power. He is out in the open for all to see. That is what *Star Wars* shows us, and that is what history shows us.

By contrast, the agents of *The Matrix* are not out in the open. They do not lead anyone. They are, in fact, not even known by the people whom they govern. The power they have is entirely covert and clandestine. While, of course, covert operations to secure political goals have been around since time immemorial, the governance of an entire population by covert methods is deeply unusual, especially in the late stages of civilisation where power and governance are channelled through the cults of personality that rule over the homogenous mass of people who live in the mega-cities.

The Matrix, therefore, has a very unusual Dominant Minority. But we can also see a big difference in the way the general public is represented in the film. In *Star Wars*, the general public is the homogenous mass of late civilisation represented by the stormtroopers in their matching uniforms and identical behaviour patterns, following the hyper-masculine example set by their macrocosmic Father, Darth Vader. What are we to make, then, of the people who live in the matrix and who should, in theory, be the ones who manifest the power of the Dominant Minority? They are not following in the footsteps of Agent Smith because they do not know that Agent Smith exists, nor do they know that the matrix exists. Whatever else we want to say about the Tyrannical Father, we know where we stand with him. He is out there in the open, leading by example. He creates Exoteric institutions and rules through them in a visible and overt fashion. The Tyrannical Father wants you to see his power. It is in his interests to show it off because he knows that the projection of power will scare off most would-be challengers and will convince the majority to comply with his wishes.

When we put it this way, we can start to see how *The Matrix* does begin to fit the definition of a Dominant Minority because, even though the agents do not gain power through the overt compliance of the public, they do gain power through their covert compliance. The concept of *power* is explicitly used in the film since we know that the matrix is itself one giant ruse to keep the people distracted while they fulfil their role in generating actual power, electricity. We should know by now that we need to interpret this fact symbolically and that one of the obvious symbolic meanings would be political power.

The Tyrannical Father rules through a formal, Exoteric role that sits atop institutions that are also formal and Exoteric in nature. He is almost certainly a military dictator, and the roles around him are military roles like generals. The Tyrannical Father manifests his power at the Exoteric. But in the matrix the exercise of power is entirely covert. Therefore, it has no Exoteric manifestation. That is why the agents are completely unknown to the public. Thus, the absence of the Tyrannical Father in *The Matrix* also amounts to the absence of the Exoteric altogether.

It is for this reason that if we try to formulate the archetypal calculus for

Neo in *The Matrix* as we did earlier for Luke Skywalker in *Star Wars*, we find gaps in the table:-

Neo	Microcosmic	Macrocosmic
Esoteric Initiation	Elder (Morpheus)	Rebel Elder
Shadow Initiation	??? (Corporate Job)	???
General public living in the matrix		
Exoteric Initiation	Shadow Orphan -???	??? – Acquiescent Orphans

The microcosmic and macrocosmic meaning of Neo's positive archetypal mission is clear and fits the exact same pattern as we saw in *Star Wars*, *A Wizard of Earthsea*, and many other Orphan Stories. Neo is called to Esoteric initiation via a Rebel Elder, which will complete the Orphan-Elder pairing, leading to a successful transition to the Adult archetype. All that makes sense. What is not clear is the nature of the shadow option that Neo has. We know it entails his boring corporate job, but what does it mean at the macrocosmic level? The Dominant Minority is represented by the agents, but the agents do not manifest any particular archetype, and certainly not the one we expect to find, which is the Tyrannical Father.

If we think more about the agents, we realise that what they actually represent is the system itself i.e. the matrix. Does this mean that the system is the Dominant Minority and that is why there is no archetypal manifestation in the movie? That is certainly one way to think about it. In *The Matrix*, we have the Shadow Parent who is such a shadow that they are all but invisible. In this way, the absence of Neo's parents at the microcosmic level does, in fact, match the macrocosmic dynamic since Neo has been searching for the macrocosmic parent (the matrix) and needs Morpheus to show it to him.

Here we have the first big symbolic clue that can help us solve this mystery. What if the matrix is the symbol of the macrocosmic Shadow Parent? We have already noted that the operation of power in *The Matrix* is that the system uses the general public to generate electricity. But there is a variation on this metaphor used later in the film, where Agent Smith refers to the general public as "crops". Both of these work as metaphors since batteries and food are *chemical energy* in a scientific sense. Agent Smith, as the representative of the Dominant Minority of late civilisation of *The Matrix*, views humans as a form of food, and it is clear that the matrix consumes its human subjects. What does the word "devour" mean? It means to eat or to swallow. What is the non-masculine form of the Will that we have identified in our archetypal logic from earlier? It is the **devouring** feminine. Can it be that the matrix is the devouring feminine?

We see the symbolic evidence for this reading early in the film when Neo is being disconnected from the matrix and where he learns to use his "real" body for the first time. Where is Neo's physical body? It is attached to the matrix in an exact replica of the womb. We see Neo dramatically exiting the womb in a fashion that is almost identical to birth. This symbolism works perfectly to denote the idea of being born again, which is directly relevant to Neo's microcosmic story. But the macrocosmic symbolism is that Neo is being removed from the womb of the matrix – from the Devouring Mother. And that means, of course, that he had earlier been under the domination of the Devouring Mother, just like all the other people in the matrix. The matrix is the Mother and Neo and the others are the Child. The film reinforces this symbol later by showing an actual child hooked up to the matrix when Morpheus is explaining the system to Neo.

All of this is an exact match for our archetypal logic. Our fundamental pairing is the Child-Parent, and it is the failure of the break in the Child-Parent relationship which prevents the formation of the Orphan-Elder one. When Morpheus creates the Orphan-Elder relationship with Neo, he is forcing the end of an implied Child-Parent relationship that Neo must be in. We know that the Child-Parent relationship becomes common at the macrocosmic level in late-stage civilisation. For seemingly all of the history of civilisation, the parent in question has been the Tyrannical Father. What *The Matrix* shows us is that the Mother is just as capable of being the dominating parent, although her manner of dominance is very different. That is what the direct symbolism of the movie shows. It is also what the broader symbolism shows.

The Tyrannical Father rules over the body. The Caesars of Rome did not care a jot what any of their subjects thought. They were not interested in the mind. It is the Devouring Mother who rules not through physical force but through control of the mind. That is why gaslighting is one of the main tactics the Mother uses to keep control of her child. Neo is the gaslit Orphan who has been lied to his whole life and whose mission is a quest for the truth. It is Morpheus who removes him from the Devouring Mother in order to tell him the truth.

We can now fill in the blanks in our archetypal table:-

Neo	Microcosmic	Macrocosmic
Esoteric Initiation	Elder (Morpheus)	Rebel Elder
Shadow Initiation	Shadow Parent - (Corporate Job)	Devouring Mother (the matrix)
General public living in the matrix		
Exoteric Initiation	Shadow Orphan – Devouring Mother	Devouring Mother – Acquiescent Orphans

Although we can only speculate, there are two probable reasons why the writers of The Matrix were unable to represent the archetype of the Devouring Mother. One of them is a symbolic and archetypal issue. In the modern West, we know what the Tyrannical Father looks like, and we know how to represent him in an archetypal sense. What we lack in western culture is an archetype that represents the devouring feminine.

This was a point that was made by the poet Robert Graves, who, like Jung and others, believed that the emerging question of the feminine was a major turning point in western civilisation. According to Graves, the West has lacked an archetype for the devouring feminine ever since ancient times. Our primary archetype for the feminine has been the Virgin Mary, and she is an archetype that is wholly good and virtuous. She symbolises the positive form of the Mother. We have known how to represent the positive form of the Mother, but we have lacked an archetype for the shadow form, for the Devouring Mother. This contrasts with other cultures, particularly India, where the devouring feminine is represented by the goddess Kali.

Thus, we can speculate that the reason why the writers of *The Matrix* were unable to find an archetypal representation for their Dominant Minority, which manifests the Devouring Mother pattern of Will, is because western civilisation does not have this idea in our cultural symbolic library. We know perfectly well how to represent the Tyrannical Father since so much of modern western civilisation has been a rebellion against and rejection of that archetype. But we don't understand the Devouring Mother. That is why the writers of *The Matrix* had to represent her as a kind of null entity – a system.

But there's another reason why there is difficulty in portraying the macrocosmic manifestation of the Dominant Minority of western civilisation and that is because the system itself, and *The Matrix* is very correct to call it a system, is highly unusual and perhaps unprecedented. *The Matrix* actually does a very good symbolic job of characterising the broad properties of that system. It is to those properties that we will turn shortly in Part 4 of this book, as we come back to the "real world" and look at how the pattern of dominance of the West has evolved.

Summary

The observations from the previous section may be hard for some to swallow. We have become used to stories, and especially films, as being nothing more than entertainment with perhaps a little bit of "social commentary" thrown in for good measure. The idea that storytellers can capture fundamental truths about the world we live in is something that would be foreign to many people. Nevertheless, that is what we are assuming with our analysis, and that is why we have paid such extensive attention to stories in this book. Storytelling is an integrated art form. In the greatest of writers, it goes beyond what can be understood and comprehended by the conscious mind. It necessarily draws on the whole of our being, including the hidden parts of the psyche. The great writers transcend themselves and their time through the use of timeless archetypes. In doing so, they are able to say something important about their own time in comparison with the eternal. That is why great stories resonate, both when they are written and long after.

We have seen that each of the three Orphan Stories we have analysed in depth belongs to a specific phase of the civilisational cycle. We can make this clearer by plotting them all on the same diagram, as follows:-

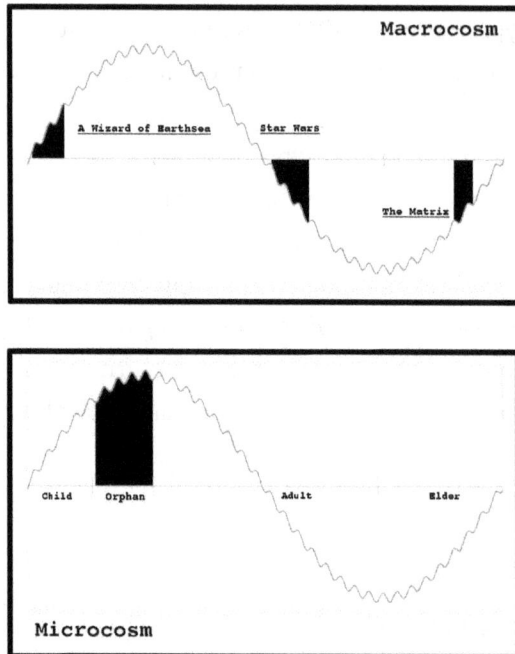

In *A Wizard of Earthsea*, the Orphan Story of Ged takes place in the decentralised and heterogenous world of early civilisation, where the political institutions of society are weak and the Esoteric is what holds together the various communities. In this world, Ged's Esoteric initiation requires no rebellion against either a Tyrannical Father or a Devouring Mother because the Dominant Minority has not yet formed. The civilisation is ruled by the Creative Minority, of which Ged will later become a member when he transcends to the Elder archetype and begins to initiate the next generation.

Both Luke Skywalker and Neo's Orphan Stories are different in this respect since they take place against the backdrop of the Dominant Minority and the choice between Esoteric initiation with the Rebel Elders or Exoteric initiation into the Universal State of late civilisation. We saw that George Lucas' representation of the Tyrannical Father dynamic is exactly correct according to the archetypal logic and the lessons of comparative history, which show that the Universal State of late civilisation is always a military dictatorship.

Finally, we saw that *The Matrix* breaks this mould. The crucial point for us to understand is that it breaks the mould in a way that is not arbitrary but is in keeping with our archetypal logic requiring a Dominant Parent in the late stage of civilisation. What's even more important, however, is that it breaks the mould in the same way that modern Western civilisation has broken the mould. We live in a time where a Universal State reigns, but it is a Universal State that is very different from the historical norm. It is so different that many people are unaware of it. Just like the people in the matrix, the operation of power goes unnoticed.

Archetypally speaking, the Dominant Minority that rules over our Universal State is not the Tyrannical Father but the Devouring Mother. All of this implies, of course, that we are living in an Age of the Orphan.

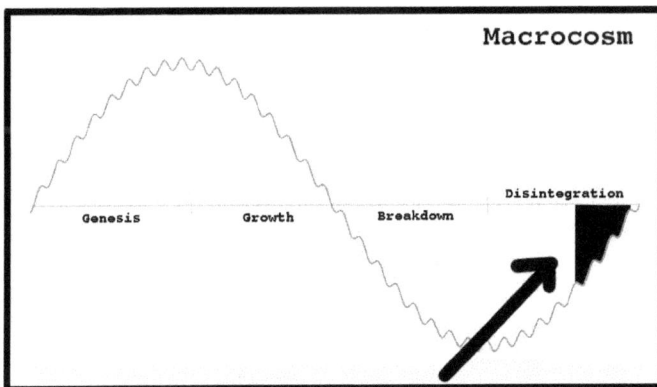

We are here:

In the next and final section of the book, we return to the "real world" as we sketch out the nature of the Universal State of western civilisation and why it manifests the Devouring Mother instead of the Tyrannical Father.

Part 4: The Universal State of America

Our analysis for much of this book has relied exclusively on the comparative historical scholarship of the British historian, Toynbee. Toynbee's methodical approach allowed us to incorporate history alongside the other schematic concepts that formed our integrated model. This has given us a useful abstraction and a way to talk about the relationships between microcosm and macrocosm.

Of course, we don't experience life as the working out of a set of abstractions. Nobody grows up thinking, "I'm currently going through an Orphan metamorphosis" or "I'm in the middle of a Hero's Journey". Even if we did consciously think about it that way, the difference it would make would likely be minimal. We interact with the world based on our entire being, and our entire being comprises far more than just the little voice in our heads. It's for this reason that the way in which each of us navigates through the challenges of life, especially the archetypal transformations, reveals our character and our personality. We learn something about ourselves that we weren't conscious of. That is why the phases of life really are Hero's Journeys since they involve a confrontation with and incorporation of the Unconscious. For most of us, the Orphan phase of life is the first time this happens. It is our first Hero's Journey.

It was a second comparative historian, a contemporary of Toynbee, Oswald Spengler, who realised that the same was true at the macrocosmic level. A civilisation has character and personality. It resonates at the Esoteric level of being. Accordingly, the way in which a civilisation responds to its challenges also reveals something about it. Toynbee was correct to see the challenge-and-response dynamic as crucial to the survival of a civilisation at the Physical level of being. But the challenge-and-response dynamic also reveals the deeper beliefs of a civilisation; its character or soul.

It was this Esoteric aspect of civilisation that was the main concern of Spengler. Toynbee was the rigorous, cautious, and methodical scholar. Spengler was the romantic who was apt to get carried away on flights of fancy. Where Spengler excelled was in a phenomenological description of culture. Spengler wanted to know not merely what pattern the overall arc of civilisation took; he wanted to know what it felt like to be part of a specific civilisation and how that was different from what it felt like to be part of other civilisations.

Of course, in a more general sense, it's true to say that both Toynbee and Spengler were practicing a form of Esoteric history. Most historical scholarship takes the form that we remember from school. It is the recounting of facts. Such-and-such a battle was won and lost. Such-and-such a ruler came to power. Such-and-such a dynasty was established. We can call this the Exoteric approach to history. It is concerned with what can be seen from outward appearances and empirical data.

The Esoteric approach is concerned with the patterns that underlie appearances. Toynbee concerned himself with the broad patterns that we have already noted. Spengler was concerned with the even more Esoteric question of what were the formative concepts of a culture and how were they related. He believed that these formative ideas were born out of a connection with a specific geography. This notion fitted in well with both 19th-century materialism and the romantic movement's worship of "nature". Accordingly, Spengler also made much of the concept of "instinct". He believed we have a kind of cultural instinct which we inherit from our society and whose genius manifests itself in the core themes of a civilisation. The instinct is formed at the beginning of the civilisation and stays with it even after it has spread to new geographic regions.

There is at least one issue on which Toynbee explicitly disagreed with Spengler and that is around the nature of civilisation and, specifically, whether the death of civilisation is inevitable. Spengler had used a biological metaphor to characterise that death. For him, it was as if the civilisation lost its life force, just as we do as individuals in old age. Toynbee criticised this approach, but his alternative explanation was that civilisations "commit suicide". This idea is equally problematic from a logical point of view. Spengler had a fatalistic view of the matter, which was well in keeping with the German romanticism of his time, while Toynbee wanted to deny that civilisations must die; all we had to do was stop them from committing suicide.

It's important to understand that these issues were not merely academic for the two men and those who read their histories. One of the results of the great works of comparative scholarship that became possible in 19th-century Europe was the realisation, made explicit through detailed analysis, that European civilisation was just one among many, that the history of Europe was not unique, and that European civilisation could, almost certainly would, "die" just as had other civilisations throughout history. These realisations came during a time when the technological changes wrought by science and the industrial revolution were changing the nature of society in profound ways. On the one hand, there was giddy and naïve optimism; on the other hand, feelings of despair perhaps best captured by the philosopher who made that subject his own, Kierkegaard.

Both of these developments are predicted by the proletarianisation process that Toynbee described and that we have dubbed the Age of the Orphan. Disinheritance can lead to a feeling of freedom and optimism when the bonds of the past are broken and attention is turned towards a bright future. Another pathway is despair. It can be no coincidence that the romantic/existentialist movement mostly took place in continental Europe because much of the continent was a latecomer to the form of politics and economy that we now take for granted but which was still relatively new at that time: the combination of nation state and industrial capitalism. It is worth dwelling on this point briefly since it can help to explain the difference in attitude between the British and German historians, Toynbee and Spengler. It will also be directly relevant to the direction of our own analysis as we proceed in this final section of the book.

Germany as Hamlet

Although a historian, Spengler's work fits within the romantic/existentialist movement, and he incorporated a number of its themes into his scholarly and non-scholarly books. With the publication of the first volume of his great work, *The Decline of the West*, Spengler went from obscurity to being almost a celebrity. As with other scholars of his time, his work became popular in Nazi circles, and this is not accidental since the Nazis also borrowed a number of themes from the romantic movement, especially in its nationalistic form. Nationalism in Germany had arisen as part of the push to unify the German-speaking peoples into a single nation state. This process proved problematic. It took Germany many decades to try and enact the restructuring necessary and finally required the diplomatic genius of Bismarck to make it happen. In Bismarck's famous "blood and iron" speech, we hear the unmistakable sound of the hyper-masculine which would manifest in the two world wars - further evidence that the Age of the Orphan had arrived.

What we find in 19th-century Germany is the onset of two of the archetypal outcomes we have spent a great deal of time analysing in this book. The one we all know about is the hyper-masculine, since that became an urgent geopolitical and military reality in the 20th century. But what preceded that in the more refined intellectual circles of the 19th and early 20th centuries was the lamentation at the loss of authority and tradition. It is because of the esteem held for scholarship in the German-speaking lands that we have some of the most elevated expressions of the existential angst associated with the Orphan archetype in the writings of Kierkegaard, Walter Benjamin, and Nietzsche, to name only three.

The Germans had found themselves in a position where they needed to unify for geopolitical reasons. This required the dismantling of the existing political apparatus and the authority it had based on tradition. Much of the work had already been done Napoleon and so we can usefully frame the event as a Hero's Journey with Napoleon providing the Call to Adventure. This is not a spurious analogy since many people at the time really felt as if there was a new beginning taking place. It was the frustration that came from the perceived failure to act by the political class which provided the impetus for much of the nationalist movement. The Germans needed to dismantle tradition and replace it with something created from scratch. Much of the drive for this came from the intellectual class. Thus, we have the strange spectacle of scholars and intellectuals trying to write a new German identity into existence. The composer Richard Wagner, for example, wrote a number of essays with this goal in mind, including one called "What is German?"

These seemingly harmless scholarly questions about identity would later become a huge political and military crisis. Nationalism was only one of the responses to the conundrum; other -isms included Marxism, socialism, communism, anarchism, and nihilism. From a mainstream political point of view, it was nationalism which would ultimately win the day, as it would throughout most of Europe. It is not well remembered how much grief this caused in Europe itself, and not just via war.

If we remember that the Orphan's mission is to move to an Adult identity in the four domains of economy, politics, religion and sexuality, all of these imply an existing cultural framework. What happens when that framework gets changed? Identities become uncertain. That's what happened in central and eastern Europe. Cultural and political identities were realigned based on little more than a common language. There were now countries for people who spoke German and for people who spoke Italian etc. That pattern might have worked for nations like Britain and France but it did not work in central Europe, where the Holy Roman Empire and the Austro-Hungarian Empire had been multi-lingual and multi-national from the start.

The result was that millions of people became stateless, and millions more found themselves suddenly outsiders in places where their ancestors had lived for centuries. There were real political ramifications too. Hitler partly justified his annexation of the Sudetenland in order to "protect" German-speaking peoples in that region. It is less well remembered that Poland, Hungary and Slovakia also took the opportunity to acquire land at that time to protect "their own people". The abstract, philosophical identity crisis of the 19th century became a life-and-death identity crisis in the 20th.

In almost literal terms, we can see that this was the Age of the Orphan.

Millions of Europeans found themselves orphaned from the places where their ancestors had lived. Suddenly, they were without a *fatherland*. Historians may analyse this in purely political terms, but what we can see in the writings of the 19th century is that the political manifestation came after the Esoteric one. All of this lends weight to our archetypal analysis, which aims to view these events not from the isolated standpoint of politics or warfare but from a holistic point of view.

It is against this backdrop that we must understand the work of Toynbee, but especially of Spengler. The different attitudes of the two men towards the question of the death of civilisation reveal a crucial difference between their nations at the time that they were writing. In Germany, far more than in Britain, there was a genuine existential angst at play in the 19th and early 20th centuries. The question was not just that civilisations die, which is an abstract and rather academic one. The question was: doesn't this mean that western civilisation will die? It is one thing to confront the death of civilisation as an abstraction. It is a very different thing to confront the death of the civilisation you are a part of. Spengler and many of his countrymen clearly believed they were living through a time where the death of their culture was at stake.

We have just pointed out that there was a German identity crisis beginning in earnest in the 19th century. German nationalism was one attempt to piece together a new identity with reference to old Nordic mythology and other means. Spengler's work took the same underlying drive and used it to create a work of genius. He wanted to define once and for all what western civilisation really was and, in doing so, to also clarify Germany's position. No doubt, this was also a very important reason behind Spengler's meteoric rise to fame. His was a message others wanted to hear. His drive to uncover the hidden meanings of western civilisation was surely related to the strength of the identity crisis that was felt in Germany.

That identity crisis and the scholarly and philosophical way in which it manifested follow a pattern we have already seen in our Orphan Stories and one of those in particular is *Hamlet*. Eventually, Hamlet will act. But, first, he attempts to work through his problems in a philosophical fashion. Germany was a nation of philosophers and scholars. It was the scholars who would try to solve the German identity crisis. Like Hamlet, their failure to do so would end in acts of self-destructive violence. The story of Germany is the story of Hamlet, a desperate attempt to fashion one's own identity and reach "maturity" in circumstances which made that almost impossible.

Of course, there really does seem to be something of Hamlet in the German character. The historian, Wolfgang Menzel, wrote in 1828, "The Germans do not do much, but they write all the more." The Germans, like Hamlet, preferred to think before they acted. Just as Hamlet had been blocked from attaining the Exoteric identity he was destined for, Germany was blocked from attaining the modern form of European political and economic maturity which had come to be embodied in the nation state and industrial capitalism. Germany was the nation of great composers, philosophers, artists, and scientists. This Creative Minority was no longer what was needed. What was needed was Bismarck's *blood and iron* which could very well be the catchphrase of the Dominant Minority.

For reasons that will become clearer later, the correspondence between Britain and Germany here is not accidental since Britain really was playing the role of Claudius to Germany's Hamlet. That is, Britain was trying to stifle the emergence of the new form of German nationhood, which included its late arrival to the game of industrial capitalism. It was trying to prevent Germany from *coming-of-age.*

All of this may sound rather poetic and quaint, but we must remember that our analysis implies a direct correspondence between microcosm and macrocosm. When we say that Germany was like Hamlet, we really are saying that the same dynamic was at work. That's why the collective psychology of Germany in the 19th century mirrors that of Hamlet. But the correspondence went beyond the merely psychological to include, most importantly, the resort to ruinous violence.

Are such correspondences just coincidences? Are they metaphors designed to make incredibly complex events understandable? Our analysis implies that they are not, and that macrocosms need to be understood in the same way as microcosms. Let us now make that claim explicit.

Re-evaluating the Archetypes of the Macrocosm

To assist with our new perspective on the macrocosm, we can make use of a German thinker who was a big influence on Spengler and whose ideas are also directly relevant to our current purpose. We're talking about the philosopher, Friedrich Nietzsche. What we will need to do in this section is make a re-evaluation of our model in the vein of Nietzsche's *re-evaluation of values*. It turns out that the model we have developed so far has some biases built-in that we need to make explicit.

Remembering our archetypal table of the microcosm:-

Archetype	Level of Being		
	Physical	**Exoteric**	**Esoteric – Dominant Faculty**
The Child	Childhood	Son or daughter	Imagination
The Orphan	Puberty	Student, friend, protégé, initiate	Intellect
The Adult	Adulthood	Husband/wife, parent, citizen, employee/boss, churchgoer	Will
The Elder	Old Age - Death	Retiree, Mentor, Teacher	Soul

We noted that the Adult phase of life corresponds to the exercise of Will. Here is an obvious case where Nietzsche is relevant because it was Nietzsche's intellectual mentor (Elder!), Schopenhauer, who introduced the concept of Will in the 19th century. Nietzsche later modified the idea and called it will-to-power. Now, we don't need to get bogged down in a detailed discussion about what Will is and is not. Let's just highlight a few points that are relevant for our purposes.

Firstly, the will or will-to-power concept fits within our overall scheme when it is used either as a metaphysical principle of existence as in Schopenhauer or in a more limited biological or psychological fashion as Nietzsche sometimes implied. One of the variations of the idea that became popular in intellectual circles in the 19th century was called will-to-knowledge. We can see that this maps to the Orphan phase of our table via the faculty of Intellect. Meanwhile, will-to-power in the sense of a striving for the feeling of growth or power, maps to the Adult phase of the table.

What this implies is that there is a generic force called "Will" that promotes the growth of the individual which gets modified by the archetypal phases of life. Thus, during the Child phase, we would call it Will-to-imagination; Will-to-knowledge would belong to the Orphan; Will-to-power to the Adult; while a Schopenhauerian negation of Will would belong to the Elder. At base, all of these are the same Will-to-life which drives us forward through the archetypal phases.

Will-to-power has sometimes been interpreted specifically as the outward striving for resources in either a biological or political sense. We can see that this maps directly to both Toynbee and Spengler's description of the second half of the civilisational cycle as the civilisation expands outwards via military conquest. Thus, will-to-power is a perfect description of what happens beginning with the third phase of the civilisational cycle.

Here we have one of those "coincidences" which is indicative of archetypal phase changes. Nietzsche introduced his will-to-power at the exact time when western civilisation was embracing that at the geopolitical level. Moreover, he did so from Germany, a country that was desperately trying to restructure itself in order to join the geopolitical game that had been taking shape in the 19th century. As much as Nietzsche might have despised it, the attraction of the Nazis to his ideas makes obvious sense since will-to-power matches overt imperialism.

What is more interesting is the way in which these developments are mirrored in Nietzsche's own writings. In his later works, Nietzsche began to praise Rome over Greece for its "manliness". Meanwhile, the tone of his writing became ever more belligerent. The paradox is that Nietzsche despised the nationalism that was rising in Germany and had no love for the new German nation that Bismarck had put together. Consciously, Nietzsche held one position. Unconsciously, he seemed to be influenced by the zeitgeist taking form around him.

In very much the same way that Luther became a conduit for the zeitgeist of his era, even in the elements of that zeitgeist that he himself hated, Nietzsche seemed driven by some external force to give voice to a force that could have come from the civilisational cycle itself: the voice of the hyper-masculine. Thus, Nietzsche constructed for himself a philosophy based on a kind of Tyrannical Father. He wanted a philosophy that could "rule".

There is one specific example of this that is worth quoting at length since it touches on most of the themes we will be exploring in this final section of the book. It is passage 362 from *The Gay Science*. I am using the Walter Kaufmann translation and have edited it to highlight the most pertinent parts for our discussion:-

"Our faith that Europe will become more virile. — We owe it to Napoleon... that we now confront a succession of a few warlike centuries that have no parallel in history; in short, that we have entered *the classical age of war*,...the national movement out of which this war glory is growing is only the counter-shock against Napoleon and would not exist except for Napoleon. He should receive credit some day for the fact that in Europe the *man* has again become master over the businessman and the philistine – and perhaps even over "woman" who has been pampered by Christianity and the enthusiastic spirit of the eighteenth century,....Napoleon, who considered modern ideas and civilisation itself almost as a personal enemy, proved himself through this enmity as one of the greatest continuators of the Renaissance; he brought back again a whole slab of antiquity...and who knows whether this slab of antiquity might not finally become master again over the national movement..."

When Nietzsche refers to the "classical age of war", he is surely talking about the third and fourth phases of the civilisational cycle. His belief that this meant a revival of the Classical civilisation will become crucial to our analysis shortly, and we will deal with it extensively then. For now, we need only highlight one other crucial line from the above passage, which is that Nietzsche saw "man" once against becoming master over "woman". But we already know that the opposite occurred. It would not be the masculine form of Will that would dominate, but its feminine counterpart. It is no coincidence that this was tied in with the defeat of Napoleon and the subsequent defeat of the "masculine" will-to-power that was taking form in Germany when Nietzsche wrote the above passage.

We have the benefit of hindsight, and so it's easy to think badly of Nietzsche for his erroneous prediction. But that error was shared by many, including Spengler, and it was based on what appeared to be rock-solid evidence from history, which Nietzsche was intimately aware of since he was a scholar of the Classical. We have gone into detail about how the Tyrannical Father leads an era of war during the second half of the civilisational cycle. That is what Nietzsche was expecting to happen next in Europe. For several decades, at least, he was correct.

What differentiates Nietzsche is that, even more than Spengler, he embraced this development. We can clearly see from the above passage that Nietzsche saw it as a good thing, and this is tied in with a number of other elements in his thought. One of those elements is an idea he called the *re-evaluation of all values*. In our context, what this means is the re-evaluation of the second half of the civilisational cycle to no longer present it in a negative fashion but in a positive one. What Nietzsche was saying was something like, "we are living through the time when the Will must be exercised; we should do so without a guilty conscience."

This re-evaluation accounts for much of Nietzsche's philosophy, including his analysis of Christianity as the slave revolt against the master morality of Rome. Within our terminology, Christianity was the revolt of the Orphans of late civilisation against the Dominant Minority; that much is true. Nietzsche argues that history has been written, through Christianity, from the viewpoint of the slaves and not the masters. He invites us to think of the matter from the point of view of the elites. The Dominant Minority does not think of itself as evil. It carries out its Will with a clear conscience. Nietzsche would say that there is no such thing as the shadow form of the hyper-masculine. There is only a healthy expression of Will. Those who resent the Will are those whose own Will is lacking. The Tyrannical Father does not call himself such because he lives the fulfilment of his own power.

Nietzsche's re-evaluation encourages us not just to take the viewpoint of the elites but also of the macrocosm itself. If we allow that the macrocosm follows the same path as the microcosm, then the macrocosm must also go through its archetypal phases. The arrival of the third phase of the cycle is as inevitable as the arrival of adulthood for each one of us. That is the point which Nietzsche implies and which Spengler later made explicit.

What the re-evaluation concept allows us to see is that there was a bias in Toynbee's analysis, as evidenced by his use of the terms Breakdown, Disintegration and Dominant Minority. Calling the third phase of the cycle Breakdown would be like calling the Adult period of our own lives breakdown. In some sense, it is true, and we even have concepts like the midlife crisis which point to a negative connotation for this period of life. Nevertheless, we don't call the Adult phase of life Breakdown and so why should we do it at the macrocosmic level? What happens when we change these terms to more neutral ones that correspond to the human lifecycle? We get something like the following table:-

Microcosm	Macrocosm
Child	Genesis
Orphan	Growth
Adult	Maturity
Elder	Old Age

How does this terminological change affect our understanding? We are no longer calling it the Breakdown phase but the Maturity phase. It's not a Tyrannical Father manifesting the hyper-masculine; it's a Mature culture manifesting its Will. The arrival of the third phase of the civilisational cycle is then the arrival of the Will as the dominant faculty at the civilisational level. It is the Adult phase of the civilisational cycle, the phase of maximum strength and influence. For those who end up on the wrong side of that Will, the civilisation becomes the Tyrannical Father but that is just one perspective on the matter.

It is true that the arrival of the macrocosmic Maturity phase really does seem to require that the individual citizens of the civilisation sacrifice something of their own archetypal development, and here we see another strange "coincidence" in the philosophy that emerged around the time when western civilisation was making its transition to Maturity. At just this time, philosophers such as Locke, Rousseau and Hobbes appeared. One idea they all had in common was that they saw that civilisation seemed to involve a reduction of freedom of action from the point of view of the individual. The individual gives up the freedom of the *state of nature*. It is in their interests to do so because of the benefits they receive from society. The ideas of Locke, Rousseau and Hobbes just happened to match the phase of the cycle where the relatively self-sufficient peasantry were being asked to give up that self-sufficiency in order to concentrate power for the civilisation to reach its Maturity phase. Here was a philosophy which put that sacrifice into words and paved the way for a renunciation based on a new *social contract*. (As we will see, the use of legalistic and business terminology here is not accidental).

Perhaps the philosophers of the Enlightenment were right in saying that civilisation always requires the individual to sacrifice something. Whether that sacrifice really does become more pronounced in the second half of the cycle is hard to know for sure, and so, once again, it may just be our bias at play when we claim that the second half is worse on this score. Continuing with our re-evaluation of the macrocosm, the phrase Dominant Minority also takes on a new connotation. It is simply the expression of the Will of the civilisation which is exactly what we would expect to see in the Mature phase just as the Adult phase of life is when we, as individuals, achieve our maximum of worldly influence, when we know what we are doing and how to do it. Moreover, Will is all about stepping into the unknown. It is about acting with imperfect information and, thereby, having the courage to move forward into realms where the Intellect cannot predict outcomes. This explains why the second half of the civilisational cycle involves a reorientation away from the past and towards the future. The Intellect is concerned with what has been. The Will reaches forward into what has not yet become.

Furthermore, the acquiescence of the Orphans in the third phase of the cycle is necessary in order to achieve a concentration of Will at the collective level. The civilisation in its early phases is decentralised and heterogenous, but also politically and militarily weak. It is incapable of concentrating force to any great extent. It is a simple matter of physics that force projection increases with the concentration of energy. To con-centr(e)-ate means to bring to the centre which is exactly what happens as the seat of power shifts to the mega-cities of late civilisation.

In short, all the developments that Toynbee and Spengler describe as occurring in the third phase of the civilisational cycle are exactly what we would expect to occur if the third phase mapped to the Adult period of the civilisation; the manifestation of Will. But this concentration is also exactly what happens to us as individuals. What makes the Orphan transition difficult is that we must give up the infinite possibility of childhood for the limited horizons of adulthood. What we win in the process is the concentration of our own power as we become skilled and proficient in a specialised domain. The same thing happens to civilisations. Of all the pathways that could have been taken, one must be chosen. In one sense, this is the end of "growth". In another sense, it is the concentration of power brought about by the exercise of Will.

This is where the fatalism of Nietzsche and Spengler actually casts them in the role of Elders on the subject of civilisation. What an Elder must do is lead the Orphan through the transition from infinite possibility to a relatively fixed life path. They lead the Orphan to the end of the Growth phase of life and into the concentration phase (Adult). Nietzsche and Spengler were making the same claim at the civilisational level. In a roundabout way, they were playing the civilisational Elder. We will return to a discussion of the manner in which they were doing so later.

If the Will belongs to the Mature phase of the macrocosm, what about the final phase, which we have labelled "Old Age"? If we are correct that the macrocosm also goes through the archetypal phases, we would expect this phase to map to the microcosmic faculty of Soul? That is exactly what both Toynbee and Spengler found. The final phase sees the arrival of what

Toynbee called the Universal Church and what Spengler called the Second Religiosity. The Universal Church is born out of the proletariat, who do not become active participants in the Universal State and therefore are not part of the manifestation of the Will tied to the Dominant Minority. These are the Rebel Priests and their followers, and the faculty they map to is that of the Elder: Soul.

We can now make these correspondences clear and map out an archetypal table of the macrocosm as follows:-

Microcosm	Macrocosm	Primary Faculty	Macrocosmic Manifestation
Child	Genesis	Imagination	Creative Minority
Orphan	Growth	Intellect	Creative Minority
Adult	Maturity	Will	Dominant Minority - Universal State
Elder	Old Age	Soul	Dominant Minority - Universal Church

With our Nietzschean re-evaluation, we can see that the correspondences between microcosm and macrocosm go even deeper than we first thought. The cycle and its archetypal phases seem to be identical. If that's true, then we can posit that the macrocosm goes through its own moments of transcendence from one phase to another, just as it does for the individual. But that is almost the exact argument that Toynbee and Spengler made. Historical events are not random. Rather, they fit within a larger pattern of development that matches the microcosm not just in a biological sense but in the Esoteric sense as well.

And this brings us right back around to the point where we started this final section of the book. The existential angst of the 19th and 20th centuries, including the collective psychological phenomena that Jung observed with the two world wars, of which we have seen a precursor in the writing of Nietzsche, were driven by the seismic shifts caused by the arrival of the Mature phase of the macrocosmic cycle. As both Toynbee and Spengler knew, what was going on was the battle over the formation of the Universal State of western civilisation. Schopenhauer and Nietzsche arrived on the scene at just the time when the German-speaking peoples were trying, through *blood and iron*, to concentrate their power into a collective expression of Will. Of course, they were not alone. All of western civilisation was doing the same thing. It was the battle for the formation of the Universal State.

Historians treat such matters from a political and military viewpoint. What we can see from our integrated perspective is that there is a collective psychological correspondence that has all the hallmarks of a confrontation with the Unconscious. This suggests that the archetypal phases of the macrocosm are Hero's Journeys just as they are in our lives. That is what was driving the collective psychology of the world wars in Europe. That collective psychology is a mirror for our own personal psychology. The Hero's Journey comes up from our individual Unconscious, while the collective Hero's Journeys comes up from the collective Unconscious.

This idea entails a modification of Jung's concept of the Collective Unconscious, albeit one that is in broad agreement with some of his later work, including *Aion* and *Answer to Job*. We now posit that the Collective Unconscious is not just a static collection of archetypes but is also profoundly influenced by the archetypal phase of the macrocosmic cycle. Just as puberty, for example, confronts each of us with a challenge from the Unconscious, so too does the archetypal transition from the first phase of the civilisational cycle to the second, and so on.

The German identity crisis of the 19th century and its resolution in the *blood and iron* that led to the two world wars are prime examples of the Collective Unconscious drive motivated by the Mature phase of western civilisation. Historians have henceforth analysed these through primarily political, economic and military lenses. We are fortunate to have had the evidence of the scholars of the 19th century but, perhaps more importantly, of a psychologist of the calibre of Jung, for whom it was clear that there was a collective psychological element to both world wars. Our archetypal analysis integrates all these perspectives by noting that the 19th century was the time when western civilisation was entering its Maturity phase and that this was the link that unifies the collective psychological with political, economic and military events. We will see further examples as we proceed with our analysis.

To summarise, we now posit that what we have called the phases of the civilisational cycle are archetypes of the macrocosm that function in the same ways as the archetypes of the microcosm. Just as the transition points between the archetypes are the most difficult and dangerous for us as individuals, the same is true of the macrocosm. And just as the archetypal transitions are Hero's Journeys involving a confrontation with the Unconscious for each of us as individuals, so too do civilisations have their own confrontation with the Collective Unconscious. All of which is to say that we need to think of civilisations as really being the same *kind of thing* as individuals. At the Physical level of being, they have a metabolism and they grow over time; at the Exoteric level of being are the institutions of society; and at the Esoteric level of being are the collective conscious and unconscious minds, as well as the higher Esoteric in the form of metaphysics, Spirit and Soul.

What we will be doing in this final part of the book is applying this idea to modern western civilisation. We have already proposed that the 19th century was the beginning of the Mature phase of the cycle (although arguably it had happened earlier than that and it was the nations of continental Europe who were feeling the pressure of trying to *catch up*). All of this is indicative of the macrocosmic Call to Adventure associated with the transition to Maturity, which has been completed in our time since we have assumed, following the analysis of Toynbee and Spengler, that we are now in the Universal State which represents the stable part of the Mature phase. Thus, the 19th and early 20th centuries were the difficult archetypal transformation that has now been decided and has resulted in the Universal State in which we now live. The Orphan/Growth transition then becomes the Reformation, and we will go into detail about that shortly. That gives us the second and third archetypal phases of the macrocosmic cycle of modern western civilisation. What about the first?

What is perhaps peculiar in relation to the modern western civilisation is that we know in great detail about its Genesis phase, and the reason for this is because that Genesis has been an obsession of our civilisation right from the beginning. If civilisations are just like individuals, then civilisations can have "parents". That is exactly how Toynbee characterised the relationship between modern western civilisation and the ancient civilisation we call the Classical. If civilisations have a psychology that mirrors the human individual, and if civilisations can have parents just as we can, wouldn't we expect to see the same psychology between the macrocosmic parent and child? This claim may sound outlandish, and yet there is ample evidence for it in the relationship between the modern European civilisation and its ancient "parent". Can it be a coincidence that it is the modern European civilisation that came up with the notion of the *Oedipus Complex*? We know better than to believe in such "coincidences". As we are about to find out, the relationship between the Classical and the modern western civilisations really is one that has been fraught with *daddy issues* right from the start, and these have very much shaped the world in which we live.

In short, what we will be doing in the final part of the book is describing the history of modern European civilisation from a macrocosmic archetypal point of view. We begin at the beginning with the relationship between the modern and the Classical civilisations that initiated the Genesis phase. We will then move on to the Orphan/Growth phase as represented by the dramatic events of the Reformation and, finally, to the Mature phase, which is the one we are all living through and which is marked by the establishment of the Universal State. Let's begin.

The Father of the Faustian

We argued earlier that Spengler's magisterial work, *The Decline of the West*, was primarily motivated by a desire to understand and document the culture of western civilisation. For that reason, it is to Spengler that we now turn in order to sketch out the most important characteristics of our civilisation. Spengler's work is more than one thousand pages long, and we certainly don't have the time to cover it in any great detail here. Fortunately, we're only going to need a handful of Spengler's concepts, the first of which is the name he gave to western civilisation. He called the modern western civilisation beginning around the year 1000 AD the *Faustian* in reference to the well-known story of *Faust* made most famous by Goethe. Spengler's choice of name is revealing for two key reasons. We'll get to the second one later. The first relates to Goethe's work itself.

One of the main themes of the second part of Goethe's *Faust* was the working out, albeit in highly symbolic form, of the relationship between the ancient Greek and the modern European civilisations. This had been a prime issue in Goethe's own life. At age 37, Goethe had taken an extended trip to Italy, which later formed the material for his book called *Italian Journey*. The trip was clearly a turning point for Goethe's own life, while the book itself was widely read and was clearly a big influence on Spengler, and Nietzsche too. Whether Spengler knew it, he had named the modern western civilisation after a book whose main symbolic purpose had been to make sense of the relationship between the modern western and ancient civilisations.

Spengler's name for the modern European civilisation is, as far as I know, a novel one which he coined. The name he used for the ancient Greek and Roman civilisation, however, was one that was in common use and which we saw earlier in our Nietzsche quote. It was called the *Classical*. We said that Germany was having an identity crisis in the 19th century and that Spengler's work needs to be understood against that background. But we could go a step further and say that Faustian civilisation has been having an identity crisis right from its inception. That identity crisis was born out of the very peculiar relationship the Faustian had with the Classical.

Many historians consider the Faustian civilisation to be an extension of the Classical in a straight, linear fashion, albeit separated by the *dark ages* when the light of civilisation was almost extinguished. Spengler insists time and time again and provides ample evidence to back up his claim that this is not true. He demanded that the two civilisations be thought of as separate entities. Part of the thrill that comes from reading Spengler is that he is able to explain what Faustian culture is and why it is different from the Classical. He helps us understand our own culture. The implication is that we do not understand it. Why do we not understand it? A big part of the reason is because so many of the surface forms of Faustian culture, what we have called the Exoteric, are taken from the Classical.

The examples are almost too numerous to mention. Just consider how many times in this book alone we have found that a key word in our analysis comes originally from either Latin or Greek. Most of the vocabulary of our jurisprudence, our political concepts, and our science and mathematics are taken from the Classical languages. For centuries, the Christian Mass was conducted in Latin while men were quite literally put to death for daring to translate the Bible into modern languages that could be understood by the average person. Consider neoclassical buildings and art, the dominance of Classical philosophy (for centuries, Aristotle was referred to simply as "the philosopher"), the desire on the part of the kings of Europe to have a (mostly imaginary) lineage that could be traced back to the Greeks and Romans. The list could go on and on.

We might be tempted to say that the Faustian civilisation simply borrowed from the Classical what it found useful. But the influence is far more pervasive than that. The Faustian was both literally and figuratively born in the ruins of the (western) Roman Empire. It was in the late stages of that empire that the Christian church became the state religion of Rome and it was the remains of the administrative and religious apparatus that included the Church that somehow survived the fall of the western Roman empire. In fact, and this is a key point, the Church created the nascent Faustian civilisation by stitching together an alliance of barbarian warlords of northern and western Europe under the rubric of Christianity.

Since we live in a post-Reformation world where we take the separation of church and state for granted, we find it hard to understand that the bishops, priests, and Popes of the ancient world and the early Faustian were not just religious leaders. They also coordinated non-religious functions, including education, scholarship, and administration. In fact, the church was still responsible for many of these domains all the way up until the 19th century. Most of the administrative functions that are nowadays handled by the state bureaucracy were handled by the church for most of the history of modern

216

Europe going back to late Rome. It is for these reasons and more that many historians analyse the Faustian as the continuation of the Classical.

But, again, we see something more than mere pragmatism or continuity at play in the inheritance of the Classical by the Faustian. The glory of Rome was still strong in the minds of the warlords of northern Europe following the collapse of the western empire, and those same warlords, and possibly many scholars and churchmen too, wanted to be associated with Rome. To take just one example, there later arose the story of how Britain had been founded by a certain *Brutus of Troy* descended, as the name suggests, from the Greeks who fought at that famous location. Henry VIII would later use this myth to justify his own position as a king descended from the Greeks. This practice was not limited to the British. On the continent, similar stories were invented to show that the various kings and nobles were descended from the greats of antiquity.

Since the Christian church had been incorporated into the Roman state towards the end of the western Roman empire, we can get some appreciation for why the kings and warlords of northern and western Europe were able to be converted to Christianity by the bishops and priests. Being associated with the church was being associated with Rome. The stronger warlords then became the muscle which convinced the remaining holdouts to join the club, often at the pointy end of a sword. It took several centuries for the process to complete, with Scandinavia being the last to yield, but, eventually, a unified grouping emerged where essentially all of western Europe was united in Christianity under the leadership of the Pope in Rome. It would not be too misleading to call the result a caliphate, with the Pope as *caliph*.

In short, the Faustian had been tied to the Classical right from the beginning. The strength of this bond is evidenced by the fact that, all the way into the 20th century, we see European leaders reaching back to the ancient civilisation for justification and inspiration. Most of us would be familiar with the *Hitlergruss*, the holding of the arm straight out, usually accompanied in the movies with the cry of "Heil Hitler". That was originally the Roman Salute, and it has its origins in antiquity. Napoleon made extensive use of Classical references including beginning a trend of furniture and jewellery creation based on Classical examples. When he became emperor, he had two crowns made for himself. One of them was a replica of a Roman crown. Mussolini played the same game by promising the Italians a return to the glory of Rome.

Spengler, writing in the early 20th century, lamented how various scholarly disciplines were still in thrall to Classical concepts that, in his opinion, had long been superseded. This was no doubt due to the fact that the Church had been in control of modern scholarship from the beginning. In fact, the modern university was born out of the Church. Cambridge and Oxford were both administered from Rome in their early days. We have noted how the Church exercised its authority over scholarship by executing various heretics for, among other things, trying to translate the Bible from Latin into the vernacular. For centuries, the Church had an iron grip on the intellectual life of Europe, not just the spiritual.

All that began to end with the Reformation, and both Spengler and Toynbee's work can be seen as a result of that break since the very style of history they practiced implies something new in scholarship. The Classical style of history, which is still used to this day, has been called the "great man theory of history". We might also call it Exoteric history since it is mostly concerned with events and facts that can be observed externally. By contrast, both Spengler and Toynbee were practicing a form of history that is Esoteric since it is concerned with finding patterns beneath the surface. It is, in fact, a Faustian style of history - something genuinely new and not a carryover from the Classical world.

In the case of Spengler, in particular, this phrase *Faustian history* has a meta-meaning. Spengler was not just practicing a new kind of history that needs to be understood within the larger culture of the Faustian; he was then applying that history to Faustian culture itself. Thus, Spengler's work fits within the re-evaluation implied by our preceding discussion. If the 19th century was the Faustian coming into its Mature phase, how fitting that it should discover a form of history that was specific to its culture and use that history to gain a better understanding of itself and also of the Classical which had, until then, dominated it.

Here, again, we see evidence for our claim that the macrocosm matches the microcosm. The Orphan phase of life is about self-understanding, which only comes from separation from the Parent. This is exactly how Toynbee characterised the relation between the Classical and the Faustian. He had said that the former was the Parent to the latter. It follows that the Faustian would need to separate itself from the Classical in order to understand both itself and the Classical. That is what was going on with comparative history. It was what was going on across the board in the 19th century.

The Orphan must break with the Parent in order to understand itself as a separate entity. One steps out of the shadow(!) of the Parent and becomes oneself as an Adult. But this differentiation from the Parent is exactly what we have just described in the works of Goethe's *Faust* and *Italian Journey* and also in Spengler. It was also a central concern in the work of Nietzsche and others. What we see time and again in these great works of art and scholarship is the need to clarify what the Faustian is relative to what the Classical is. It is the Child – Parent psychology playing out at the macrocosmic level.

Spengler's insistence on the uniqueness of the Faustian as separate from the Classical, and his thousand-page book to prove it, represent the Faustian civilisation stepping into its Mature phase. The Faustian finally understood itself as separate, unique, and worthy. In the macrocosmic cycle, Spengler was aiming to push the Faustian culture to maturity via a work which both identifies the uniqueness of the Faustian and the Classical. But that is exactly the archetypal mission of the Orphan: to discover one's own identity. Spengler was the Orphan, born into an Age of the Orphan, and pursuing the same mission at the macrocosmic level.

That such a work should come from a historian is no surprise since the Faustian was founded upon a historical consciousness that came from being surrounded by the ruins and legends of Rome. Spengler noted that this fascination with history was lacking in other cultures, including and especially the Classical itself. The Faustian was built on history, even if originally in the form of fictitious genealogies linking the barbarian warlords of northern Europe back to the glory days of Greece and Rome. We see the same mentality at play in the Puritans of Britain and the USA who truly believed themselves to be descendants of the tribes of Israel. Prior to Goethe, Luther had made a famous trip to Italy which changed the direction of Faustian culture. The crusaders had made similar journeys to the holy land. Right from the start, the Faustian referenced itself against the Classical.

This borderline obsession with the inheritance from the ancient world has given the Faustian culture its unique stamp. The Classical civilisation was Exoteric and extroverted. The Faustian grew up literally and figuratively in its shadow. Since it was hidden beneath the Exoteric forms of the Classical, the Faustian became Esoteric by default. It took a scholar and historian like Spengler who was willing and able to look beneath the Exoteric surface, to see the Faustian for what it is. But we can go a step further and say that only a historian born and raised in the Faustian culture could have come up with such a history. Esoteric history belongs to the Faustian because the Faustian is the Esoteric civilisation.

And here we come upon a very curious fact. Perhaps because Spengler was preoccupied with showing that the Faustian was unique and independent of the Classical, he did not classify the relationship between them as a Child – Parent one. In fact, he insisted that the Faustian be thought of as completely different. He did, however, come up with a concept that might have been applicable to the relationship between the Faustian and the Classical except he defined it in a way that made the application seem incorrect. The idea is one he borrowed from geology. It is called *pseudomorphosis*.

Per Spengler, pseudomorphosis occurs when a dominant culture imposes its institutions and practices on a subordinate one. Since we are using that familiar word, *dominant*, we can go a step further and say that this situation always occurs when there is a Dominant Minority in place. Thus, a pseudomorphosis implies a civilisation in its later stages that has achieved military and political supremacy over others. We know that, for most of history, this entailed a Tyrannical Father archetype dominating over a subordinate people. The subordinate culture does not go away but becomes, in our language, Esoteric; hidden beneath the dominant. Because the subordinate culture is being supressed, Spengler believed a pseudomorphosis is always accompanied by the underlying emotion of hatred which arises among the members of the subordinate population towards the dominant.

There are a couple of important things to note about Spengler's concept of pseudomorphosis right off the bat. Firstly, it's a perfect description of exactly what was going on in Germany in the 19th and early 20th centuries. What was attempting to be overlaid onto the German-speaking peoples was a form of politics and economy that had been born in Britain. Much the same thing had happened in France during the Revolution since the ideas that sparked that uprising were very much inspired by the British example. The difference in the cases of Germany and France is that the drive to make the change was not coming from a dominant force outside the culture but from within the culture itself. Here is the first way in which we need to broaden Spengler's concept of pseudomorphosis: the *dominance* can come from within or without.

The second point to make is that Spengler's concept of pseudomorphosis, including the hatred felt by the subordinate party, is exactly the same dynamic we described in our earlier analysis of the Orphan. *Hamlet* is the story of the hatred that occurs when an individual is kept under the domination of another and prevented from maturing into the Adult archetype. Hamlet hates Claudius because Claudius has usurped his Exoteric position. That's how it works at the microcosmic level. Spengler's concept of pseudomorphosis shows that the same thing holds at the macrocosmic. The subordinate culture feels the hatred of Hamlet towards the dominant, which has usurped its Exoteric institutions or, more probably, replaced them altogether.

But we have also seen other examples of this same dynamic, including the hatred of the proletariat towards the Dominant Minority in the latter stages of the civilisational cycle, where the societal Tyrannical Father leads the Universal State to dominance. It's the same hatred which Freud posited as a possible outcome of the Oedipus Complex where the son comes to hate and rebel against the father. It's the same hatred Nietzsche identified as that of the slave towards the master. Clearly, there is a more general principle at play. Dominance can lead to hatred. It makes no difference whether the dominance is "external" or "internal".

But hatred is just one of the possible outcomes of a relationship of dominance. We know from Freud that another potential outcome is idolisation and hero worship. That is what Freud observed in familial relationships, and it forms one pathway through the Oedipus Complex. But it is also exactly what we have just described in Faustian civilisation's attitude towards the Classical! The Faustian idolised the Classical in the way a son might worship his father. Since we have already defined the Faustian – Classical relationship as that of Child – Parent, and since we have claimed that the same psychology holds at the macrocosmic as the microcosmic, this idolisation is to be expected. It is one possible outcome of the macrocosmic Oedipus Complex. We will see the other possible outcomes shortly.

Clearly, however, the Classical civilisation was not dominant over the Faustian in a Physical sense. That would be impossible since the Classical had "died" before the Faustian was born. What sort of dominance relationship held between the two civilisations? We have two other levels of being that we might refer to in this regard: the Exoteric and the Esoteric. We know that the Exoteric institution which created the Faustian was the Church and this was left over from the late Classical. From the Church comes all of the higher Esoteric principles on which the Faustian was created, as well as the aforementioned Esoteric aspects of idolisation and reverence towards the Classical civilisation. All of this can be summarised under a Child – Parent archetypal relationship, and, just to get even more meta, that relationship is built into the Christian theology as two parts of the trinity: Father and Son. Thus, the Classical civilisation exerted both an Exoteric and an Esoteric form of dominance over the Faustian at the beginning of the latter's existence.

Spengler had described pseudomorphosis as a dominance relationship between two living cultures, but the Classical civilisation was "dead" at the beginning of the Faustian. When we say that the Classical dominated over the Faustian, we are not talking about a direct, political, or military dominance, which is how Spengler used the concept. The dominance of the Classical over the Faustian was a spiritualised and sublimated domination. It was Esoteric from the very beginning. The Classical was the spiritual Father to the Faustian. Another meta-meaning in this respect is the fact that the Pope was the central figure of the nascent Faustian civilisation and the word Pope comes from *papa* meaning "father".

Thus, it makes perfect sense that many centuries later, Freud made the Father – Son relationship the core of his psychoanalysis. More generally, though, the reason why psychoanalysis could arise at all was because Faustian culture had created a schism between the conscious and unconscious minds. The Exoteric world of the Faustian claimed to be the Classical. It was the world of the Father, of Rome and Greece. The Faustian became the spiritualised, Esoteric son. But it was a son who could not grow up; who could not manifest the Exoteric. Like Hamlet, the Faustian was forced into introversion, the Esoteric. The reason why Spengler needed to look beneath the surface in order to find the Faustian was because it was still being dominated by the surface forms of the Father civilisation. Why would psychoanalysis arise during the Adult phase of the Faustian? Because the Faustian civilisation was still trying to process its *daddy issues*; still trying to *grow up*.

Here, again, we see another important point captured in the etymology of the words we are using. We call it the Classical civilisation. The word *classical* means "of the highest rank". It's from the Latin word *classicus* which referred to the top rank of Roman society. The entire premise of calling the ancient civilisation *Classical* is that it was superior - yet one more example of the spiritualised dominance the ancient civilisation held over its Child.

When Spengler used the term *pseudomorphosis*, he had in mind the kind of domination that the Romans exerted over the peoples of what he called the Magian culture in the eastern Mediterranean and Middle East. The Romans were not exactly shy about making their dominance felt by the peoples they conquered. As a result, violent uprisings were not uncommon. Feelings of resentment and hatred are quite natural in such circumstances where slavery was common, as was mass slaughter when it was required. Like with everything else in Roman society, the dominance was overt. It took place on the Physical and Exoteric levels of being. What the Romans had no interest in dominating were the minds of the people whom they had conquered – the Esoteric level of being. They had what we would consider a very tolerant attitude on such matters and encouraged local customs and religious rites to be upheld.

If we expand the concept of pseudomorphosis to include the Esoteric level of being, we allow for the psychological forms of dominance that modern psychoanalysis discovered. We can also see that the Esoteric form of dominance applies to the Classical – Faustian relationship. That relationship was not one based in hatred and resentment but rather in idolisation and hero worship, at least in the early days. Does it even make sense to call such a relationship one of *dominance*? Here we find yet another etymological meta-meaning that justifies our analysis. The word *dominate* also comes from Latin where it is from the word *domus* meaning *house*. Roman fathers were the heads of the household and had complete legal and physical power over their family members. Domination is literally born out of the commanding position of the Father carried over from Roman times.

Thus, we find that our assumption that the relationships of the microcosm hold also at the macrocosm works perfectly as a description of the link between the Classical and Faustian civilisations. The Classical is the Freudian Father to the Faustian Son. In the history of Faustian civilisation, we see the two main Oedipal responses towards the Father. In the beginning, there was idolisation and hero worship. Then came the Reformation and the rebellion against the Father. We will explore that in more detail shortly. Finally, there is the third outcome, which Freud analysed as the healthy response. The child eventually comes to see both itself and the father as individuals. This is exactly what we have described as one of the main themes of the Orphan Story. The transcendence to the Adult archetype is predicated on a successful resolution to the Oedipal tensions. Failure leads to destruction, as in the case of Hamlet.

We have said that the 19th century was the time when the Faustian was coming-of-age and we can see clearly that Spengler's work must be viewed as part of the process by which the Faustian was finally coming to see itself as independent of its Father, the Classical. There are numerous other examples of the same process from this era. Napoleon blew away the edifice of the Holy Roman Empire. That empire had lasted a thousand years and was predicated on a Pope crowning a barbarian warlord of northern Europe as king of the Romans! When Nietzsche later announced that "God is dead", he was symbolically referring to the Faustian's own Orphan Story and the need to confront the death of the civilisational Father. There are other examples we will look at later.

The extraordinarily long "childhood" of the Faustian civilisation where it was dominated by the forms inherited from the Classical has given Faustian culture its unique quality. Spengler touches upon this time and time again in his analysis and sums it up as follows: "The spirit of Classical history and the spirit of western history can only be really understood by considering the two souls as in opposition." We know now that this opposition is the opposition of Hamlet trying to break free from the grasp of Claudius. It's the Faustian trying to find its own identity. Because the Faustian developed for so long underneath the Classical, what happened was that it found its identity literally and metaphorically *underneath*. But *underneath* is just another word for the Esoteric. If the Exoteric structures of society had been inherited from the Classical, the Faustian would have to become Esoteric. That is where its identity could be created and have some chance of developing.

Thus, when the Faustian "comes of age" in the 19th century, we see a plethora of scientific breakthroughs, all of which were concerned with what lies beneath the surface. We have already mentioned the psychoanalysis of Freud and Jung which is the psychology that lies beneath the surface of the conscious mind. The comparative scholarship of van Gennep and Joseph Campbell looks for structural patterns beneath the surface. The great interest in linguistics in the 19th century was predicated on finding the grammatical rules that lay beneath the surface manifestations of language. There is Schopenhauer and Nietzsche with their concept of the Will; an invisible (Esoteric) force driving nature. Darwin found an invisible (Esoteric) driving force behind evolution.

Meanwhile, there were great advances in mining, geology, and archae-ology that were literally about digging beneath the surface. The industrial revolution was founded on coal and other fuels that needed to be dug up from the ground. There was an explosion of interest in the occult in the 19th century, which also seeped into popular literature. We see an Esoteric focus in practically all the great scientific discoveries of the West culminating, perhaps, in quantum mechanics, which dug so far down into nature that it fell out the bottom.

And, of course, both Spengler and Toynbee's histories were about looking at the patterns that lie beneath. Time and again throughout his book, Spengler pulls up some hidden concept and raises it before us to say, "see, this is what the Faustian really is." But what is even more revealing is Spengler's point that the Faustian is in opposition to the Classical. This opposition is such a common pattern that it cannot be accidental. It points to a long teenage rebellion phase that was itself spiritual and sublimated.

We can summarise the differences between the Faustian and the Classical, as follows. Most of these are taken from Spengler and they are, as he noted, all oppositions:-

Classical	Faustian
General Public	Elites
The Body	The Mind
The Present	Past and future
Exoteric	Esoteric
Community	Individual
The Deed	The Idea (dogma, ideology)
Extrovert	Introvert
Appearance	The Mask
Conscious	Unconscious
Noon day sun	Midnight
Popular	Elitist
Leaders and Heroes	Impersonal forces
Self-Evident Facts	Requires explanation and theory

The Faustian is the occult civilisation hidden beneath the Classical in a pseudomorphosis. In psychological terms, it is the civilisation of introversion; it is Hamlet chasing the ghost. From the beginning, it was elitist since it was the bishops and popes who alone had the sacred knowledge passed down from antiquity and from God. Since the modern university was birthed by the Catholic Church, our scientists, scholars, and experts are the modern day bishops and popes and they retain the elitism that has been present from the start.

We can summarise all of this as an archetypal relationship between Child – Parent that holds at the macrocosmic level. This relationship was Oedipal in nature right from the start because it was sublimated into the Unconscious. The 19th-century then becomes the Orphan Story of the Faustian, the time when the Faustian made the transition to the Mature archetypal phase of the civilisational cycle. It is also deeply fitting that this coming-of-age was accompanied by the idea of the death of civilisation, including the death of the Faustian itself, since that is part of the Orphan's journey. Only a civilisation so dominated by the "Father" could have learned this lesson. Everybody knew that the Roman Empire had been mighty, and everybody knew that it had perished, nevertheless.

It is a mark of how profoundly the Faustian was influenced by its Father that the death of the Classical was still being processed in the 20th century. That is why it forms a central point of Spengler's work. That is why Toynbee had to wrestle with the question of civilisational death. Perhaps comparative history itself could only have been created in the Faustian civilisation which needed to process the meaning of the death of Rome. In the process, the Faustian was finding the self-confidence to finally distance itself from the Father. It could finally see the Classical for what it was, and thereby it was able to see itself too.

This brief introduction to the nature of the Faustian "soul", as Spengler put it, gives an extra dimension to our analysis. We all go through phases of life that are, in an archetypal sense, the same. But the way in which we deal with the archetypal challenges is what reveals our own character and soul. We posit that the same is true of the macrocosm. Spengler's great contribution was to show the ways in which the civilisations differ from each other. He argued that the key features of the Faustian, just like all other civilisations, were born from the geography where the culture originated. Perhaps there is some truth in that. But, at least in relation to the Faustian, we are going to argue that the relationship with the Classical civilisation was far more important and, in particular, the Child – Father relationship inherited from the ancient world.

At each of the major archetypal turning points of the Faustian, the relationship with the Classical was key. This is self-evidently true of the beginning of the Faustian which was built on the idolisation of the Classical. The next major turning point is the rebellion against the Father. It's time to talk about the Reformation.

The Reformation: A Civilisational Teenage Rebellion

We noted in Part 3 the brilliant trick that George Lucas played in the Star Wars trilogy by making Darth Vader both the father of Luke Skywalker and also the representative of the Dominant Minority, combining microcosmic and macrocosmic elements of the story into a single relationship. We would assume that such perfectly symmetrical symbolism only exists in the fictional realm, where writers are unconstrained by the limitations of *the real world,* and yet we see a very similar correspondence at play in the realm of history, where the major macrocosmic turning points are channelled through a single individual whose own archetypal battle mirrors that of the macrocosm. The Hero's Journey of the person in question becomes the Hero's Journey of the collective.

Napoleon once commented how he felt as if he were being driven on by a force much larger than himself. If that force was the archetypal energy of the macrocosmic transition of the Faustian to the Maturity phase of the cycle, we can see how the French general, as an exponent of Will, is an obvious candidate for that energy. While Napoleon's rise can and has been analysed in political and military terms, we can also see an obvious collective psychological element at play, not just in the cult of personality around the man but in what preceded him. If the macrocosmic archetypal transitions also include a challenge from the Unconscious, the French Revolution and especially the Terror must count as exemplars of a confrontation with the Collective Unconscious. Napoleon was the "solution". He was the attempt on the part of the Faustian to transcend the challenge. In any case, we can see in Napoleon's life obvious parallels with the macrocosmic archetypal dynamic that was taking place.

The Growth phase of the macrocosm corresponds with the Orphan phase of the microcosm, so it should be no surprise to find the desire to transcend the relationship with the Parent at that point of the cycle and, where that transcendence is held back, as in the case of Hamlet, to find that the pressure can build until it explodes into violence. It is exactly that which we see in the Reformation. The hero of the movement, who really was a hero in the everyday sense of the term, was Martin Luther. Luther's personal Hero's Journey began during the Orphan phase of his own life and involved a rebellion against his own father. He would later lead a macrocosmic rebellion against the societal Father, the Pope.

There can be no doubt that Luther's personal Hero's Journey involved a confrontation with the Unconscious. Luther used the medieval Christian theology that he was raised in by calling that challenge one *from the devil,* and he would later find the devil everywhere in the world around him. The vehemence of Luther's personal battle even startled his fellow monks and priests when, in rebellion against his father's wishes, Luther quit university, where he was studying law, and joined a monastery. Whatever else can be said, Luther confronted the challenge from his Unconscious in a direct fashion. He would later apply the same passion to the macrocosmic challenge that made him famous.

Luther was the archetypal Orphan born at the time when the Faustian was going through its own archetypal Orphan phase. He was destined to turn his rebellion against his own father into a rebellion against the archetypal Father of Faustian civilisation itself. It was the popes (the holy "father") who created the Faustian civilisation in the first place. It would be the Pope who Luther would rebel against. Since we live in the aftermath of his rebellion and a culture very much shaped by it, we struggle to understand how much courage it must have taken. Plenty of heretics had been put to death by the Church before Luther. As the son of an average family born into an average town in the relative backwater of Germany, Luther should have expected the same fate.

A big part of why that never happened was because Luther, like Napoleon, had tapped into something larger than himself. Once again, we see clear evidence of a collective psychological event that coalesced around the young man. This is clear evidence of an archetypal dynamic at play, especially since the ramifications of Luther's rebellion were mostly not what he would have wanted. What we see in both the dynamic between Luther and his father and the societal Father of the Pope is the Faustian Orphan fighting to emerge from beneath the overbearing influence of its Father, the Classical.

We have said that the Classical culture was extroverted, Exoteric, public, and based on actions and deeds. All of these properties are present in the way that the Greeks and Romans practiced religion. That religion was based on public action. More specifically, it was based around rites of practice - the exact same kinds of rites that we studied extensively earlier in the book. There was essentially no dogma involved in Classical religion. The Romans did not care what you believed or what you happened to think about religious matters. In fact, they had a distrust of religions that were too "deep". What they did care about was that you observed the rites and ceremonies prescribed by religion. The father of the household had a leadership role in carrying out daily religious rituals, but all members of society were expected to fulfil their ritual obligations.

The rites of passage in the Classical world mostly took place in sacred locations such as temples. The construction of temples and other religious buildings was part of ritual observance. As the Roman sphere of influence expanded, the Romans encouraged local populations to continue to conduct the rites of passage related to their local gods while also requiring the observance of the rites of the state religion. While there were, of course, plenty of religious myths in circulation, the written word was of almost no importance to Classical religion since the vast majority of the population was illiterate. What was of utmost importance were deeds - the following of the rites of passage.

The Faustian was built on the template inherited from the late Classical, so it should come as no surprise to find that the Catholic Church was very much focused on ritual observance. The seven sacraments of the Church are all rites of passage carried out by the priest as Elder. Right from the start of the Faustian, however, we see the seeds of what would become the religious revolution of the Reformation. In the 11th and 12th centuries, there was an explosion of monastic activity. The monasteries became centres of religious learning based very largely around the reading of scripture. They would eventually give birth to another institution which was unknown to Classical antiquity but which became a core feature of the Faustian: the university.

The monasteries and universities came to see the book, not the rites of passage, as the foundation of religious practice. The importance of the Bible grew over the centuries as work in translating the original text from ancient Greek found that the version used by the Church, the Vulgate, was riddled with errors. But what became a more pressing concern to the theologians and scholars of the universities was the way in which the Church controlled which parts of the Bible were transmitted to the faithful. The belief grew that the Church was giving an incorrect interpretation of the meaning of Christianity. A movement arose to fix the errors in the original translation and then to translate the Bible into vernacular language so that the average person could have direct access to the word of God.

The Church had taken to dealing with heretical ideas through the mechanisms of the Inquisition, so it's no surprise that early translators of the Bible into vernacular language such as Willian Tyndale were put to death for their troubles. Of course, this only strengthened the aura that surrounded the matter since the impartial onlooker often concluded that there must really be something of importance involved if people were prepared to be killed over words in a book. The battle lines were drawn. The Church wanted to repress the written word and stick to the rites of passage in the practice of religion. The growing Protestant movement wanted to promulgate the written word to all. Can it be a coincidence that the printing press should arrive at just this time to be one of the formative technologies that would decide the matter in favour of the written word? Luther didn't think so. He called the printing press a gift from God.

The ancients practiced their religion through ritual, but the theologians of the 16th century had a different vision. They wanted the average person to be able to read and recount Bible stories. Erasmus hoped the farmer "might sing snatches of Scripture at his plough, that the weaver might hum phrases of Scripture to the tune of his shuttle, that the traveler might lighten with stories from Scripture the weariness of his journey."

But the Protestants were not simply about the embrace of the written word alongside the rites of passage prescribed by the Church; they were actively against those rites. As John Foxe complained, "the church was solely concerned with outward ceremony and human traditions. People spent their entire lives heaping up one ceremony after another in hopes of salvation, not knowing it was theirs for the asking. Simple, uneducated people who had no knowledge of scripture were content to know only what their pastors told them, and these pastors took care to only teach what came from Rome ..."

Note that most of the big names in the Reformation including Luther, Erasmus, Tyndale, Foxe and others, were products of the universities and therefore evolved out of a tradition unknown to the mainstream Classical civilisation. What we see in the Reformation, therefore, are the beginnings of the elements of the Faustian culture that would later come to maturity in our time. Importantly, those elements were a rebellion against the practices inherited from the Classical civilisation.

That the Reformation was driven largely from the cities and towns and not from the countryside is no coincidence, since the transfer of power to the cities is indicative of the centralisation that leads to the Mature phase of the macrocosmic cycle. Since it was based on knowledge of the written word and membership in the university, we can say that the Protestant movement was elitist in focus, even though it purported to speak on behalf of all and even though one of the results of its teachings was a series of peasant rebellions. It was also introverted since the act of reading the Bible, like all reading, is an introverted activity. Again, this is in contradiction to rites of passage, which are public and social by nature. The movement away from the rites of passage and towards the reading of scripture was therefore a movement of the culture away from the Exoteric and towards the Esoteric. Since the Exoteric was what had been inherited from the Classical, we can see why the Faustian so reliably inverts the Classical. The true Faustian was born out of a rebellion against the Classical Father.

The transition away from ceremonial observance and towards the written word is also directly relevant to the two forms of connection we established between the microcosm and macrocosm in our integrated model way back in Part One of this book. In our model, we accorded equal weight to both the rites of passage and the Hero's Journeys as follows:-

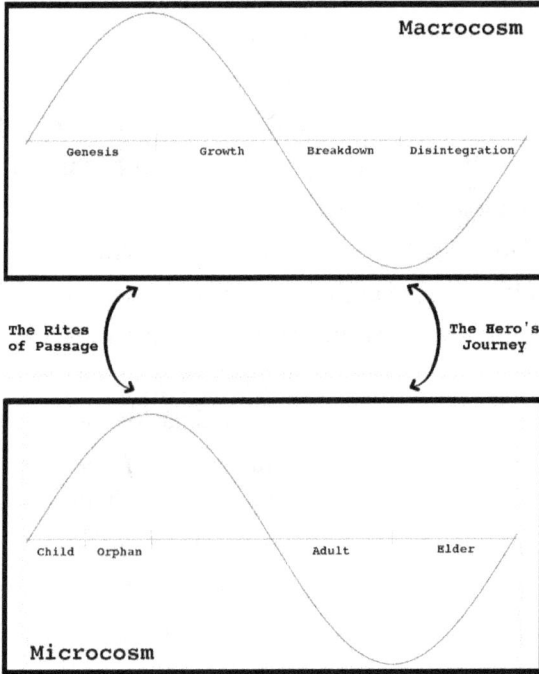

Since the stories of the Bible are Hero's Journeys, the Reformation shifted the basis of religious observance away from rites of passage and towards Hero's Journeys. This practice incubated in the monasteries and universities for centuries beforehand, but it now arrived as a general social force, fuelled by the adoption of the printing press, which was just the technology needed to make it happen.

In this development, we also find an answer to a question we asked back near the beginning of the book: why are there no Elders in the modern West? Elders require rites of passage. If you get rid of the rites of passage, you get rid of the Elders. But we can be even more specific. If you swap rites of passage for Hero's Journeys, the author of the Hero's Journey becomes the sublimated Elder. The Protestants believed the Bible was the word of God and that everybody could have access to God as Elder directly through the Bible. You didn't need to go through the worldly Elder in the form of Popes, bishops, and priests.

Of course, the word of God still needed to be translated into the vernacular in order to make any of this happen, and so we might also say that it was the translators of the Bible who became the Elders since they were the ones who had to channel the word of God. In that case, Luther himself becomes an Elder since he was the author of an apparently magisterial translation of the Bible into German. Suddenly, we see the rebellion against the Pope in a different light. It was not simply a rejection of the Pope and the Church but a replacement of both with something very different. That very different something is what we are calling the true Faustian which emerges, as Spengler pointed out repeatedly, in opposition to the Classical.

Thus, Spengler's naming of the two civilisations also takes on a new meaning. The Classical comes from *classicus*, an actual class of people in Rome who really were societal Elders. Beginning with the Reformation, the Faustian threw off the Elders left over from the Classical pseudomorphosis. They were replaced by the printing press and the book i.e. the Hero's Journeys. The writers, translators and scholars henceforth became the sublimated societal Elders of the Faustian. After what did Spengler name this Esoteric and introverted civilisation based on stories? After a story! *Faust*.

This also explains why so many of our stories, as we have seen earlier in our Orphan Story analysis, feature the Elder archetype, even though that archetype is missing from the broader culture. We initiate ourselves through Hero's Journeys. We have sublimated our Elders into story form as fictional characters or as the authors themselves. The monks and scholars of the monasteries and universities had incubated this form of initiation via their Bible studies and then spread it to the rest of the culture beginning with the Reformation.

What does Jesus say in Mathew 10:35 - "For I have come to turn a man against his father, a daughter against her mother, a daughter-in-law against her mother-in-law". But we already know that the one who breaks up the Child – Parent relationship is the Elder. If the story in the Bible is correct, Jesus was an Elder in his own time. He then became an Elder to a whole civilisation through the written word of his Hero's Journey conveyed down through the centuries. The Protestants did not need an Elder in the Pope; they had one in the Bible.

It barely needs mentioning how important the written word and the power of universities have become to Faustian civilisation. In our time, there is as good as universal literacy, and about one-third of the population attends university. Only in such a society could newspapers have become a general tool of political communication (or propaganda, depending on how you look at it). All this follows from the rebels of the Reformation. Luther used the printing press to get around the Papal censor. He shattered the partnership that existed between the Church and the kings of Europe in the pre-Reformation era, where the Church functioned as the public relations agency. If a king wanted to get a message in front of all his subjects, only the Church was in a position to make that happen with any degree of certainty. Luther and the printing press changed all that, and it's fair to say that at least some of the kings who watched Luther's star rise were well aware of the political possibilities that were thereby opened up.

There can be no question that Luther, a university man himself, in large part helped to shape this aspect of Faustian culture. But Luther was also central to another development, one that he would have very much disapproved of. We know that he would have disapproved because it was the basis of his rebellion against his own father. Luther's father was a member of the newly emerging merchant class. He was what we would nowadays call a businessman. He wanted his son to follow in his footsteps by becoming a lawyer. That was originally why Luther went to university, he was studying law. But Luther rebelled against his father and against the mercantilist life path that had been laid out for him and went to join a monastery, thinking that this would bring him closer to God. What did he find at the monastery? Mercantilism!

The monasteries of Europe, and the Church in general, were incredibly wealthy by the standards of the day. Part of the reason was that they were using the labour of the monks to create goods for sale. For Luther, this was a sacrilege against the religious mission which the Church proclaimed for itself. Later, when Luther went to visit Rome, he saw the absurd luxury that this system created for the Church authorities, including and especially the Pope. Leo X was not shy about showing off his wealth, and, while it is true that a lot of the Church's income went into creating some of the great works of architecture and art, much of it also went into the kind of debauchery that hearkened back to the Caesars of the Roman empire.

The Church was arguably the first multi-national corporation, although it also functioned as a quasi-government since it was also able to levy taxes. When money got short, as it had during the time when Luther was visiting Rome, the Church raised extra capital through the sale of indulgences. We know of Luther's objection to this practice on theological grounds, but imagine it from the point of view of a king in northern Europe. Money is already tight, and the projects you might like to invest in to improve your kingdom can't be afforded. Then the Pope launches a brand new scheme to sell indulgences, and all your peasant folk rush off to empty their pockets into Church coffers, which then get transported thousands of miles away to Rome.

Therein lay the larger problem. The Church was draining money out of general society and channelling it into some combination of debauchery and idleness. Some monasteries did provide services to the local community, many did not, and some of the monks who enjoyed the perks of the scheme were as indiscreet as the Pope. Their behaviour had not gone unnoticed by both kings and common folk. In the later words of the American revolutionaries, it was taxation without representation, all held together by the threat of eternal damnation if you went against the Church's wishes.

One of the reasons the kings of Europe came to support the Reformation was because they wanted to free up the capital held by the Church and remove the Church's ability to siphon money out of the general economy. They saw that the popularity that Luther enjoyed could be used as a political force to achieve that outcome. That's exactly what happened next, and it happened mostly in the Protestant North. Henry VIII led a particularly vociferous campaign that closed down all the monasteries across England. This worked to free up large amounts of capital. Just a few decades later, mercantilism went into overdrive under the reign of Queen Elizabeth.

Here we have the second pillar of the modern Faustian that emerged because of Luther, although definitely against his will. It barely needs to be said how important this development has become to the world we live in. Mercantilism was the precursor to modern capitalism and has become the basis for the economic and political ascendancy of the Faustian civilisation. It is no coincidence that its full flourishing required the Church's power to be broken. Somewhat ironically, both Luther and Luther's father turned out to be correct, and both have been vindicated by history. It is both the mercantilists and the lawyers, along with the university scholars, who now dominate the mature Faustian civilisation. We have both Luther and his father to thank.

There is one final act of rebellion that emerges in the Reformation that has reached maturity in our time, and that forms a third pillar that completes the political, economic, and religious aspects of the mature Faustian identity. We have seen how the disobedience against the macrocosmic Father, the Classical civilisation, created the primacy of the written word in Faustian religion, which also opened the door for the full development of the Faustian economy in the form of capitalism. The third area it unlocked was in the domain of politics.

The Faustian was built upon the fusion of late Roman politics and the Christian religion. This involved the repackaging of a concept from the Classical society, where rulers were thought to be descended from gods and sometimes became gods themselves. Julius Caesar is a prime example. He was made a god shortly after his death. The Faustian Popes reformulated this notion as the *divine right of kings*. The king was not a god but received the blessing of God through the Pope. Although the kings of northern Europe probably never foresaw it, when they denied the Pope, they undermined the authority that came with the divine right of kings. They had sawn off the

Esoteric branch upon which they were sitting.

As we saw earlier in the book, the Father is built into the Christian theology. Over a long period of time, it had been made commensurate with Greek philosophical assumptions and then integrated into the Roman state, where it seems to have been a replacement for the cult of Caesar, which we earlier analysed as a cult of the Father. This archetypal worship of the Father had been carried over into the early Faustian. Even after the rebellion of the Reformation, we still see books like Robert Filmer's *Patriarcha, or the Natural Power of Kings* which attempted to uphold the divine right of kings via reference to the patriarchs of the Bible. Filmer explicitly argued that the state is a family with kings as fathers and subjects as children!

The denial of the Father in the theological sphere already had a political aspect to it. It is perhaps not so well remembered that Luther and the other Protestants wanted to establish a system where church leaders would be elected by the congregation. The seeds of modern democracy were already present, but these democratic tendencies were suppressed by the kings of Europe, who did not want to lose their political power. Well, perhaps *suppression* is too light a word. Somewhere between one hundred and three hundred thousand peasants were killed in the uprisings that accompanied the Reformation, an early tremor presaging the political earthquakes that followed in the next centuries.

With the divine right of kings gone, it was only a matter of time before the kings themselves would go. Just one hundred years after the death of Luther and the liquidation of the monasteries by Henry VIII, the king of England got his head chopped off. At his trial, Charles I invoked the divine right of authority granted to kings:

"*No earthly power can justly call me (who am your King) in question as a delinquent ... this day's proceeding cannot be warranted by God's laws; for, on the contrary, the authority of obedience unto Kings is clearly warranted, and strictly commanded in both the Old and New Testament...*"

Note the wording here: *obedience to kings*. That is the obedience of the old world, the unquestioning obedience due to the Father. The exact same argument had been used by Henry VIII when the peasants revolted against his shutting down of the monasteries. Robert Filmer's characterisation of the state as Father was no metaphor. It was how people really thought about these matters. Henry VIII had demanded obedience and got it. Charles I was not so lucky. When we say that the execution of Charles I is the rejection of the archetypal (Tyrannical) Father, in a psychological and political sense, this is not a metaphor. In Filmer's terms, the "children" had grown up. Although Britain was not the first country to have a parliament, the model developed after its civil war became the template that would later spread to other western nations and which has come to maturity in our time with the universal suffrage that the Protestants had originally wanted for their churches.

The archetypal pattern that underlies the developments that we now consider to be an integral part of Faustian culture in its maturity should now be clear. The Reformation was the rejection of the Father that had been inherited from the Classical world. But that Father was already a complex symbol, fusing elements from the Classical culture with the Jewish tradition via the Bible. This brings us to a fourth and final aspect of the Faustian that has come to maturity in our time. The collapse in religious attendance in the post-war years follows the fact that belief in Christianity also collapsed among the educated classes of Europe in the 19th century. Interestingly, this was something that Calvin had noted was built-in to the Protestant belief system when he said, "there remaineth nothing else for the rest but the reproach of atheism."

It is not well remembered how much anxiety the removal of the Father/Elders by the Protestants caused. We will avoid a theological explanation for why that is, since it would take us too far off course. But we can state as a simple psychological fact justified by the evidence that Protestant priests used to complain that members of their congregation would come to them with crippling anxiety. At least part of that anxiety was caused by the removal of the Elder as a source of authority. For those who could not make the transition to the written word and the sublimated Elder of the Bible, this was a real psychological burden that many could not carry. Although it's not what Calvin meant, atheism was understandable as a response. Another response which was more common in the early days was the progressive watering down of the Protestant message to make it more palatable. Both of these trends have now played out in our time with the continued decline of the importance of the church.

From all of these examples, we can see that the rejection of the Father is what allowed the Faustian to emerge during the Reformation and has shaped the civilisation in its Mature phase, which we still live in. In them, we find the attributes that define our modern world: atheism, materialism, science, the primacy of the university and the written word, newspapers, parliamentary democracy, capitalism. Alongside these, we find the more general properties we outlined earlier to describe Faustian civilisation: introversion, the primacy of Hero's Journeys over rites of passage, Esotericism, the mind over the body, the elites over the general public etc.

Only by understanding that the Faustian was built on a rejection of the Father and only by acknowledging that the Father was already an incredibly complex symbol combining political and religious elements from the Classical (Greek, Roman and the Jewish) tradition can we understand the paradoxes that have formed the world in which we live. What happens when you negate the Father? Do you thereby win "freedom" or do you just swap one form of authority for another? What we can see through the history of the Faustian beginning especially with the Reformation is the alternation between the rebellion against the Father and the idolisation of him. It is no coincidence that the idolisation has always correlated with a form of explicit authoritarianism (obedience to the Father) or that the rebellion has always been against that form of authority. Both Oedipal responses have been present over the centuries.

It is this dynamic which has set up the paradox of the modern world: it is based upon a rebellion against a Father who was himself born in the transition to Dominant Minority of the Classical civilisation and whose dominance was then Esoterically established over the nascent Faustian. What happens when the civilisation which has rejected the traditional archetype that represents the Dominant Minority itself comes to manifest its own Dominant Minority? What form of authority does that entail? We sketched out the answer to this question in symbolic terms at the end of Part 3 with our discussion of *Star Wars* and *The Matrix*. We have now laid the groundwork to fill in the details from a historical point of view.

Recalling our archetypal table from earlier:-

Microcosm	Macrocosm	Primary Faculty	Macrocosmic Manifestation
Child	Genesis	Imagination	Creative Minority
Orphan	Growth	Intellect	Creative Minority
Adult	Maturity	Will	Dominant Minority - Universal State
Elder	Old Age	Soul	Dominant Minority - Universal Church

We can now fill in the parts of the table that we have just analysed for our own civilisation; the Faustian:-

Microcosm	Macrocosm	Primary Faculty	Macrocosmic Manifestation	Manifestation (Faustian)
Child	Genesis	Imagination	Creative Minority	Catholic Church (Classical Pseudomorphosis)
Orphan	Growth	Intellect	Creative Minority	Reformation
Adult	Maturity	Will	Dominant Minority - Universal State	----
Elder	Old Age	Soul	Universal Church	----

The Reformation maps to the Orphan phase of the cycle, and we have traced out how it has set the stage for the Maturity phase that we now live in. The central event of the Maturity phase is the formation of what Toynbee called the Universal State. In the Classical civilisation, this was the emergence of the Roman empire and the transition of Rome from republic to military dictatorship. It was this exact transition that the military dictators of our time, Napoleon, Hitler, and Mussolini, were trying to re-enact, and it can be no coincidence that they explicitly referenced back to the Classical in order to do so. Even Nietzsche, in our quote from earlier, welcomed the return of the "slab of antiquity" presaged by the "classical age of war". The Oedipal idolisation of the Father is the attempt to mimic him exactly.

It is clear that the would-be Tyrannical Fathers have not succeeded in forming the Universal State of the Faustian. Given what we have just written, this should not be a surprise. The Faustian had rebelled against the Father beginning with the Reformation and so it would have required a complete about face to re-embrace the Father in its Mature phase. Nevertheless, the Mature phase implies the exercise of Will and the arrival of the Dominant Minority.

The Faustian civilisation solved this paradox by creating a new form of authority and a new pattern of dominance. It would not be military dictatorships which would form the full expression of the Faustian Will in its Maturity phase. To know what would form the expression of that Will, we have to look for what it was that defeated the Tyrannical Father.

Britain and the Origins of Informal Empire

In Britain (and also the Netherlands) was born the pattern which would eventually form the basis of the Universal State of the Faustian and which we now take completely for granted: parliamentary democracy and capitalism. The foundation of the British Empire from the beginning was not direct military conquest but trade. It was an empire built not by emperors, generals, kings, or queens but by what we would nowadays call *businessmen*. This was not an accidental occurrence. We have seen how Luther's father was a member of the emerging mercantilist class. The policy of mercantilism was pursued quite deliberately in Europe, and the nations that had easy access to the sea - Britain, Spain, Portugal and the Netherlands - had an advantage. The merchant class were the precursors to what would later be called the bourgeoisie, or capitalists.

We can see that the legal, political, and economic basis for modern capitalism was already in place as early as 1600 when the East India Company was founded as a joint stock company with private money for the purposes of competing with the Dutch, Spanish and Portuguese for the lucrative spice trade. Nowadays, we take limited-stock companies (corporations) completely for granted. But the East India Company was a very different, very unusual, institution in its initial manifestation. It had its own flag, its own governance structure, its own army, its own universities to train its staff, and even its own currency. It was a multi-national corporation, and yet, it had all of the Exoteric markers that we would now ascribe to an independent nation state. In fact, for quite some time, the Company had a larger standing army than the nation that had given birth to it. It used that army to conquer large parts of India and otherwise secure its global interests.

As if all that wasn't weird enough, the Company "did business" with two separate ruling classes on two separate continents. It had a charter from the British crown and was nominally representing British interests overseas. At exactly the same time, it was acting as a de facto government for the Mughal emperor in India, whose visage even appeared on some of the coins the Company produced. The Mughal rulers found it in equal parts perplexing and humiliating to be made to sign treaties not with royalty or national leaders with the usual pomp and ceremony reserved for matters of state but with lowly merchants in grubby offices. They were forced to do so because the armies of the Company had conquered their own. In the East India Company, there was a nominally private corporation waging war against, and then serving as an effective government for, a foreign emperor while returning the profits back to England.

Although there was a certain level of political opposition to this at home, while the money kept flowing, neither the British government nor Crown seemed to care much about how the Company operated in its overseas business dealings. However, in 1773, we saw what was certainly the world's first corporate bailout as the Company asked the Bank of England for what was, at the time, an enormous amount of money to keep it afloat. Since the Company was "too big to fail", the British government complied but thereafter decided to get more involved to prevent similar outcomes in the future. It required a governor-general to be appointed to represent the interests of the British government in India. Even then, the governor-general was appointed by the board of directors of the East India Company. Already at this early stage, we see the intertwining of parliament and corporate interests, which still exists to this day. It was an early formation of what is now sometimes called *the deep state*.

Although this pattern is deeply unusual on historical grounds, we can nevertheless see how it makes sense within the history of Faustian civilisation that we have just sketched out. The rebellion against the Father was also a rebellion against the Ruler. The English had decapitated their Ruler, Charles I, and replaced him with parliament. For internal political reasons, they later decided to reappoint a king, but it was on terms dictated by parliament. The Ruler archetype was reinstated, but the role became increasingly ceremonial over time. The real power lay behind the scenes. The same pattern was then repeated in India. Nominally, the Mughal emperors fulfilled the Ruler archetype. But the real power lay with the East India Company as the effective government.

All of this fits perfectly with our earlier characterisation of the Faustian civilisation as being occult, Esoteric and introverted. The Faustian has always been about the Mask. It was this that Luther had rebelled against in the form of the Church which wore the mask of holiness but, behind the scenes, was basically the first multinational corporation. Appearance and reality were not the same thing, and, for Luther, as for most people throughout history, this was an intolerable state of affairs.

We must remember, however, that this had been the case right from the beginning of Faustian civilisation. Charlemagne was not a *king of the Romans* in any real sense. The Holy Roman Empire was not holy, Roman or an empire. The terminology, the symbolism, all the Exoteric forms, were brought over from the Classical and overlaid on a culture which operated completely differently. For Luther, the discovery of this was an existential crisis. For Spengler, it was simply the nature of the Faustian as an occult civilisation that existed beneath the Exoteric forms and operated through them.

Thus, the deeply weird institution of the East India Company actually makes sense once we understand that the Faustian civilisation has always been about the Esoteric that lies beneath the surface. Whether an English king or a Mughal emperor was sitting on the throne made little difference from the Company's point of view. In the operation of the East India Company, we see the origins of the specific manner in which modern power came to be exercised and still is exercised to this day. That power no longer rests in the Ruler (the Father) but in the opaque network of corporate, parliamentary, and diplomatic interests that sit beneath him. It was this network which built the British Empire, and that's why the British Empire never had an emperor. It simply didn't need one.

Britain may have been the first empire in history to create what historian Jeremy Black has called an *Informal Empire*. This empire ran not on direct military conquest but on trade. Here again, we see yet another inversion of the Classical. The Romans benefitted from the trade that their empire facilitated, but the power of the empire was always based in the military. Thus, the word *empire* comes from the Latin *imperator* which was originally the title given to the commander of a Roman army.

What is an Informal Empire? A form of command without a leader; without a Father figure. We could substitute the word *informal* with any of the other adjectives we have used to describe the Faustian. An Informal Empire is an Occult Empire, an Esoteric Empire, an Introverted Empire. In psychological terms, it is an Unconscious Empire because nobody until fairly recently has been able to recognise it for what it is, and this almost certainly includes most of the people who were actively involved in building it. Empires have emperors. That is what the mind looks for. When it cannot find it, it assumes that whatever is going on must not be an empire.

Of course, the British did know they were running an empire, and that's because they were still engaged in other forms of imperialism that were recognisable. Thus, when Rudyard Kipling wrote *The White Man's Burden*, this was an encouragement to Americans to pursue an old-fashioned form of imperialism through military conquest. The final stanza is worth reproducing:-

Take up the White Man's burden—

Have done with childish days—
  The lightly proffered laurel,
   The easy, ungrudged praise.
 Comes now, to search your manhood
   Through all the thankless years,
 Cold-edged with dear-bought wisdom,
   The judgment of your peers!

"Have done with childish days". In our archetypal terms, this can be considered a call to the Orphans to become Adults and exercise the Will of "manhood". Since it deals with the macrocosm, it is the call for the civilisation itself to reach its own Maturity as an expression of its Will. It's all very reminiscent of our Nietzsche quote from earlier.

There are two lines in the middle of the poem that are also worthy of attention:

Take up the White Man's burden—
  No tawdry rule of kings,

No tawdry rule of kings channels the implied rejection of the Father. Kipling does not refer to the judgement of a Father but of *your peers* once again, referencing the network of interests that has been the basis of the Faustian during its Maturity phase. The fact that Kipling was writing the poem as an argument against the anti-imperialist movement in the United States will become a crucial point in our later analysis.

Most historians would agree that the British Empire's dominance was certified by its defeat of Napoleon. When we analyse that defeat from an archetypal point of view, we see something that fits perfectly with our earlier analysis. Remembering the two Oedipal responses of the Faustian in its relationship with the Classical Father. We have the idolatry trend and the rebellious trend, which began in earnest with the Reformation. We have seen that the Informal Empire of the British was based very much on rebellion. The British more than any other European power (except, perhaps, the Dutch) had thrown off the Father in the form of the king.

Napoleon's rise was initially part of a movement in France that had an identical goal. The Republican movement was heavily influenced by the British example and by British ideas. Napoleon was originally part of a group of Kipling's *peers* fighting for republicanism, but he ended up manifesting not an empire of peers but an old-fashioned military dictatorship based, as Nietzsche pointed out, on the Roman paradigm. He tried to become the Tyrannical Father. It was, of course, exactly when he made that transition that he lost a great deal of support, including, most famously, from Beethoven. What Napoleon ended up doing was trying to create a Universal State in Europe based on the Classical example. His defeat by the British was the defeat of the old paradigm by the new pattern of Informal Empire which henceforth became the dominant force in Faustian politics.

About a century later, we see yet another attempt to create a Universal State in Europe based on the Classical example. This time there was not a single Tyrannical Father figure but several, including the two most famous, Hitler and Mussolini. Once again, both of these men included explicit references back to both Rome and the Holy Roman Empire. Just like Napoleon, both Hitler and Mussolini emerged out of a movement of *peers* only to become Tyrannical Fathers, just as Stalin did in Russia and Mao did in China.

Since historians focus on the dramatic military aspects of these developments, what is often missed are the developments beneath the surface. As good Faustian thinkers, we know that it is there that we must look to understand what was really going on.

Napoleon had ushered in the era of Total War. One of his innovations was to have extensive and well-organised supply lines. Another was conscription. These allowed him to form massive armies with which to overwhelm the enemy. One of the side effects, however, was to significantly blur the lines between combatants and non-combatants. Was a civilian who had a paid job supplying the army a combatant or a non-combatant? Perhaps more important than the abstract moral question was the fact that armies built on long supply lines were now dependent on the civilian population. Beginning in the 18th century, military power was increasingly tied to the power of the general economy of a nation. Accordingly, one way to wage war against an enemy was to target their economy, and that meant indirectly targeting civilians.

This led to a form of geopolitical competition that was also very strange by historical standards. With the advent of Total War, the line between combatants and the general public became blurred. As the industrial revolution proceeded, this blurring became even more pronounced since the ability to wage war became synonymous with industrial capacity. In response to these developments, sabotage became an invisible, occult, and Esoteric (there's those Faustian adjectives again!) form of warfare. Any reduction in the capacity of a potential enemy to wage war, for example, in the stifling of their economy, was a small "victory" in the larger competition. But competition no longer began with the commencement of hostilities and ended with a peace treaty. The shift to industrial economies and Total War created a kind of permanent state of economic warfare.

Thus, with the British defeat of Napoleon, the fight for supremacy moved very much into the Esoteric realm of the Informal Empire. From a military point of view, the 19th century was incredibly peaceful by historical standards. In fact, "war" had been sublimated into the economic realm, where Britain now held the major advantage over its continental rivals. Even Germany eventually competed with Britain in the new paradigm of Informal Empire by looking for trade and financial partnerships across the globe, but Britain's head start gave it an edge.

A very large part of the workings of Informal Empire involved restricting the trade and financial opportunities of competitor nations. Commercial sabotage included more overt practices like piracy (privateering) and reached a dramatic new phase with the Boston Tea Party which was an overt act of trade vandalism. With the advent of modern finance, Informal Empire has become increasingly esoteric in nature. It even seeped into the peace treaties that followed defeat in war ,which increasingly came to resemble commercial contracts. For example, among the terms and conditions of the Treaty of Versailles, there were a number which required German banks and companies to relinquish ownership of various assets, including the Deutsche

Bank's share in the Baghdad railway. We can see that war, business, and finance had become intertwined. It became impossible to say where one began and the other ended. It could well be said that war had become the extension of business by other means, a pattern that the East India Company had established.

Kings and emperors down through history ruled in an extroverted, Exoteric fashion. It was in an emperor's interest to project his power as much as possible to dissuade challengers from trying their luck. The imperialism of the Faustian has occasionally taken such an Exoteric form. But, for the most part, it has been Esoteric. Whatever else can be said about that Classical world, it was out there in the open. Everybody knew who the boss was. In the Faustian form of empire, there is no boss; no *tawdry rule of kings* to use Kipling's phase. There is a network of interests - a group of peers. Importantly, the configuration of that network is always changing, which creates the dynamism that is the system's great strength. That great strength is also a source of angst. It is this ever-shifting, ever-changing dynamic with the absence of formal authority which gives the Faustian civilisation a peculiar underlying anxiety, trapped like Macbeth and Banquo in the misty forests where the line between illusion and reality becomes all but invisible.

To the misty fogs of the Faustian forest must be added the ever-increasing amount of ideology that came to accompany the game of politics. A classic example is what historians Ronald Robinson and Jeremy Black have called the "imperialism of free trade" pursued by Britain in the 19th century. This was a series of treaties, banking arrangements, diplomatic efforts, and business connections through which wealth was transferred back to the imperial centre, but it was overlaid with a thick veneer of scholarly debate, much of which, it has to be said, was pursued with honest conviction. The universities that gave birth to the Reformation now became the system which produced the ideology. Of course, they also trained the lawyers, accountants, and other technocrats who would put it into action.

Arguably the most important of those technocrats, and the group that became increasingly influential as the Informal Empire matured into its final form, were the bankers. Here we have one of the more obvious ways in which the rejection of the Father led to the emergence of the modern paradigm since the sin of usury had been upheld, for the most part, by the Catholic Church. That is why the work of providing banking services had been left to the Jews of Europe. Although Luther was against usury, other Protestants including Calvin had a more relaxed view, and thus the Reformation also opened the way for banking to ascend to the central place it now holds in the Informal Empire of the Faustian Universal State.

Once again, it was no coincidence that this process accelerated in the 19th century and, while the Jews were still prominent in the banking industry at that time, as Hannah Arendt pointed out, the blaming of the Jews for the banking crises of the 19th and 20th centuries happened at just the time when banking had gone mainstream and it had become acceptable for non-Jewish Europeans to become bankers. The scapegoating of the Jews gave those bankers the perfect cover for their own malfeasance. In any case, the crucial point is that banking had now become central to empire and it's no coincidence that the Pound sterling had become a primary source of British power and that attacks on a nation's financial system were added to the methods of economic sabotage and warfare.

Spengler was well aware of these new forms of economic warfare, but here we see another curious oversight on his part. Despite being a historian of genius and despite having written one of the great works of history in the Faustian style, Spengler saw in the new form of warfare not a uniquely Faustian form of dominance, even though he had brilliantly identified modern finance as being a specifically Faustian invention. Rather, Spengler, following in the footsteps of Nietzsche, predicted a return to the military paradigm. Spengler called this *Caesarism*. How ironic that the man whose work had done so much to define the nature of the Faustian as separate from the Classical would hearken back to the Classical in such an obvious fashion! It cannot be a coincidence that this is one of the few things that Spengler got wrong (although, of course, there is always the possibility that he will be proved right in the future, even though circumstances make that look highly unlikely).

Of the new form of Informal Empire, Spengler wrote in his book, *The Hour of Decision*: "There is no telling how this economic war will end, but it is certain that it will finally restore to the State as *authority* its historical rights, based on voluntary...and highly mobile armies." Spengler's emphasis on that little word, *authority,* is crucial here. He desired an authority based on military prowess, just as had existed in ancient Rome. To be sure, it was also the form of authority that Napoleon had tried to exert, and it was the form of authority that Hitler attempted to exert again in the years after Spengler wrote his book.

We have seen that the desire for the Father, for the authority figure, was present in ancient Rome at the time of the formation of the Universal State. That this desire should once again reappear at the same point in the civilisational cycle for the Faustian is not surprising. Our archetypal logic predicts it, in fact. But even the would-be Tyrannical Fathers of the Faustian were explicitly not Caesars. Spengler criticised the machinations of Informal Empire as being born in the proletarian rebellion against authority. But so, too, were the military dictators who arose to challenge the new paradigm. Napoleon was an outsider, born in Corsica to rebel parents. He was not of "noble" background. He was proletarian. The same was true of Hitler, Stalin and Mao. Mussolini and Lenin were middle-class at best. All of the would-be Caesars of the Faustian were themselves proletarian.

Moreover, they were all intellectuals in a way that the Roman aristocracy would have found deeply dishonourable. Mussolini, Lenin and Stalin were newspaper editors and, apparently, very fine journalists. Lenin graduated top of his class before being kicked out of university by the authorities. Even Hitler famously wanted to attend art college. All of them became involved with grassroots intellectual movements. They were, in most respects, the opposite of what Spengler believed Caesarism represented as some kind of innate aristocratic instinct born out of good breeding. Of course, the same is true of Spengler who was born into a family of modest means and lived for many years in poverty. Similar to Stalin and Mussolini, he eked out a living as a teacher and occasional writer for magazines. All these men were the product of that uniquely Faustian institution: the university.

The rise of these intellectuals into positions of old-fashioned "authority" is almost certainly a result of the innate collective psychological desire for somebody to take control of a world that had ceased to make sense. That was also the reason for all the complicated intellectual theories that the intellectuals of that era were immersing themselves in. It was a desire to understand a world that had become so complex precisely because it had ceased to rely on centralised authority. This astonishing complexity could never have been achieved through the rigid, hierarchical political system implied by a Tyrannical Father. Thus, the overthrow of the Father was a necessary prerequisite for the Informal Empire to emerge.

We have already noted the psychological and existential angst that this new, Esoteric form of dominance created in the collective psyche. The feeling of being adrift, of the loss of authority, and of the loss of shared cultural bonds was felt most strongly on the continent. A pattern that we see time and again throughout the 19th and 20th centuries was a burning desire to throw off the Father on the one hand and then a reactionary force that looked for the Father to save the day. The French Revolution allowed the rise of Napoleon. The German mini-revolution of 1918 opened the door for Hitler. The Russian Revolution led to Stalin. The Chinese civil war gave rise to Mao.

We have to remember that, even in England, the rebellion against the Father had been led by somebody who was arguably a tyrant in his own right. Cromwell fought off the more radical egalitarian forces that were at play and probably prevented the worst excess that would later be seen on the continent. It was his personality that held the country together, while the vacuum created by his death led parliament to put a king back on the throne. Even England was not ready to do without the Father entirely.

England, however, gave birth to a country that would be ready to throw off the Father. It was a country born out of the spirit of the Reformation and which had inherited all of the British institutions needed for the exercise of Informal Empire. Can it be a coincidence that the nation in which the rebellion against the Father was the most pronounced has ended up becoming the Universal State of Faustian civilisation?

Spengler had correctly identified the pattern of the Informal Empire but could not see that it was a specifically Faustian form of dominance. Who would defeat Napoleon and then later Hitler? It was the Informal Empire begun in Britain and then brought to perfection in the nation born from the British template. It was the nation that had thrown off the Tyrannical Father most strongly and was, therefore, the most prepared to practice the new pattern of dominance. It was the United States of America.

The Defeat of the Tyrannical Father

Spengler may have been wrong in his prediction about the form that the Universal State of the Faustian would take, but he was dead right on another point. He said that the Universal State of a civilisation is not formed as a conscious or deliberate plan by the people who will eventually take up the mantle. On the contrary, it is more correct to say that the Universal State is forced upon a nation. This notion fits with our interpretation of the macrocosmic cycle as being a set of archetypal Hero's Journeys. The Call to Adventure in the Hero's Journey is offered to the hero; it doesn't originate with them, at least not with their conscious mind. We have already seen how the battle that Luther had with his own Unconscious tapped into the Collective Unconscious of his time and blew up into an archetypal transition for the entire Faustian civilisation. We would expect to see a similar pattern at the time of the transition to the Universal State representing the Maturity phase of the civilisation and we already know that the two world wars were exactly that. Thus, the formation of the Universal State is also a Hero's Journey – a challenge from the Unconscious.

It is a curious fact that both Toynbee and Spengler failed to predict the exact form that the Universal State would take, even though they had both anticipated its arrival. We have seen that Spengler's error of thinking that the Universal State would reproduce the Classical form was a popular idea in Germany at that time and was shared by Nietzsche. Toynbee was closer to the mark, at least on surface appearances. He predicted something similar to the global institutions of the United Nations; a kind of global pact based around a shared constitution. The fact that both men were superficially wrong and that Spengler got himself caught up with the Nazi movement, has no doubt done much to discredit both in the post-war years, where, we are told, it is now the *end of history*. However, in true Faustian style, we know that we need to look beneath the surface appearance to find out what's going on. When we do so, we do indeed find that the Faustian has created its Universal State. Since we have the benefit of hindsight, our job is easier than Spengler and Toynbee's, although it has still taken an entire book to lay the analytical groundwork necessary to decode the mystery. As usual, the Faustian requires a theory in order to be understood. Seemingly self-evident facts only mislead.

One of the main pillars of our integrated model has been the difference between the Exoteric and Esoteric which maps, albeit imperfectly, to the difference between consciousness and the Unconscious. What is visible is what is conscious. What is invisible is harder to bring to consciousness. In psychological terms, the Hero's Journey requires the confrontation with what is not yet visible and is therefore difficult to bring to consciousness. In bringing in to consciousness, one integrates it at all levels of the Self.

We have touched numerous times on the uniqueness of the historical consciousness of Faustian civilisation. This bringing to consciousness of history was present right from the very start in the form of the ruins of the Roman Empire and the Catholic Church as the Exoteric institution that created the Faustian. We have relied on Toynbee and Spengler for our analysis, but around the turn of the 18th century, the work of the Italian, Giambattista Vico, and the Frenchman, Charles Rollin, had already outlined the concept of the cycle of civilisations in some detail. The Faustian was born with the knowledge that the mighty Classical civilisation had perished. It subsequently extrapolated that knowledge to civilisations in general, including, of course, the Faustian itself.

This historical consciousness was present and very influential in the birth of the United States and the subsequent way in which the US has understood its position in the world. The idea of American exceptionalism is predicated on historical consciousness since the *exception* is against the historical norm. Thomas Paine gave expression to the sentiment when he stated in *Common Sense* that the US was an opportunity for a brand new beginning. The USA was founded on the belief that Europe was descending back into the kind of tyranny that signalled the decline of civilisation. The perception of George III as the Tyrannical Father was related to this since the tyrannies of the past were driven by just this archetype. The "independence" that the colonists sought was not just from the Tyrannical Father but from the historical decline that his arrival was seen to precipitate.

All of this was a continuation of the rebellion against the Father that had begun with the Reformation, and it is no coincidence that the colonies had more than their fair share of Protestants and Puritans. It was this reason that Thomas Paine was still using the divine right of kings as a punching bag in *Common Sense* to unify the colonies around the idea of a new nation. The following quote is representative of the way in which he portrayed the matter:

"And a man hath good reason to believe that there is as much of king-craft, as priest-craft, in withholding the scripture from the public in Popish countries. For monarchy in every instance is the Popery of government."

We can see in this statement the logical conclusion of the point we made earlier which is that the kings of northern Europe had undermined their own authority when they disintermediated the Pope. The British had put a puppet (archetypal?) king back on the throne for internal political reasons, but the American colonists had no such need. They were prepared to go all the way and realise the logical outcome of what had begun with the rejection of the Pope during the Reformation. They were finally throwing off the Tyrannical Father once and for all. The historian, Kenneth Lynn, put it this way:-

"The psychologically painful experience of overthrowing the father figure of George III and of breaking the historical connection between the colonies and the imperial *parens patriae* was led by colonists who had not been tyrannised over by their own fathers, and who in fact were accustomed to thinking of parental authority as a guarantor of filial freedom and self-realisation."

Within this short passage are several key points. First is the theme which has been the foundation of our analysis: that the emergence of the mature Faustian has been predicated on the rejection of the (Tyrannical) Father. Second is the correspondence between macrocosm and microcosm. The rejection of the Father was not just a macrocosmic event; it was predicated on fundamental changes that had occurred at the level of the family. These changes were not arbitrary. In Rome, the father was the head of the household and exercised what we would consider a tyrannical level of control and legal authority over his family. Luther's rebellion against his own father and later the Pope needs to be seen as the rejection of this kind of authority. A century or two later, the position of the Father had changed. As Lynn notes, the American colonists had been raised in a new kind of culture where the Father did not play the role of tyrant in the household, and they then demanded the macrocosmic Father to do the same.

The third point to make is perhaps even more crucial as it relates back to the negative freedom implied in the declaration of independence. The colonists of the USA believed they were rebelling against tyranny **and** imperialism and that their nation was therefore founded upon a rejection of both of those concepts. This belief was based not just on the behaviour of the European kings but an understanding of history. Wherever imperialism had appeared, it was correlated with the Tyrannical Father. To reject the Tyrannical Father was, therefore, to reject imperialism in general and to create a society where imperialism would never take hold. That was the conscious understanding of what had happened.

The problem with that idea is that we see the emergence of Informal Empire right from the beginning of the United States. In fact, the United States was founded on exactly the kinds of commercial, trade, and financial weaponisation that sits at the heart of the battle for Informal Empire. For decades before the military hostilities began in the War of Independence, the colonists had taken a series of measures that were designed to win political concessions by hijacking British trade. These measures worked to achieve the repeal of several acts in the British Parliament. The Boston Tea Party was actually the last and most serious of these measures. It was an act of commercial sabotage that represented such an escalation of the economic and trade war that the British Parliament felt obligated to respond with even harsher measures, which became known as the Intolerable Acts.

What led eventually to military hostilities was the progressive ramping up of all the practices of Informal Empire which revolve around the nexus of commerce, trade, and politics. The revolutionary war was conducted as much off the battlefield as on it. Even during the military hostilities, much of the battle was economic in nature. The British took control of American ports in order to prevent both exports and imports, thereby reducing the colonists' income. Meanwhile, the colonists attempted to block any trade with the British army on American soil. When the French joined the war, the British used similar tactics aimed at blocking trade to the French-controlled sugar plantations in the Caribbean.

These economic tactics on the part of the British worked to a very large extent. The American colonists were short of cash due to an inability to levy taxes and the massive inflation caused by trying to pay for the war by printing money. The founding fathers made the reluctant decision to approach another Father figure, Loius XVI, knowing full well that they were in danger of swapping one tyranny for another. Louis XVI was happy to help because he was still bitter about the French defeat to the British in the Seven Years War. The Spanish also provided significant assistance since they were interested in weakening British power as well. American political "independence" was won at the cost of economic and financial dependence. In the aftermath of the war, the nascent United States had significant debt obligations back to Europe, and these were a serious concern for the new nation.

Here, the Americans had an incredibly lucky break. Louis XVI may have been an enthusiastic supporter of the colonists for his own political, and perhaps egotistical, reasons. There was just one problem: France was bankrupt. The fiscal fallout that fell on France for supporting the Americans ushered in the French Revolution, enabling the Americans to skip out on their debts to the French. Even then, the failure to pay was a cause of significant diplomatic tension that resulted in military hostilities between the French and Americans, and which may have escalated if it wasn't for the fact that France was descending into political chaos. As a final ironic twist on the story, Britain was happy to restore trade links almost immediately after the war and thereby became the main trading partner with its old colony, a position which France had assumed it would achieve as a reward for its assistance.

The point of all of this is that, although the US might have become politically independent, it was still tied back to old Europe for trade, and the economic dependence created by trade could be manipulated for political reasons. That is the game that all parties in the War of Independence played. Much of the support provided by France and Spain to the American colonists was channelled through nominally private companies. This allowed the French and Spanish to clandestinely support the cause for about two years before formally joining the hostilities. All of this − the use of trade and commerce to support war efforts, the sabotage of trade and commerce to hurt an enemy, the encouragement of debt obligations to win political concessions from an "ally" − belongs to the practice of Informal Empire, and we can see that the US already knew exactly how to play that game before it achieved formal political independence from Britain.

That's why the Boston Tea Party was a perfect symbolic event for what was really going on. In the years leading up to the event, the East India Company had gotten the British Parliament to give it a monopoly on the trade in tea. This created a market failure. The price of tea in Britain went up, which is what usually happens when one company has a monopoly, but the British public realised they could buy tea cheaper from the Netherlands. Parliament tried various tax and tariff responses to try and fix the market failure they created, and the American colonies were one avenue to address the problem. Britain had assumed the colonists were dependent enough to accept whatever Parliament ordered. Thus, the already complex interplay between parliament and commercial interests was already in full swing.

There is one more aspect of the Boston Tea Party that is of key symbolic importance. As we have just implied, the tea that was dumped in the harbour had been supplied by the company that we know was central to the formation of Informal Empire; the East India Company. A naïve reading of the affair might lead one to assume that the colonists were against the Company. In fact, the opposite was true. Prior to the war, a number of leading colonists looked to the East India Company as an example of "self-rule"; one that they might like to emulate. This would be a weird thing to believe if the East India Company had been a modern corporation, but we know from our earlier discussion that it behaved in most ways exactly like a nation state. One of the markers for that was its flag.

No better symbol of the influence that the Company had on the American colonists can be found than the fact that the original flag of the US, the grand union flag, was practically identical to that of the East India Company. It had the now famous red and white stripes in the body, with the Union Jack in the canton. After the war of independence, the Union Jack was swapped for the familiar stars, giving the stars and stripes. The symbolic importance of this is hard to overstate, but it should not be that much of a surprise, since we have already established that the colonists saw trade as the basis of their freedom, and the East India Company was a paragon example of that "freedom".

There are several key points to make about these matters. The first one is the aforementioned difference between what was conscious and unconscious in the minds of the general public. Consciously, the colonists believed they were rebelling against the Tyrannical Father in the form of King George III and that this rebellion would win independence from Europe which was believed to be more broadly descending into the kind of tyranny that signaled civilisational decline. The United States was to be a fresh start based on freedom. What was unconscious (for most people) was that political freedom had been won in large part using a variety of covert and clandestine tactics that we have grouped under the label Informal Empire. These were not believed to be techniques of politics and therefore were not categorised in that way, even though it was clear that trade, economics, and finance were already being weaponised to achieve political outcomes.

The second point is that this is an almost identical pattern that we saw earlier with Luther. The word Protestant itself comes from the word "protest". The Protestants did have some new and interesting ideas for the practice of faith, but these were not couched in positive terms but negative terms of a rebellion against the Pope just like the American colonists had to couch whatever positive vision they had as a rebellion against King George III. Luther had used the relatively unknown technology of the printing press to achieve his goals, and the American colonists had used the relatively unknown practices of economic and trade warfare to achieve theirs. What Luther did was to swap one theology for another, and what the colonists did was to swap one form of politics with another, but both of them had to be done through rebellion rather than in a more positive fashion.

All of this follows from the larger point we have been making about Faustian civilisation. The dominance of the Father carried over from the Classical meant that the Faustian had to rebel against the Exoteric and Esoteric forms inherited from the ancient world. Because of the strength of the Classical influence over the Faustian, when the Faustian finally broke through into the expression of its own ideals, it framed these in a negative sense, not as goods in their own right but as rejections of the Tyrannical Father. Thus, the main body of the US Declaration of Independence is a list of grievances against King George III, and we all know of Luther's list of 95 grievances nailed to the door of the church. This is all part of the general pattern which Spengler identified whereby the Faustian is always in opposition to the Classical. This is so because the Faustian had to first break free of the Classical before it could realise its own forms. It was the Child civilisation that had gotten stuck in the Orphan phase and which needed to escape from the dominance of its Parent.

A third and crucial point follows from this, which is that the United States' rebellion against King George III was not a rejection of Faustian civilisation itself. On the contrary, it was a perfect expression of that civilisation. It was, in fact, the Faustian civilisation reaching its maturity in a political sense, just as Luther's rebellion against the Church had been the beginning of the mature phase in a theological one. The United States is an exemplar of all the main characteristics we have come to describe as being the true Faustian, which only could emerge once the Father of the Classical had been rebelled against. We have already seen how the colonists were adept at practicing the new forms of politics in the form of trade and economic disputes mediated through parliament. In the political and legal sense, America was born with all the elements which have come to maturity in our time and that we completely take for granted.

We saw earlier how Faustian culture had rejected rites of passage and replaced them with the written word. It is no coincidence that the prodigals and pilgrims of early America were highly literate for their time. It is for this reason that a book like Thomas Paine's *Common Sense* could be so influential in the formation of the country. One year after its publication, its sales figures equalled 20% of the US population. Luther had utilised the technology of the printing press in his rebellion against the Pope. The Americans would utilise it to rebel against the King. What could be more Faustian than the fact that the United States was founded on written documents? The Declaration of Independence and the US Constitution are the political equivalents to Luther's 95 theses nailed to the church door. With them, the Faustian civilisation realises its maturity in a political sense. The British constitution had remained largely unwritten. It was up to the Americans to put it in words.

Numerous other countries duly followed suit. In the early 19th century, almost every country in South America wrote their own declarations of independence to break free of Spanish rule. We see the practice as far afield as New Zealand, where the *Treaty of Waitangi* has the exact same format as the US document, albeit for very different political purposes. In archetypal terms, the declaration of independence was the phase change from Orphan to Adult. The Faustian civilisation declared itself to be independent of the Father held over from the Classical.

Thus, in the nascent United States, we see all the elements of the true Faustian present. The emphasis on the written word, the legal, political, and economic frameworks to enable mercantilism, the Enlightenment ideals of science and progress, parliamentary democracy, and more. Crucially, we see the game of Informal Empire being played right from the beginning. It was a game that the United States would become highly adept at, and it is the game on which the Universal State of the Faustian is now based. It was because the Faustian had the consciousness of history that the American colonists and others could believe they had put an end to the tyrannical exercise of

Will while also practicing a new form of Will. That new form of Will could only be practiced openly once the Father had been denied in the fullest terms possible.

It is this new form of Will that has come to predominate more and more as the Faustian has reached its Maturity phase. How shall we characterise a form of Will that has been defined negatively as a rejection of patriarchal authority? I had accidentally stumbled across the answer in my book, *The Devouring Mother: The Collective Unconscious in the Time of Corona*, and we have already outlined the basis for the answer in our distinction between the Tyrannical Father portrayed in *Star Wars* and the Devouring Mother of *The Matrix*. Before we come to the last part of our analysis and outline the specific way in which the United States established the Universal State of Faustian civilisation, we first need to talk about the hyper masculine and the devouring feminine.

The Masculine vs. the Feminine Will

It is noteworthy that philosophical debates around the exercise of power in the 19th century were still hung up on the historical paradigm of the Tyrannical Father. The argument was often framed under the concept of "paternalism". To what extent it was permissible for the government to exercise a Tyrannical Father pattern of dominance over a citizen was debated by the philosopher John Stuart Mill. If a man was going to cross a bridge that was about to collapse, we were within our rights to violate his "freedom" and exercise a paternal form of Will to save his life by preventing him from crossing, using violence if necessary. The power of the Tyrannical Father could be exercised, but only as a last resort.

Even as liberal a thinker as Mill allowed an out-clause for the exercise of paternal power in relation to the native tribes of the various places where Europeans had established the Faustian civilisation. It should not surprise us in the slightest that the framing of this was done using an explicit Child – Parent metaphor. The savage tribes were the "children" to the European "adults". Although a Faustian government could not act as Tyrannical Father to its own citizens, it was allowable for it to do so in relation to the childlike peoples of the world.

On this subject, we have a crucial piece of information that distinguishes the exercise of paternal authority from the informal kinds of authority we have associated with trade and commerce. Importantly, it is from the earliest days of the new nation, the USA. In several of his private letters, Thomas Jefferson laid out a plan for how to approach the issue of the native Americans. He recommended undermining the autarky of the native tribes by removing the basis of their self-sufficiency while simultaneously offering the olive branch of "trade". The goal was to make the native American population dependent, especially through the accrual of debts, after which Jefferson hoped the two peoples could become one through assimilation.

Jefferson's strategy was predicated on the observation that the alternative to this indirect approach was direct confrontation that could only result in the slaughter of the native American population due to their inferior military technology. On that question, he turned out to be one hundred percent correct. It was the more direct approach that prevailed for much of the westward expansion of the United States. Perhaps the most extreme example was the Mexican American War where Ulysses S. Grant lamented his participation in the one-sided butchery of the native population. Jefferson correctly saw the choice as between assimilation through trade and annihilation in battle.

It is no small irony that exactly the same calculus would later face Faustian civilisation itself. The advent of Total War had already blurred the boundary line between soldiers and civilians. Alongside advances in military technology, this made the slaughter of civilian populations a part of war. As it turned out, the US was at the forefront of that development too, with its own civil war resulting in a shocking number of casualties among civilians. The practice would only become more intense until we get to the mass bombings of civilian populations on both sides in WW2 and, of course, the big one: the atomic bomb attack on Japan.

We may see in this the blind force of chance or technological "progress", but just as the printing press had given Luther the edge over the Pope, so too does it seem incredibly coincidental that military technology should make the old form of Tyrannical Father domination redundant. That was, of course, something that Nietzsche and even Spengler could not foresee since both died before even the idea of the bomb was concocted. With the advent of the atomic bomb, Jefferson's choice between military-based slaughter and assimilation through trade was now an existential one for the whole world. Informal Empire was now the only game in town.

What happens when the Tyrannical Father is denied but a civilisation must exercise power nonetheless? We already outlined the answer to this in Part 3 when we noted that the alternative form of dominance was the feminine one embodied in the archetype of the Devouring Mother. Curiously, the difference here is the difference between Freud and Jung. Freud was concerned almost solely with the Father while Jung, perhaps in order to differentiate himself from Freud, became far more interested in the Mother. Jung would later join a number of other thinkers of the 19th and 20th centuries in identifying the rise of the feminine in general as a major turning point. The Faustian civilisation was moving into its Mature phase and that requires the exercise of Will. By a simple piece of logic, if the masculine form of Will had been ruled out, what was left was the feminine. Can it be a coincidence that the feminist movement should arise in the 19th century just at the time when the Faustian was reaching its Adult phase? Can it be a further coincidence that the United States would be at the forefront of the same movement?

Jung himself noted the relationship between the rejection of the Father and the emergence of the feminine Will in his book, *Psychology of the Unconscious*:-

"Up to this time indirect hints point only to the mother, which is nothing remarkable in an American girl, because Americans, as a result of the extreme detachment from the father, are characterised by a most enormous mother complex, which again is connected with the especial social position of woman in the United States. This position brings about a special masculinity among capable women, which easily makes possible the symbolising into a masculine figure."

Jay Fliegelman explores this same dynamic from a literary point of view in his book *Prodigals and Pilgrims: the American revolution against patriarchal authority, 1750-1800*. Of the parental philosophy of the early United States, he writes:-

"Yet at the same time, Lockean pedagogy encouraged a new parental solic-itude, an engaged and emotional commitment to one's children and their future, which militated against both rational relations between generations and the final parental letting go. In violation of its own rationalist emphasis, it encouraged the manipulation of heart and mind as well as manipulation of will. Thus did it, especially in its Rousseau-istic modification, suggest the terms of a new emotional or affectional authoritarianism by which the old-style family might, in effect, be constituted. Parents who could manipulate their children's emotions and bind their hearts need not resort to more overt imposition of their will."

Here we have the entire Devouring Mother dynamic at both the microcosmic and macrocosmic levels spelled out in wonderful purity. The Tyrannical Father is about the overt imposition of will. The Devouring Mother is about the manipulation of emotions, captured perfectly in the phrase *affectional authoritarianism*. It is authority masquerading as solicitude, which translates into permissiveness and enabling behaviour. The overt imposition of will, the traditional role of the father in a patriarchy, is saved as a last resort.

There is another key phrase in the above passage which brings us right back to our earlier analysis about how the Child – Parent relationship must be broken in order to allow the Orphan – Elder to develop. Fliegelman notes that the new Lockean pedagogy "militated against both rational relations between generations and the final parental letting go". The failure of the *parental letting go* is exactly what we saw in our analysis of the Orphan Story. It leads to the failure of the Orphan – Elder pairing. However, the Elder had not gone away altogether. We know from our earlier discussion of Luther that what had filled the void were Hero's Journeys. And here we have another one of those impossible coincidences because Fliegelman's book is a literary analysis. It's about Hero's Journeys!

It is no coincidence that the United States was founded on a strong Protestant and Puritan ethic. The Elder had been sublimated into the written word of the Bible. This was then secularised into the written word of education, which now became crucial in the raising of children. But the written word and the education itself, at a time before state-provided mass education, were in the control of the parents. Thus, the Parent had become the sublimated Elder through their control of the education of their adolescent child. In fact, they were now in the role of priest in relation to the societal Elder of the philosopher. Meanwhile, Locke and Rousseau were filling the new role of societal Elders working through the written word. Both philosophers were writing for a new class of parents who were going to fill the void left by the Protestant rebellion against the Elders of the Classical pseudomorphosis with the written word.

What we see from the beginning of the United States, and which was also prevalent in Britain and other Protestant nations of the time, was the microcosmic movement of the Parent into the role of sublimated Elder through the auspices of education. This was the logical conclusion of Protestantism which had gotten rid of the formal Elder role and replaced it with an Esoteric form. Parents has become Esoteric Elders. If this is true, then it follows that the arrival of mass education run by the State manifested the same paradigm at the macrocosmic level. The State became the sublimated and Esoteric Elder to the societal Orphans. Since this mostly happened in the late 19th and especially the 20th centuries, this matches the exact archetypal progression we have been documenting: the exercise of macrocosmic dominance through the State takes the form of the Devouring Mother, a sublimated and Esoteric form.

Still, the new paradigm had not done away with the Father altogether but rather limited his involvement to the early phase of life. Here we see a perfect fit with our archetypal differentiation between Child - Parent and Orphan - Elder. Locke had recommended an old-fashioned, strict discipline during the ages that we have denoted by the Child archetype. He specified a gradual relaxation of Tyrannical Father discipline around the age of 7, after which education would take over from obedience. The overt imposition of paternal Will had not been done away with altogether, only limited to the Child phase of life. With these changes, the Faustian had extended and given an importance to the Orphan phase of life that is perhaps unique in history. With the massive extension of education in the post-war years, the Orphan phase of life now lasts well into the twenties for most people in the modern West.

Thus, Faustian culture around the time of the foundation of the USA did not do away with paternal authoritarianism altogether. Rather, it relegated it to the Child phase of life, after which education would take over and was to be conducted along the lines laid out by Rousseau and Locke. It was no longer based on obedience to authority. Education was to be conducted along the lines laid out by Rousseau and Locke. It was no longer based on obedience to authority. Rather than being directly instructed, the child should be allowed to find "its own way" to the conclusion. The child would be kept on track through the manipulation of the learning material it was exposed to. The Elder role, an exoteric and extroverted relationship, had been sublimated. Rather than an overt relationship as occurred, for example, in ancient Sparta, the child was made to believe that it was finding its own way while the sublimated Elder was behind the scenes pulling the strings like the Wizard of Oz.

We are not here to judge either the moral or practical worth of this change. The key takeaway from our archetypal point of view is, firstly, that these developments were already implied by the Reformation with the Protestants swapping the authority of the Pope for the authority of the book. Secondly, this ties in exactly with the archetypal logic we outlined earlier, especially in relation to the Child – Parent and Orphan – Elder relationships. Thirdly, and most importantly, what we see is a new form of authority and a new pattern of dominance. The pattern of dominance exerted by the Tyrannical Father is the overt imposition of Will. This was deliberately eschewed in favour of a form of Esoteric power based on the manipulation of the emotions. It was the *affectional authoritarianism* of the Devouring Mother.

It can be no coincidence that the shift in educational strategy was accompanied in the US by the formation of movements such as the *Republican motherhood* or the *Congress of Mothers*. We have seen that paternalism was a dirty word, synonymous with the Tyrannical Father. Maternalism, on the other hand, became a term applied to a collection of social movements originating in the United States around the Mother – Child relationship including parental involvement in education. This education was often framed as an extension of the Mother – Child relationship.

Note also that this pattern of dominance was inherent in Jefferson's plan to deal with the native American tribes. Rather than an overt imposition of dominance over them, he wanted to subliminally guide them to the goal of assimilation through the encouragement of indebtedness via trade. Manipulativeness is built-in to this pattern of dominance since the whole strategy can only work if the subject remains unaware of the ulterior motive. If John Stuart Mill had proposed a paternal pattern of dominance in relation to native tribes, Jefferson's was a maternal pattern, one based on solicitude, but one that wilfully created dependence.

The Devouring Mother pattern exists when the relation of dependence between Child and Parent extends beyond the time when it is healthy. We have seen a perfect example of this excessive dependence in the story of Hamlet. The risk of the new style of education and the enhanced parental control that it implied was that there were few formal markers of independence. Ironically, the United States itself had to get around this problem by formally and overtly declaring its independence and writing a document to make it official. At the microcosmic level, as Fliegelman noted, the new practices blurred the line between the Orphan and Adult phases of life and made the Devouring Mother relationship more likely to occur. Even Locke had pointed out in his influential book, *On Education*, that this was a trap that mothers were prone to fall into.

Whatever we think of Jefferson's approach, he at least believed that the native Americans would become "adults" after assimilation and would thereby take up equal rights with the rest of Americans. In that sense, his plan was a way to get the natives to "grow up". It was a plan that fitted into the new educational philosophy. That can work if the "parent" really does want the child to grow up. What if, for whatever reason, they do not? What if the new form of domination became permanent? Then it would turn into the Devouring Mother, a never-ending form of dependence.

The Tyrannical Father form of dominance is the overt imposition of Will well beyond the time when that is appropriate. It is the dominance of King Lear. The maternal pattern of dominance is to continue affectional author-itarianism beyond the time when it is appropriate. It is the dominance of Claudius and Gertrude over Hamlet. That is how it works at the microcosmic level and also at the macrocosmic.

With this, we have our answer to the question: what happens when you deny the paternal pattern of Will and dominance? The answer is that you foreground the maternal pattern. In the Faustian civilisation, and especially in the United States, with its overt rejection of the Tyrannical Father, it is the devouring feminine which has become the pattern of dominance employed by our Dominant Minority. It is a dominance based on dependence - exactly the kind of dependence Jefferson was trying to induce among the native Americans.

The paradox is that the United States was founded on "independence" and here we find a key truth which Jefferson clearly knew and so must have the other elites of his time. The US may have won political independence through "free trade". But trade is not free. Trade makes one dependent. In the case of the nascent United States, it remained dependent on Europe for trade. That dependence would last all the way until the present day, even though it has now taken a very unusual form which we will get to shortly. The US was never able to break away from *old Europe* completely. The operation of Informal Empire had kept it attached. That is why, to say it again, the United States is the continuation of the true Faustian, not a rebellion against it.

There is one final aspect of the pattern of dominance of the Informal Empire that needs to be addressed. Jefferson knew he had to keep his proposal in relation to the native Americans a secret. That's why it appears only in his private letters. In just the same way, the Lockean and Rousseauean educational paradigms are predicated on the student not being aware of the larger picture. Rousseau even used the phrase *invisible hand* to describe his educational philosophy (again, the Elder had been sublimated, made invisible; Esoteric). What happens when the hand is made visible? What happens when Jefferson's plan is made known to the native American tribes? The whole thing falls apart. The entire paradigm is based on manipulation and gaslighting. As long as the manipulation is used as a means to an end, it can still "work". But humans have a bad habit of allowing the means to turn into the ends.

What happens when the student finds out "the truth"? The practice of affectional authoritarianism and Informal Empire can easily lead to resentment once the manipulated party learns they have been deceived. This is especially true in the political realm in which these new forms of "education" were employed. Faustian civilisation had sublimated the Elder role, which meant that the exercise of authority had to be made invisible. The Dominant Minority operated discreetly behind the scenes to exercise a subliminal pattern of dominance not just in relation to its own public but also in relation to its political rivals. Thus, France and Spain both covertly aided the American colonists for years before making their allegiance overt.

Fliegelman noted that the new form of affectional authoritarianism worked against rational relations between the generations. But the same thing began to happen at the macrocosmic level between geopolitical rivals. It is perhaps partly for this reason that when overt warfare did break out, it started to take on a more brutal form. And when peace was concluded as it inevitably had to be, the resentment generated not just by formal warfare but by the clandestine forms of Informal Empire lingered and spoiled the chances of rational peace deals. Consider the insistence of the French that the Treaty of Versailles have a clause blaming the Germans entirely for the war. This was an obviously ridiculous statement and was objected to by both the Americans and the British, yet it was left in the treaty as an appeasement. The only thing it achieved was to enrage the Germans and lead directly to the Second World War. Rational relations had, indeed, broken down.

The practice of Informal Empire made motives obscure at just the time that the world became more complex. The second and third-order effects of actions make it almost impossible to know whether the "enemy" is harming you on purpose or whether they are just pursuing some other goal and accidentally caused you harm. In some cases, the second and third-order effects blow back on the nation pursuing the action in the first place. The French had supported the American colonists in order to weaken their enemy, Britain. In doing so, they ended up causing their own government to collapse in revolution.

Is it too much of a stretch to see the use of deception in the exercise of authority and power as being behind the rise of psychoanalysis? Whatever else you want to say about the Tyrannical Father, you know where you stand with him. The relationship is overt and out in the open for all to see. The affectional authoritarianism of the Devouring Mother, on the other hand, by making the exercise of authority invisible, opens up the realm of the Unconscious. The battle becomes Esoteric and philosophical. It is Hamlet chasing the ghost. It is Neo searching for the matrix. It revolves around the struggle to understand what is really going on.

The psychological aspect of the Faustian had been there since the time of Luther. For him, the Pope was the devil, upholding an Exoteric façade of holiness when the Esoteric reality was very different. The Informal Empire plays the same game. It creates an Exoteric façade to hide the Esoteric reality. What is shown to the conscious mind and what is hidden in the Unconscious are two different things. This was always the case right from the start of the Faustian and so, in some ways, the development of the Faustian has been the long working out of the extremely complex relationship with the Father that has been there right from the start. The Faustian was wrestling with its *daddy issues* long before Freud gave them a name.

The reference to psychoanalysis here also allows us to make sense of the fact that the masculine and feminine patterns of domination are not mutually exclusive, even at the microcosmic level. In Jungian theory, the Soul takes the opposite gender to the biological one. Thus, a man has a feminine Soul called the *anima* and a woman has a masculine Soul called the *animus*. Even for the individual, the question is one of balance and proportion. Clearly, the rise of the feminine patterns of dominance did not do away with the masculine forms altogether. Rather, these were applied as a last resort. The tendency towards feminine patterns was markedly enhanced in the US since its rebellion against the Father had been more extreme than anywhere else in the Faustian world and gave rise to Jung's *Mother Complex.*

Of course, by the end of the two world wars, the masculine pattern of dominance had become an existential threat to humanity itself with the advent of modern military technology. It could be argued that the masculine form of dominance died on the battlefields of the two wars. What was left was the Informal Empire and the exercise of *affectional authoritarianism.* We are now ready for the final part of the story.

The Universal State of America

Empires are supposed to be won in battle. That is what history tells us. That is what the word itself means, since it comes from *imperator*, a title given to a Roman general. Empires are created by the great warriors and rulers imposing the masculine pattern of dominance via physical and military superiority. The founders of the United States were students of history, and their concern with "standing armies" and the "tyrants" who ruled them proved that they were good students. The Constitution of the United States was in large part designed to act as a bulwark against tyranny, with various checks and balances in place to protect against the Tyrannical Father. Out of this same ethic came the longstanding US policy of non-interventionism, inspired by George Washington's farewell speech and carried on in various forms throughout the 19th and early 20th centuries. Thus, when the US began to make overt moves towards old-fashioned militaristic imperialism in the late 19th century, this caused a big political pushback, including the formation of the Anti-Imperialist League, which had many notable members.

It was the policy of non-interventionism and the strong support it had from a large section of the US public that kept the country out of the beginning of both world wars. After the shambles of the Treaty of Versailles and the fact that debts owed to the US were not repaid in the aftermath of World War 1, the ethic of non-interventionism strengthened into an isolationism that came to dominate in the US between the wars. With an abundance of natural resources, a large population, an enviable strategic and geographical location, and a host of other factors, it could be argued that the US was better placed than any nation to pursue the ideal of autarky. At least, that's what many Americans believed.

The problem was the same one we have already noted: trade implies interdependence. That was true of the trade in commodities that dominated when the US was founded. It became even more true with the industrial revolution. Industrial capitalism created an oversupply of goods. Capitalists needed to find markets for their goods, and that meant selling into other countries. Meanwhile, nations running industrial economies needed access to the natural resources required for production. On top of all that, was the problem of unemployment that oversupply caused.

These developments, alongside the increasing sophistication in financial systems and other auxiliary domains, drastically complexified the political and economic landscape, which meant the interplay between nominally public interests managed by parliament and nominally private interests that often bought influence in parliament. The Boston Tea Party was a prime example of this network of competing interests. The East India Company had used its political influence in the British parliament to win a monopoly on the trade in tea. Having created a market failure, the parliament then sought to apply band-aid solutions, one of which was dumping tea into the American market. The subsequent dumping of the physical tea into the Boston harbour was a perfect literal gesture of the more abstract economic and political problems that were at stake. The Declaration of Independence blamed King George III for all these problems. In fact, it was not the Tyrannical Father that was at fault. These were all teething problems with the relatively new practices of Informal Empire.

In the years leading up to World War 2, the isolationist ethic that had become popular in the United States collided with the complexity and interdependence of the global economic system to create yet more market failures that led to war. Following the stock market crash of 1929, the US Congress passed the Smoot-Hawley Act of 1930, which implemented tariff barriers with the ostensible goal of protecting US industries. Just as the

American colonists had retaliated against what they perceived as unfair British trade policies, other countries retaliated against the Smoot-Hawley Act. A trade war began, that resulted in a precipitous decline in global GDP, which fell 10% on the back of a 50% decline in global exports. The result was the Great Depression. Isolationism had run head first in the cold, hard reality that the global economy was fundamentally interdependent.

Several main trading blocs formed in the aftermath of the protectionist measures. Europe split into two main blocs, one based around Germany and the other around the British Empire, while America had its sphere of influence in Asia and South America. Hitler's solution to the Great Depression, which had caused 33% unemployment in Germany, was massive expenditure on weaponry with the plan to use it to try and solve Germany's natural resource deficiencies through military conquest. Whatever else can be said about that, it solved the unemployment problem. Germany had almost no unemployment by the start of WW2, while US unemployment remained in double figures for the rest of the 1930s.

In response to the obvious build-up for war that was happening in Europe, the isolationists in the US Congress passed a number of measures designed to keep America out of the hostilities. Several bills called the Neutrality Act were passed, which expressly forbid the sale of arms. This came after a public outcry over arms sales during World War 1, and the fact that much of the debt accrued to the US during that war was never repaid. There was also the fact that the then US president, Woodrow Wilson, had gotten the US into the war against the wishes of a large proportion of the public.

We now arrive at a key point in the story. The non-interventionist policy was grounded in the very foundations of the United States from the pen of none other than George Washington himself. It was written into the foundational document of the country, the Declaration of Independence. In the mind of the general public, there was no contradiction between trading with other countries while remaining politically neutral. The truth was otherwise. The US was reliant on Europe for trade, just as it had been right from its inception. The Great Depression had shown that.

In accordance with the non-interventionist belief, the general sentiment in the US was against involvement in the world wars. It was up to the two presidents, Wilson and Roosevelt, to find a way around that sentiment. Both had to work within a political system that had been expressly designed to prevent Tyrannical Father-style authoritarianism and with a public that never would have accepted that, even if it had been possible. It should be no surprise to us that the two presidents set out to win compliance using the exact same methods that American parents had been using towards their own children. That is what our microcosm-macrocosm assumption holds, and it is a pattern we have seen time and again throughout this book. As above, so below.

We know that American parents had been employing Fliegelman's *affectional authoritarianism* right from the start of the United States. It was the Rousseau-style of education that worked by manipulating the emotions and the will to lead the student to the outcome that the teacher wanted. Wilson and Roosevelt would follow the same methodology. The public was to be made to think that it had reached the conclusion that involvement in the war was necessary through its own volition. This was going to require the extensive use of *affectional authoritarianism* in the public domain.

The methodology was especially blatant in the case of Woodrow Wilson. His slogan for re-election in his 1916 presidential campaign was "He kept us out of war". Nevertheless, Wilson knew perfectly well during his campaign that the US would enter the war, and that's exactly what happened immediately after he was re-elected. To win over a sceptical, if not outright hostile, public, Wilson created the *Committee on Public Information*. This was a state-sponsored propaganda bureaucracy that organised the production of movies, newspaper articles, and advertisements, recruited celebrities and volunteers, and generally did whatever was necessary to win public support for the war. The US government was now practising *affectional authoritarianism* against its own citizens, as were other western governments. All of this was amplified by new communication technologies. The written word, which had been so crucial in Luther's time and during the founding of the United States, was now on the verge of being superseded by film and radio.

All of this hearkens back to Spengler's key point. The Universal State is not formed willingly but against the conscious will of the people who must take up the mantle. In the Hero's Journey context, it arises as a challenge from the Unconscious that must be transcended. The collective consciousness in America said that they could stay out of the world wars. The reality, the challenge from the Unconscious, said otherwise. The tension between political independence and trade dependency had been there from the start. The US claimed its political independence based on a policy of "free trade".

But trade makes one (inter-)dependent, not independent. That's what the Great Depression had shown very clearly. The US economy was dependent on trade. Without it, the Great Depression would become a permanent state of affairs. The isolationist sentiment was at odds with reality. Wilson and Roosevelt could not overtly impose their Will on a public that had rejected the Tyrannical Father, so they turned to the covert methods of *affectional authoritarianism*. Crucially, those methods could now be contrasted directly with the Tyrannical Fathers of Europe strutting around in their military uniforms.

Whether the US needed to get involved in World War 1 is debatable, but the calculus for World War 2 was much clearer. In his memoirs, Khrushchev wrote that Stalin had told him many years after the war that he believed that, if it wasn't for US assistance through the Lend Lease program, the Soviet Union would not have been able to survive the initial Nazi onslaught, since the Nazis had captured many of their major food-producing regions. The same is certainly true of Britain. In other words, without US assistance, the Nazis would have achieved their war aims and turned Europe into a single political and economic bloc under German domination.

By the end of the war, the calculus was the same but with the roles reversed. The Soviets were fully mobilised and had already captured eastern Europe. What was to stop Stalin rolling over the rest of the continent? Western European nations were sitting ducks, and they knew it. They begged the US to retain a military presence. Setting aside all the moral arguments involved in the decision, on purely self-interested grounds, could the US have sat back and allowed Germany or the Soviet Union to establish what would have been a unified economic region at least as powerful in economic terms as the

American? That was the Call to Adventure offered to the United States, and it came from the Unconscious part of the American psyche.

Note the crucial fact that is implied in these calculations: the Universal State of the Faustian was predicated on the control of economies. That included the ability to set the terms of trade and, increasingly, to control auxiliary functions like banking. The Informal Empire which was originally based on trade, had, by the 20th century, become increasingly predicated on more and more sophisticated forms of banking. The mercantilist trade of earlier times had been conducted in gold and silver bullion, just as it had all the way back in Roman times. This created a limit on the volume of trade. The difficulty in acquiring bullion played a large role in the Opium Wars. The East India Company had solved the problem by trading opium with China, something it had access to due to its presence on the subcontinent and surrounding areas.

By the 19th century, a further innovation was to allow trade in paper that was backed by gold and silver. Trade in paper had been famously tried in France in 1716, and spectacularly failed. In the resulting collapse, many of the French aristocracy lost their shirts. By the 19th century, bankers had managed to get a grip on the new system, and it's no surprise that the Bank of England was at the forefront. Whatever else can be said about these developments, they made international finance far more complex, opaque, and Esoteric, leaving the way open for both sabotage and the strange and unpredictable emergent phenomena that complex systems produce. The resentment around the control of banking was projected onto the Jews, but, as we noted earlier, they were just a convenient scapegoat. In reality, banking had become an integral part of the Esoteric pattern of dominance related to the operation of Informal Empire and the United States was at the forefront of that development.

Just as the US war of independence had been an economic and trade war long before it became a military conflict, the two world wars were as much battles between competing systems of Informal Empire; the fascist and communist systems of Germany and Russia, respectively, the British commonwealth and the United States.

To say it again, history tells us that empires are won in war. But we have already sketched out how two parallel forms of warfare had been emerging for centuries before the world wars. There was the old-fashioned military kind of war, and there was the new economic war using the methods of the Informal Empire. Over time, the practices of Informal Empire came to predominate. It is fitting, then, that the way in which the United States "won" World War 2 had much more to do with economic warfare than military.

Roosevelt set out to change the isolationist public sentiment one step at a time. Firstly, he side-stepped the bans on arms sales brought in by the Neutrality Acts by convincing the nation to allow sales on a cash and carry basis. US allies, mostly Britain, would be able to buy armaments as long as they paid in gold and took all the risk on shipping. The scheme worked, but drained Britain's gold reserves so fast that they were in danger of running out. This led to Roosevelt's next idea, which was called *Lend Lease*. The scheme allowed payment-free supply of goods and went beyond armaments to include provision of what ended up being mostly non-military products, including large amounts of foodstuffs. Crucially, Lend Lease was made available to the USSR too. By the time the war was over, about a quarter of all Lend Lease transactions had been with the USSR.

If we accept the premise that, without Lend Lease, Germany would almost certainly have defeated the Soviet Union and probably also Britain, it follows that the USA beat Nazi Germany not by fighting on the battlefield, although that did happen later, but through economic warfare. But it goes further than that. What had happened before and during the war was that all the combatant countries in Europe, including the Soviet Union, had turned their economies exclusively towards wartime production. The United States, as a non-combatant, then stepped in to fill the void in relation to non-military production. That's what much of the Lend Lease program entailed. The US provided trucks, cars, industrial supplies, food, and more to the combatant countries. The resulting economic boom finally broke the back of unemployment in the US.

The United States would become the dominant imperial power and win its Informal Empire by staying off the battlefield. It earned an enormous quantity of gold via the cash and carry program. From the Lend Lease program, it accrued an even more enormous quantity of debt, especially from Britain. In the aftermath of the war, these debt obligations were used to quietly transfer the power of the British Empire across to the United States. In just the same way that Jefferson had hoped to make the native Americans dependent through debt, the US had made Britain and other nations dependent on it.

In the aftermath of the war, the US incorporated both the British and German economic and political blocs into its Informal Empire. The details of this were worked out via a series of diplomatic and technocratic conferences, the most important of which was arguably the Bretton Woods Conference which may have had the appearance of a friendly and cooperative international meeting but was de facto run by the US since its dominant economic and financial position meant that it was able to dictate the terms of the agreement. An official from the Bank of England stated of the Bretton Woods conference that it was the worst thing to happen to Britain except for the war itself. This creates the paradox that the US won its Informal Empire as much from its allies as from its enemies.

There were other enormous benefits accrued to the US during the war that went unnoticed by the general public. At the start of the war, Britain realised it was going to have to put its economy on a war footing and would, therefore, not have the resources to develop the various military technologies it had been working on. It transferred a large amount of intellectual property to the US in the hope that the Americans would be able to make use of it. Among this IP were significant advances in radar technology, jet engines, and the initial theory behind the atomic bomb. Following the defeat of Germany, the US inherited practically all German industrial, military, and scientific IP, as well as its industrial plant and equipment. A number of German scientists were quietly repatriated to the US to continue their work.

In the aftermath of the war, Britain and other European nations dismantled all formal imperial institutions. The official story was that imperialism was over. It's true that the old kind of imperialism - the formal, Exoteric imperialism inherited from the old world in the form of the Tyrannical Father

- was over. It had died on the battlefields of the war. It was replaced by the new imperialism of the Informal Empire. The transfer of power happened quietly and Esoterically through the complex agreements worked out by technocrats in the background.

Of course, there was one final battle to go, and that was between the last two blocs that remained standing in the aftermath of the war. The German and British blocs had been incorporated into the American. The Soviets had at least nominally increased the scope and power of their bloc in eastern Europe, with China also in the picture.

The reason the Cold War needed a new name was because it was a different kind of war. We already know what kind of war it was. Since the atomic bomb had made direct military combat impossible, the Cold War was simply a purer form of Informal Empire. It was fought on the complex and Esoteric battleground of economics, finance, and ideology that had been brewing in the background for centuries and which now became the main game. It is no coincidence that the Soviet Union, although present at the Bretton Woods agreement, did not agree to participate. Nor did it participate in the subsequent Marshall Plan. Stalin forbade any Soviet-dominated country from participating. Moscow countered with its own version of the plan along very similar lines. Stalin knew what Jefferson had known more than a century earlier: trade creates dependence, even or especially when that trade is "free".

We can also see in this development another pattern of Informal Empire which is, on the surface, very strange. The United States was the victor in the war and won the British and German economic blocs as a result. But it needed to pump money into those blocs in order to keep them functional. This was another realisation which came after the war, since we know that the immediate idea, called the Morgenthau Plan, was to deindustrialise Germany. As Churchill told the Americans, a Europe without the German economy was not going to work, hence the switch to the Marshall Plan. Ever since, the rich nations of the world have found it in their interests to finance the poorer ones in exchange for political allegiance, something the Soviets did in competition with the US and which China does nowadays too.

The Cold War was a war between two Informal Empires. With no possibility of achieving dominance via military conflict, the superpowers turned to proxy wars, covert regime change operations, colour revolutions, psycholog-ical warfare, propaganda, espionage, trade embargoes, and financialisation, among other tactics. It is in the conduct of the Cold War that we see the battle of Informal Empire in its purest form.

With the collapse of the USSR, we now find ourselves in what is almost certainly the final version of the Universal State of the Faustian civilisation. It is an Informal Empire with a central point in Washington D.C., but which operates as a relatively decentralised network of interests that spans the globe. The Informal Empire has no emperor. Whatever hierarchy remains is there for appearance sake only. The organisational structure of the Informal Empire is a collection of more or less important nodes in an ever-shifting array. A node that is aligned to the ideological and economic interests of the network and which serves those interests is enhanced, while other nodes are devalued or removed. All of this happens invisibly, Esoterically and mostly automatically, although sometimes a node needs to be removed by force.

The pattern of dominance of the Informal Empire is *affectional authori-tarianism*. Prior to WW2, there was still a balance between the masculine and feminine patterns of dominance. But the masculine form died on the battlefields of the war and was then rendered obsolete by the atomic bomb. What we have seen in the post-war years, therefore, is the supremacy of the feminine form of dominance embodied by the Lockean and Rousseauean theories of education which, are now practiced at the macrocosmic level by the political operatives who specialise in psychological operations to gain compliance from the public. To the Rousseauean paradigm, we can also add the lessons of psychoanalysis, another piece of intellectual property incorporated by America in the aftermath of the war and put to use in advertising and public relations. Since I outlined these developments in detail in my book, *The Devouring Mother*, I won't go into them in more detail here.

With this, we have the answer to the question that both Spengler and Toynbee had asked but which neither had predicted correctly. The Universal

State of the Faustian was indeed created after World War 2, but it took the form of the Informal Empire. We can see how the Informal Empire fits all of the key properties of Faustian civilisation. It is Esoteric and occult, based on mind instead of body; it utilises the mask to create an Exoteric front that hides deeper intent; it is predicated on a network of elites who rule covertly over the general public.

From a macrocosmic archetypal point of view, the seismic shift that happened in the 20th century is directly analogous to that which occurred in Rome. Rome had to make the incredibly difficult transition from republic to military dictatorship. That was what was necessary to form the Universal State of the Classical civilisation. It was a form manifested archetypally in the Tyrannical Father. Rome itself was a people who had inherited the Classical civilisation from the Greeks and, possibly because of that, were able to make the transition to the Universal State where the Greeks, who were still tied to the old ways, were unable to do so.

The US began to make the same transition under Wilson, which then went into overdrive under Roosevelt with the massive expansion of the State in general, including the implementation of the welfare state. With this began the method of control that has only become more pronounced to this day. The pattern of dominance that the Dominant Minority of the United States, and the Faustian more generally, now wields both in relation to its own citizens and also in relation to other countries is that of the Devouring Mother who keeps her children in a state of dependence through control of trade, finance, and information.

With this, we can now fill in another row on our macrocosmic archetypal table:-

Microcosm	Macrocosm	Primary Faculty	Elites	Manifestation (Faustian)
Child	Genesis	Imagination	Creative Minority	Classical Pseudomorphosis
Orphan	Growth	Intellect	Creative Minority	Reformation
Adult	Maturity	Will	Dominant Minority - Universal State	The Universal State of America
Elder	Old Age	Soul	Universal Church	----

With the collapse of the USSR, the Universal State of the Faustian was reached. The Dominant Minority of the Faustian civilisation, concentrated in the USA but with trade, diplomatic, and banking nodes around the world, has become the Dominant Minority for most of the globe. Just as they had done at Bretton Woods, the technocrats once again gathered to work out the new post-Soviet order. Once again, it was sold to the public using that tried and true catchphrase: "free trade". Unlike the actions of Wilson and Roosevelt which were motivated by war, the neoliberal agenda was conducted from a position of geopolitical dominance. It was a rearrangement of the world as imagined by the technocratic elites.

What we have seen in recent years is the domestic political blowback against the neoliberal agenda. The Dominant Minority has responded with a form of *affectional authoritarianism* has reached a genuine fever pitch with the Brexit and Trump votes and shows no sign of slowing down. *Affectional authoritarianism* has now turned into outright psychological warfare.

Locke had assumed that his new theory of education would lead to friendship between parent and child later in life. The child would eventually realise the wisdom its parents had shown by gently guiding it into adulthood rather than utilising the disciplinarian methods of the Tyrannical Father. It probably never occurred to either Locke or Rousseau what would happen if the "educator" had no intention to allow the child to "grow up". When the informal pattern of dominance becomes entrenched, as it has now that the Faustian civilisation has found its Universal State, it becomes the Devouring Mother. That is the world in which we now live.

The Age of the Orphan

We are all now the Orphans of the Faustian civilisation in its Universal State phase. Due to the global nature of that civilisation, it is not inaccurate to say that our Age of the Orphan encompasses the entire world. Where this will lead us in the future is unknown. As Toynbee correctly pointed out, even if we are sure that the wheel of civilisation turns only in one direction, a conclusion that is based on a very small data set of little more than twenty civilisations most of which we know next to nothing about, that does not exclude the possibility that the wheel is just one part of a larger vehicle whose direction we have not identified. To do what Spengler did and fatalistically chain ourselves to the wheel may do little more than crush ourselves underneath it.

We have seen that the Faustian inherited the incredibly complex symbol of the Father from the Classical. That symbol was itself a hybrid of at least two civilisations. The rejection of that symbol, as Nietzsche rightly saw, was a momentous event and one whose ramifications are still being felt. What our archetypal logic suggests is that the rejection of the Father is part of the archetypal phase we have called the Orphan. This leads to a meta-meaning since the Faustian is itself an Orphan civilisation. That would make the United States and the other peoples born from the Faustian, meta-Orphans. Perhaps the Age of the Orphan that follows may extend into new civilisations born under an Orphan symbol the way the Faustian was born under the Father.

Since we are the Orphans of the Faustian, it seems fitting to finish this book with one more Orphan Story. It was written during a time when the nation of its author was undergoing its own rebellion against the Father and the central premise of its plot revolves around the rejection of the Father.

Before we get to the story, there is a point worth making about what was going on in Russia in the 19th century. We have already mentioned that the would-be Tyrannical Fathers who rose to power in the 20th century were proletarians. Within our archetypal logic, we would call them Orphans. And when we look at the life stories of each of them, it is startling how similar they are to the proto-Orphan who started the whole trend, Martin Luther.

Let's do a lightning review of the biographies of the men who came to lead those rebellions.

Mao was born into a peasant family. He rebelled against his own father by breaking off his arranged marriage in order to pursue life as an intellectual. This brought him into contact with the ideas of Marx and other western figures and with the intellectual movement in China that was aiming to oust the emperor (the societal Father). Mao's father would later disown him. One biographer called him "the eternal rebel".

Lenin's father died when he was 15. This had a major influence on the boy, who became confrontational and rebellious, renouncing God. Lenin was a gifted intellectual who became enamoured of the ideas of Marx. His brother was sentenced to death for an attempt to assassinate the Tsar (the societal Father) and Lenin was kicked out of university after leading an anti-Tsar demonstration. While in exile, he translated Marx into Russian (mimicking Luther's translation of the Bible into German).

Stalin was born into a poor family. His father became a violent alcoholic, and his mother separated from her husband when Stalin was still an infant. She worked odd jobs as a maid to get Stalin through school. Stalin was academically gifted, writing what was apparently excellent poetry that became well-known in Georgia. He briefly trained for the priesthood before renouncing God. At the same time, he became involved in a "forbidden book club" and took up reading Marx. Later, he trained to become a teacher and also became the editor of a newspaper publishing Marxist ideas.

Mussolini got into trouble at school for being violent and would later become involved in various rebel movements of the time. His mother was a devout Catholic and had her child baptised, but Mussolini would later renounce God and become an atheist. Mussolini thought of himself as an intellectual and was very well-read. He was originally a follower of Marx but renounced this for nationalism. Like Lenin and Stalin, he would later become the editor of a newspaper. He was apparently an excellent journalist who also wrote novels.

Napoleon was a rambunctious child, and, although there is little record of strife with his father, it seems his mother was the dominant parent. Napoleon would later say that he believed mothers more than fathers were the critical influence on a child's development. Although known for his military exploits, Napoleon was also a writer. He wrote a novel (a love story) as well as a number of pro-republican pamphlets, which won him support within that movement which was, after all, about rebellion against the king (the societal Father).

Hitler was a rebellious child, both in school and directly against his own father, who beat him regularly. His father died when he was 14 years of age and his mother only four years later. Hitler was partly raised on money acquired from orphan's benefit programs. When that money was stopped, he lived for a long time in poverty, taking odd jobs to support himself. As most people know, Hitler wrote books, including one while he was in prison (similar to Luther and Lenin's exile) while also becoming involved with a rebellious political movement.

The common factors here are quite plain to see, and they are shared with Luther. There is a rebellion against the Father at the microcosmic level, which includes a theological rebellion. These later get translated into macrocosmic rebellions against the societal Father. The fact that all the men were intellectuals who made use of the printing press is also no accident.

The Faustian was predicated on the throwing off of the macrocosmic Father. As the Faustian spread to Russia and China, it cannot be a coincidence that the men who came to the fore of those movements had also thrown off their own fathers. All of this justifies our analysis calling this the Age of the Orphan.

Part of the reason to mention these facts is to contrast them with the life of the author whose novel we will now examine. Dostoevsky got himself caught up in exactly the same kinds of intellectual circles that Lenin, Mao, Stalin, and the others did. The literary scene of his time in Russia was a breeding ground for radical politics since the government had all but outlawed dissenting political discussion. That didn't stop the authorities from targeting the writers anyway. Although there is little evidence Dostoevsky was interested in politics, his membership in one such literary group saw him charged, convicted, and then sentenced to death. He and his fellow members were led in front of a firing squad, only to be pardoned at the very last minute.

We can see in this event yet another parallel to Luther. Luther had genuinely thought he was about to die when he was caught in the lightning storm. Coincidentally, this was during the Orphan phase of Luther's life, and the event led to alter the course of his life by breaking with his father. Dostoevsky's near-death experience was also a massive turning point in his own life. It would inform arguably the most dramatic scene in his last and greatest work, the book we are about to examine: *The Brothers Karamazov*.

Dostoevsky's experience hanging around in radical intellectual circles was also a major influence on him, and his position on them featured in many of his works. In several of his greatest novels, Dostoevsky drew the kinds of men that he found there. Raskolnikov, the hero of *Crime and Punishment*, is perhaps the greatest depiction of the disenfranchised, disinherited Orphan using the intellectual ideas that were floating around at the time as cover to commit a crime. Well before the mass crimes of the 20th century, Dostoevsky had seen what it meant for the intellectual proletarians to come to power.

In *The Brothers Karamazov*, Dostoevsky brought together the threads from his other works to give us not one but four separate Orphan Stories all interwoven into the same novel. Let us now turn to the last and greatest of the Orphan Stories to finish our book.

The Brothers Karamazov

Given all we have said about the macrocosmic rebellion against the Father that occurred first in the West and then spread to Russia and China in the 19th century, it should be little surprise that the plot of Karamazov revolves around the murder of the father of the family, Fyodor Pavlovich. It is a curious fact that none of the Orphan Stories we have looked at so far featured the murder of the Father. Luke Skywalker comes very close, egged on by Palpatine, at the end of *Return of the Jedi*, while Hamlet does symbolically kill his (shadow) Father. What both stories make clear is that the murder of the Father will bring ruin on the Orphan, and that is what Dostoevsky also spells out in Karamazov.

Fyodor Karamazov has four sons: three legitimate and one illegitimate. All four are semi-literal orphans in that their mothers died when they were young. All four are as good as literal orphans in that Fyodor Pavlovich played no part in their upbringing, and they had to be raised separately by different family members. All four are archetypal Orphans in that they have no established Exoteric (or Esoteric) Adult identities when we meet them at the beginning of the novel.

The story begins with the three legitimate brothers, Dmitri, Ivan and Alyosha returning to the home town of their father for various reasons. The illegitimate brother is Smerdyakov. Fyodor has never acknowledged that he is the father, it is simply a rumour that everybody in town has heard. Smerdyakov was raised by, and has become the assistant to, Fyodor's manservant, Grigory. He lives in his father's house as hired help with no social status or life prospects at all.

The stage is set for four Orphan Stories that will all revolve around the murder of Fyodor Pavlovich, which forms the central plot point of the story. This allows Dostoevsky to compare and contrast four different responses to the Orphan phase of life, three of which will result in failure, and one of which is the example which Dostoevsky holds before us as his ideal.

Unlike any of the Hollywood movies or even the fairy-tale Orphan Stories we have examined so far, the story of Karamazov features no dramatic action or adventure, no politics, no great heroes. It takes place in a second-tier town in a second-tier province. It features the lives of ordinary people doing ordinary things.

Having said that, there is no doubt that the plot is very melodramatic. The father, Fyodor, has very little to recommend him. He is a miser in relation to his sons while being a drunken old letch who chases after young women. One of the women he is pursuing is the one his eldest son, Dmitri, is also in love with, Grushenka. The problem is that Dmitri is engaged to be married. To make things even more complicated, the middle brother, Ivan, is in love with Dmitri's fiancée. That is just the basics of the plot of a novel that is a thousand pages long.

We know from our archetypal logic that Dmitri's marriage should be his rite of passage into the Adult phase of life. The reason Dmitri has returned to the town is to collect his patrimony, which he needs to start married life.

Fyodor, being the old miser that he is, is trying to get out of paying. This enrages the hot-headed Dmitri, who has publicly threatened to kill his father over the matter.

This is a familiar dynamic that we have seen already. Dmitri's transition to adulthood is being stifled by the Father archetype. Fyodor is holding back Dmitri's Exoteric identity in a similar way to what Claudius and Gertrude do to Hamlet. Just like Hamlet, Dmitri considers breaking out of an intolerable situation via an act of murder. Those are the basics of the first Orphan Story featuring the eldest Karamazov brother.

The second Orphan Story is that of the middle brother, Ivan, and this reflects Dostoevsky's judgement of the kinds of people he met in the intellectual circles that he hung around in and that we know gave birth to such real-life personalities as Lenin, Stalin and Mao. Like Raskolnikov in *Crime and Punishment*, Ivan represents the Orphan faculty of Intellect that is disconnected and dissociated from real life. Ivan is clearly a brilliant thinker, and he shares his ideas willingly. But he presents them as if they were half-jokes and declines to defend them when they are challenged by others. Like many a university student, his ideas are not grounded in real-life experience, and this is because Ivan is still an Orphan. He has no Adult identity and no real responsibilities in life.

Ivan's unrequited love for Dmitri's fiancé, Katerina Ivanova, speaks to the fact that he is not on any pathway to a meaningful Adult identity. It should be no surprise that neither Dmitri nor Ivan have an Elder who is guiding them towards membership in any Exoteric institutions. Neither is their father of the slightest assistance, and Ivan detests the man almost as much as Dmitri. In short, both brothers are just drifting through life.

It is in the relationship between Ivan and the third brother, Smerdyakov, that Dostoevsky makes the point he had made in his earlier novels, only now the are stakes raised even higher because it is this which leads to the murder of the Father, and it is here where Dostoevsky had so presciently seen what forces were being unleashed by the intellectuals of his day. Just a few decades later, those forces would murder Russia's societal Father, the Tsar.

Dmitri and Ivan may be drifting, but at least they have some hope of completing their Orphan mission. In Smerdyakov, we see what is essentially the inversion of that hope. Smerdyakov is the Orphan who is not only not on a pathway to an Exoteric Adult identity but who has had any chance of having such a pathway denied to him. Smerdyakov is almost a non-person. In this, he is very similar to the character of Raskolnikov, but what Dostoevsky does in Karamazov is to make Ivan become the sublimated Elder to Smerdyakov. Smerdyakov is drawn to Ivan's ideas around atheism, including, most importantly, the famous idea from the novel that if God is dead, anything is permissible. Whereas Raskolnikov was both the murderer and the thinker who justifies it, Smerdyakov is the murderer while Ivan is the thinker who inadvertently justifies it.

What happens when one Orphan, who tosses around intellectual ideas in a lackadaisical fashion, becomes an unwitting Elder to an Orphan whose life circumstances are completely hopeless and who is driven by bitterness and resentment? The answer is the murder of the Father. Dostoevsky meant this, at least partially, in a theological sense, but this fits with our earlier analysis of the Faustian where it was the Holy Father who was rejected first and the political one subsequently. That's what happened in the West. It's what eventually happened in Russia and China too. What Dostoevsky does in Karamazov is to make Ivan face the consequences of his ideas by seeing that they can be used as intellectual cover for crime.

Where this ties back to Dmitri is that he is the one who will actually be charged by the authorities with the murder since he has publicly threatened to do it, and Smerdyakov, who is a cunning operator, sets his brother up to take the rap. The result is three failed Orphan transitions. Dmitri's is the one which matches most closely to what we have seen already when the Orphan's Exoteric pathway to adulthood is blocked. Smerdyakov is the shadow Orphan in its bleakest form. Ivan is the shadow Orphan stuck in disconnected Intellect which becomes Ideology when shared with those who need intellectual cover for their crimes.

All of this relates back to what was going on in the 19th century, not just in Russia. Smerdyakov represents the Toynbeean proletarianisation process. He is what happens when the bonds between the generations are broken and where large numbers of people have been thrown on the scrapheap as a result. Among that group will be a number of people whose resentment leads to violence. We know as a simple historical fact that there were many such kinds of people involved in all the major upheavals of the 19th and 20th centuries, not to mention throughout history. What Dostoevsky saw was how ideology came to be used as a front to cover up the underlying emotional driver for such radical movements. That is what he symbolises in the character of Ivan.

In Dmitri, Ivan, and Smerdyakov, we see three failed Orphan Stories. Each is prevented from attaining an Adult Exoteric identity through a combination of their own character faults and the character faults of their father and those around them. In this way, they are tragedies in the same vein as *Hamlet*.

That just leaves the hero of the story and the only one of the four brothers who will successfully transcend the Orphan phase: Alyosha.

It should not surprise us at all to find that Alyosha is the only one of the four brothers who has an Elder who is guiding them towards an Adult identity. In this case, the Elder is literally called that since the Eastern Orthodox Church has a tradition of elders. The one who is guiding Alyosha towards his initiation at the local monastery is called Zosima, who is loved by the common folk whom he tends to and, perhaps as a result, resented by the other priests in the church. Dostoevsky characterises those priests exactly the same way that Luther did hundreds of years earlier: well-fed and far too content with themselves, living off the charity of the public.

In the first part of the novel, we see the development of the Orphan – Elder relationship between Alyosha and Zosima. We know that this is the middle phase of the Orphan Story, the Transition part of the cycle. Alyosha is working towards an Exoteric identity of elder, following in Zosima's footsteps. All seems in order for the usual progression of the Orphan Story.

But Dostoevsky subverts the pattern in at least three ways. The first is that, before he dies, Zosima instructs Alyosha to leave the church and go into the world. In other words, he is telling Alyosha not to complete the Exoteric part of his initiation. In any other Orphan Story, this would be very strange. Imagine Yoda telling Luke Skywalker at the end of *Return of the Jedi* that he should give up his training and go and travel the universe instead. The reason this works in Karamazov is because Alyosha is already a very unusual kind of character - one who, as we will see, breaks the archetypal mould to a certain extent.

What Dostoevsky does with the character of Alyosha is to portray what we have earlier called *the pure Esoteric*. One way to think about this is to think of Alyosha as the human embodiment of virtue. Right from the beginning of Karamazov, we can see that the other characters view and treat Alyosha in a very unusual fashion. The reason is because Alyosha is a paragon of virtue. This is true irrespective of the Exoteric role he is striving for. In Alyosha, Dostoevsky paints us a character who represents the best of humanity. Importantly, the other characters in the story understand that this is true, although most of them are struggling to consciously formulate what it means.

We can go a step further, however, and frame this dynamic in the archetypal logic of this book. Esoterically, Alyosha is the Child. (Dostoevsky named the character after his own child, who died as an infant shortly after he started writing the novel). What are the virtues of the Child? Optimism, trust, hope, faith, and simplicity. These are all true of Alyosha in his interactions with the other characters. Of course, all these traits are very unusual in a young man and that is what makes Alyosha different right from the start of the novel. Physically he is an Adult; Exoterically he is the Orphan on a path to becoming a monk; Esoterically, he is a Child.

What Alyosha represents to the other characters and to us, the reader, is the embodiment of above-named virtues of the Child. This allows Dostoevsky to show us a psychology that appears in all his novels. The other characters can see that Alyosha is virtuous, and they acknowledge and respect that virtue. Simultaneously, they try to corrupt Alyosha. They do so out of envy because Alyosha represents an ideal that they themselves are unable to attain. He brings shame on them and they project that shame back onto him in the form of envy. Rather than lift their own game to his standards, they try to drag him down to their level.

Alyosha represents our conscience, our innate sense of what is right, which Dostoevsky identifies with the Child and which has an obvious symbolic parallel in Christianity. The devil spends fourty days tempting Jesus in the desert. In Karamazov, it is the other characters who tempt Alyosha to join them in sin.

This sets up a unique archetypal dynamic. Alyosha is physically a man but, archetypally, an Orphan. In the normal course of events, for an Adult to manifest attributes of the Child would be, at least at a psychological level, pathological. It would be the shadow archetypal forms that Freud and Jung discovered and that we have given the general label of Dissociation. This is the story of the Orphan who shies away from the archetypal mission, introverts themselves, and dissociates from reality. It is what see in both Hamlet and Ophelia. It is Neo at the start of *The Matrix*. It is the exact trap that Smerdyakov, Ivan and Raskolnikov find themselves in.

But Alyosha is not introverting himself. He is an assistant to the work of his Elder, Zosima, and he is an active presence in the lives of his brothers, his father, and his community. In short, he is not dissociating from reality. That already marks him out as strange, but then Dostoevsky raises the stakes. Alyosha's make or break moment, the crucial final phase in his Orphan transcendence, is not a battle against an overt enemy. It is something that all of us must face in our own lives. Alyosha must face the death of a loved one. More specifically, he must face the death of the Elder, Zosima.

Alyosha is made to confront the death of Zosima not in an abstract form but in the visible, physical ramifications of death. Given Zosima's status, the other characters from the monastery expect some kind of divine intervention to manifest and preserve Zosima's body. This idea quickly becomes a kind of test of Zosima's virtue. If he really was a great man, God will preserve him. What happens instead is that his body begins to degrade immediately after his death. The failure of the test allows Zosima's enemies to smear his name and throws Alyosha into a crisis of faith. Sure enough, one of the other characters, Rakitin, takes the opportunity to try and corrupt Alyosha one more time - to break his faith for good.

The challenge which Dostoevsky sets for Alyosha is to face death. That is a common theme in all Orphan Stories but the crucial point here is that Alyosha symbolises the Child. What is at stake is whether Alyosha will give up his virtues of optimism, trust, faith, and simplicity and, like the rest of the characters in the novel, wallow in the sin of the world. That is the final test, and one which Alyosha passes. He passes not by dissociating in Imagination or Intellect, in theological theories, or mystical symbolism, but in the direct confrontation with physical reality.

What Dostoevsky shows us in the character of Alyosha is the fully-initiated Child, who is made to confront the evil of the world directly, not to dissociate from that evil, and to come through the other side intact. He is the Orphan who must face the death of the Elder without losing faith.

The scene in which Alyosha secures his transcendence is one of the great passages in literature and is worth reproducing in part:-

"But with every instant he felt clearly, and as it were, tangibly, that something firm and unshakable as that vault of heaven had entered into his soul. It was as though some idea had seized the sovereignty of his mind and it was for all his life and for ever and ever. He had fallen on the earth a weak boy, but he rose up a resolute champion, and he knew and felt it suddenly at the very moment of his ecstasy. And never, never, all his life long, could Alyosha forget that minute."

This is perhaps the greatest description of the Orphan transition that has ever been written, and it was almost certainly inspired by Dostoevsky's experience with the firing squad. In Alyosha we have the highest manifestation of the Orphan transcendence which occurs entirely at the Esoteric level of being. Alyosha does not graduate from his initiation into any Exoteric role. He does not become a man of authority, a Father, or even an Elder. His victory is to remain, in his heart, a Child and to retain the optimism, trust, and faith that come with that. That was Dostoevsky's answer to the challenges of our time. To retain the childlike virtues without dissociating from reality is both the most difficult and most important task.

Having faced the death of his Elder and come out of the other side intact, Alyosha later assists a group of young schoolboys and a family to face the death of their young son. He does so not from a position of authority.

Although he is talking with a group of boys who really are children, Alyosha refers to them as "friends". Archetypally, he is one of them. He is still a Child in the best sense of the word.

As we progress through our own Age of the Orphan and perhaps into a longer period of Orphanhood ahead, Alyosha's advice may serve us well from one Orphan to another. It is almost the last line in the last book that Dostoevsky ever wrote. It serves as his final advice to those of us who live in a world not that dissimilar to his - one of ideological power games.

"Ah, children, ah, dear friends, don't be afraid of life! How good life is when one does something good and just!"

In a time of absurd complexity (and just general absurdity), perhaps such a simple and innocent message is the torch that may light our way.

About the Author

Simon Sheridan is an author, blogger and thinker whose work utilises the concept of the archetype to provide an integrated view of what are normally considered independent domains such as psychology and politics. Simon is also the author of a number of works of fiction including novels and short stories. He lives in Melbourne, Australia.

Check out https://simonsheridan.me for Simon's blog and news about upcoming releases.

Also by Simon Sheridan

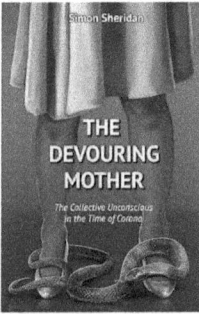

The Devouring Mother: The Collective Unconscious in the Time of Corona

Drawing on the work of the great Swiss psychologist, Carl Jung, Simon Sheridan makes the case that the archetype that has been dominant in the west for several decades is The Devouring Mother, a shadow form whose primary qualities include gaslighting, emotional manipulation and guilt tripping all in the name of protecting her children. Sheridan switches between the microcosmic and the macrocosmic to show how The Devouring Mother permeates all levels of society from interpersonal relationships and employment through to large scale political and social movements including corona.

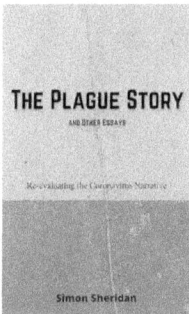

The Plague Story and Other Essays: Re-evaluating the Coronavirus Narrative

"Those who tell the stories rule society" - Plato

Societies run on stories. But in the modern west, we believe that we are above stories; we are scientific. It is partly because of this (story!) that we are often blind to the stories we tell ourselves. In this book, I analyse the structure of the story we have been telling ourselves about the corona event: the plague story. I look at how the plague story unfolded and who has been telling it. The structure of that story dictates both what has happened so far and what needs to happen to bring the matter to an end.